Captured by Aliens?

Captured by Aliens?

A History and Analysis
of American Abduction Claims

NIGEL WATSON

Foreword by
PETER ROGERSON

McFarland & Company, Inc., Publishers
Jefferson, North Carolina

This is a revised version of *The Alien Deception:*
An Exploration of the Alien Abduction
Phenomenon, 2009, self-published.

LIBRARY OF CONGRESS CATALOGUING-IN-PUBLICATION DATA

Names: Watson, Nigel, 1954– author.
Title: Captured by aliens? : a history and analysis
of American abduction claims / Nigel Watson.
Description: Jefferson, North Carolina :
McFarland & Company, Inc., Publishers, 2020. |
"This is a revised version of The Alien Deception:
An Exploration of the Alien Abduction Phenomenon, 2009,
self-published." | Includes bibliographical references and index.
Identifiers: LCCN 2020016951 | ISBN 9781476681412
(paperback : acid free paper) ∞
ISBN 9781476640365 (ebook)
Subjects: LCSH: Human-alien encounters. | Unidentified
flying objects—Sightings and encounters—New Hampshire. |
Hill, Betty (Eunice) | Hill, Barney, 1922-1969.
Classification: LCC BF2050 .W366 2020 | DDC 001.942—dc23
LC record available at https://lccn.loc.gov/2020016951

BRITISH LIBRARY CATALOGUING DATA ARE AVAILABLE

ISBN (print) 978-1-4766-8141-2
ISBN (ebook) 978-1-4766-4036-5

Front cover image of alien abduction © 2020 solarseven/Shutterstock

Printed in the United States of America

McFarland & Company, Inc., Publishers
Box 611, Jefferson, North Carolina 28640
www.mcfarlandpub.com

To the memory of Peter Rogerson

Acknowledgments

The following people have contributed greatly to my understanding of the abduction phenomenon: Peter Rogerson, John Rimmer, Robert Rickard, John Harney, Kevin McClure, Jenny Randles, Nick Pope, Hilary Evans, Peter Brookesmith, Andy Roberts, David Clarke, Granville Oldroyd, John Spencer, Stuart Miller, Richard Holland, Dave Sutton, Thomas Bullard, Rich Reynolds, Roger Sandell, Darren Slade, Mark Pilkington, Philip Mantle, Clas Svahn, Chris Aubeck and Martin Kottmeyer.

The works of Charles Fort, John Fuller, John Keel, Jerome Clark, Charles Bowen, Gordon Creighton, Budd Hopkins, John Mack, David Jacobs, Whitley Strieber and Jacques Vallee have all helped in the creation of this book.

Table of Contents

Foreword
by Peter Rogerson

Nigel starts with the Barney and Betty Hill abduction and then draws in the various threads which led to it. He chronicles the rise of beliefs in extraterrestrial flying saucers, the rise of the idea of contacting their pilots in the contactees and contactee groups of the 1950s, and the gradual rise of the abduction stories.

He sees predecessors of these in the airship tales of the late 19th and early 20th centuries (a subject of which he has made a special study), when tales of encounters and in some cases abductions by airship crews developed. These themes developed through popular culture, particularly film (Nigel in another incarnation is a film critic). But they are also based on other themes which Nigel examines in great detail including the roots in what were known as captivity narratives, tales told by "survivors" of capture by exotic human groups (Native Americans in America, Barbary pirates in Europe). Through this weaving, rather than a straightforward chronological narrative, Nigel shows how all these themes influenced one another and gave rise to the modern corpus.

Nigel examines these modern stories and notes that that is exactly what they are, stories, often fashioned by third parties such as abduction hunters out of masses of confused "testimony" often produced under hypnotic regression. Of actual hard evidence there is none—there is, for example, always some reason or other why abductions are never caught on video or CCTV though various attempts to do this have been tried. Though supporters of exotic explanations can always find some excuse for this, there is no evidence to compel us to accept their kind of explanation and plenty to make us lean toward a psycho-social interpretation.

Many of the arguments in this book will, of course, be famil-

Peter Rogerson surrounded by some of his collection of UFO and paranormal books. He was a prominent and articulate supporter of the psychosociological theory for alien abduction reports and wrote extensively on the topic for the British *Magonia* magazine (photograph by Clas Svahn, April 5, 2010).

iar to long-time readers of the British *Magonia* magazine; indeed it might well be regarded as the book of the *Magonia* position on such subjects, but for some readers this will be a new and challenging interpretation.

    This is an important book and one which I recommend.

Peter Rogerson

Peter Rogerson (1951–2018) was a librarian in Manchester for most of his working life. In 1969 he joined the editorial panel of MUFOB *magazine that supported the "new ufology" that opposed the notion that UFOs were of extraterrestrial origin. He wrote about the cultural and social aspects of ufology as well as hundreds of book reviews for* MUFOB *that eventually became the* Magonia *website. He also catalogued and referenced 5,000 UFO landing reports for his INTCAT project. Rogerson read an early version of this book, the self-published* The Alien Deception: An Exploration of the Alien Abduction Phenomenon *(2009), and his comments appeared in* Magonia, *which granted permission to reprint his review as a foreword to this edition.*

Preface

Since the 1960s thousands of people throughout the world claim they have been abducted by aliens. They are snatched from their cars on lonely roads or from their beds in the dead of night.

Some say they are examined by seemingly benign alien beings who act like human scientists, while others say they are sadistically probed and prodded by unfeeling creatures who are the stuff of our worst nightmares.

Abductees often have little conscious recollection of these events, and usually through nightmares, flashbacks and hypnosis, they eventually learn more about their encounter with the unknown.

Often they believe they have been used as part of a breeding project to create hybrid alien/humans or are the victims of secret government projects conducted in league with the aliens. Certainly they are all truly bewildered by their experiences.

Ultimately, alien abductions make us consider fundamental questions about our place in the Universe and our future evolution as a species. Are we alone in the Universe or is this just wishful thinking?

Are abductions real events that have momentous consequences for the whole of humanity or are they the product of rumor, psychosis, hoaxes, media hype and sensationalism?

Is there a grand alien/government conspiracy manipulating our minds or are we deceiving ourselves?

The famous Betty and Barney Hill abduction in 1961 can be seen as the start of the abduction phenomenon as we know it today. By exploring their case and the evidence that supports it, this book branches out to examine the historical, paranormal, extraterrestrial, psychological and media influences that explain how reports of alien abductions in the United States have flourished and spread throughout the world.

3

Introduction

Most of us have heard tales of flying saucer sightings and stories of abductees, the victims of sometimes torturous medical examinations, but how did this come about?

U.S. abduction cases and media have had the most impact on the rest of the world and that is why they are so important. Other countries do report similar cases although they are influenced by their own social and cultural variations; for example, in Britain the alien greys are not so prevalent.

The theories and types of investigation conducted by ufologists have changed considerably since I first became interested in the subject in the 1970s. The belief in the Roswell flying saucer crash of 1947, abductions and U.S. government dealings with aliens has opened the field for even wilder speculation and theories.

In the 1950s, the so-called contactees claimed to meet Space People who looked just like us. They met them in cafés, bars, and other public places without anyone else knowing that there were aliens among them.

Besides these amiable encounters, the contactees often recounted stories of being taken in flying saucer craft to alien societies on Venus, Mars, and the Moon. As we now know, this was obviously impossible. So were the contactees cranks, or were they duped by their aliens?

Up to the 1970s, most serious ufologists, who fancied themselves as "scientific," discounted any case that involved the sighting of aliens. For them it was hard enough to prove the existence of flying saucers to a skeptical scientific community without bringing in bug-eyed aliens. Talk of aliens brought to mind low-budget science fiction movies and the wild stories of sensation-hungry contactees.

Yet, if these flying saucers were some type of spacecraft, then it was logical that they would contain pilots. Therefore, when such cases got attention from the serious ufology community in the late 1960s and early 1970s, aliens were called "occupants" or "humanoids." Indeed, a special edition of *Flying Saucer Review* that took a detailed look at worldwide cases of abduction and alien encounters was titled *The Humanoids.* It quickly sold out and was released as a book in 1969.

Since the 1980s, the "greys," as they are called, have become the most popular image of alien visitors. The greys have disproportionately large heads in relation to their spindly bodies. They have large almond-shaped eyes, but their nose and mouth are small; they have no hair or ears.

During this period, American ufologist and artist Budd Hopkins categorized many of the prime elements of the abduction experience. He discovered that UFO witnesses, with no inclination of an abduction experience, often cannot account for a missing period, ranging from minutes to hours. Abductions often start in childhood, continue throughout a person's life, and are not just isolated incidents. Abductees regularly find mysterious scars on their body; they are often confused and worried by dreams or nightmares that they have had since childhood. Under hypnosis they remember being inside a flying saucer. Typical memories recall medical procedures that include the taking of sperm or ova. At times, the experience amounts to a form of ritualized rape. From his study of hundreds of reports, Hopkins believes that aliens are abducting people to create human/alien hybrids.

As might be expected, such ideas have attracted the attention of both skeptics and believers. Skeptics regard the abduction researchers and abductees as gullible fools who do not know the difference between fact and fantasy. The believers regard the abductees as tortured victims who need understanding and help after the trauma of alien encounters.

Today, ufologists tend to use the terms *alien, visitor* or *grey* to describe the beings seen in association with UFOs. Ufologists who think aliens come from other dimensions or astral planes prefer the terms *entity* or *ultraterrestrial.* In contrast, those who think the aliens are biological beings prefer the terms *E.T. (Extraterrestrial)* or *E.B.E. (Extraterrestrial Biological Entity).*

I prefer the term *alien* and use it in this text because it leaves open the possibility that any visitors may have an extraterrestrial, psychological, or supernatural origin.

I have opted to use the abduction experience of Betty and Barney Hill, which took place in 1961, as a means of understanding their experience and how it relates to abduction history, investigation, research, explanations and implications.

1

Are We the First?

The Hill Abduction

The Betty and Barney Hill abduction became an overnight sensation when details of their experience were leaked to the *Boston Herald Traveler* newspaper which published a series of articles about them in October 1965. The following year their experiences became the subject of John Fuller's book *The Interrupted Journey*, which was serialized in newspapers and magazines throughout the world.[1]

The great Hollywood film mogul Samuel Goldwyn said, "Give me a couple of years, and I'll make that actress an overnight sensation." For Betty and Barney Hill, it took nearly three years for their case to achieve this status. Before we look at how their abduction experiences were recalled and put on public display, we should look at the UFO sighting that triggered a series of events that had far-reaching consequences for the Hills and for UFO research throughout the world.

The Trigger Event

It all began on the night of September 19, 1961, when they were driving back from a short holiday in Canada to their home in Portsmouth, New Hampshire. They took a break in a restaurant at Colebrook and resumed their journey at 10:05 p.m. As they drove southward along U.S. Highway 3, they saw a light moving erratically in the sky. Stopping at a picnic ground, before they got to Cannon Mountain, they looked at the light through binoculars. They speculated that it was a commercial airliner or Piper Cub aircraft, but its movements were too erratic. It did not seem to be a helicopter, as they could not hear any sound from its motors. Through the binoculars, it looked like the body of an aircraft without any wings. Colored lights flashed along the body of the craft. Barney resorted to thinking it was a search plane or a military aircraft. Meanwhile their Dachshund, Delsey, was whining and wanted to go back in the car. Barney began thinking the object was playing games with them and that it was observing them.

The object ran parallel to their car while they drove through the White Mountain gorges. As they progressed, the craft seemed to grow larger. To Betty, it appeared to be spinning and it had a double row of windows. It was now visible as a large structure with red lights.

After passing a place called Indian Head, Barney stopped their car in the middle of the road and ran across a field to get a better view of the craft. Not hearing Betty's urgent screams for him to get back in the car, he got as close as 50 feet (15 meters) to the UFO, which was hovering at about tree height. Looking through binoculars, he saw a row of windows and five or six uniformed beings moving behind them. All of these beings moved away to work at a large control panel inside the craft, except for one who looked like a German. This being, which he thought was the leader, stared intently at him.

Not surprisingly, Barney was gripped by an overwhelming fear; nonetheless, he could not tear himself away. When the craft slowly descended, and a ladder started to appear from underneath it, he got the idea that they planned to capture them. This broke his apparent paralysis, and he quickly dashed back to the safety of the car.

As the Hills sped away from the scene, they heard a strange beeping or buzzing sound striking the trunk of the car. At this point, they experienced a tingling sensation and they were overcome with drowsiness. When they heard the same beeping sound again, they found they were at Ashland, 35 miles south of the sighting location.

In response to an enquiry from a UFO investigator, Barb Becker, in 1990, Betty Hill said that one of the humanoids had spoken to Barney and that was why he had come running back to the car shouting that they were going to capture them. The car vibrated when they heard the first set of beeping sounds, but instead of experiencing "missing time" at this moment, they drove down a secondary road. Along here, they saw what they thought was the Moon setting behind the trees ahead of them. They saw some men in the road blocking their way, and it was from that point that they remembered nothing until they found themselves driving along the road in search of the main highway. They watched the craft fly away, and then when they rejoined the highway, they heard the beeping sound again. What Betty does not mention is that this additional information came to her in a series of dreams she had about their encounter every night from September 29 to October 3, 1961.

Betty claimed that they could not talk about this puzzling experience and that they wanted to forget about it. Yet her subsequent actions contradict this statement.

Indeed, on the afternoon of September 20, Betty rang her sister, Janet, who had seen a UFO four years previously, to talk about the encounter. She also spoke to a police officer about the sighting and he told her to report it to the nearby Pease Air Force Base, and that is what she did, but she did not mention that they saw any humanoids. At first, the officer was skeptical, but he spoke to Barney and reassured him that UFO sightings were not that unusual. The next day Major Paul W. Henderson telephoned them to say that he had spent all night writing a report about their sighting.

This was recorded as report No. 100-1-61 and sent to Project Blue Book. As this is the only official report concerning this case, and it was written only a few hours after the sighting when it was still fresh in the witnesses' memory, it is worth quoting in detail. This tells us that just after driving southward past Lincoln, New Hampshire, the Hills saw a brightly lit object in front of them that quickly went northward and then southward:

> Shortly thereafter, it stopped and hovered in the air. There was no sound evident up to this time. Both observers used the binoculars at this point. While hovering, objects began to appear from the body of the "object," which they describe as looking like wings, which made a V shape then extended. The "wings" had red lights on the tips.... The object continued to descend until it appeared to be only a matter of "hundreds of feet" above their car. At this point, they decided to get out of that area, and fast.[2]

It went on to say that they heard a series of short and loud buzzing sounds in their car and that these were repeated when they reached Ashland. Besides not referring to seeing the beings inside the craft, they did not mention their loss of memory prior to reaching Ashland and hearing the buzzing/beeping sound again.

Revealing the Abduction

Only two days after the sighting Betty visited her local library to find out more about UFOs. On obtaining Major Donald Keyhoe's book *The Flying Saucer Conspiracy*, she read it in one sitting and wrote to him about their sighting on September 26, 1961.[3]

Then, as previously mentioned, from September 29 to October 3, 1961, came Betty's nightmares about their encounter. She dreamt that some men took them to a landed craft in the nearby woods and conducted medical examinations on them before returning them to the car. These dreams outlined what they later recalled under hypnotic regression. Betty tended to think these dreams were memories of real events, but Barney just thought they were vivid dreams. She had these dreams when Barney was working night shifts. After typing up her account of the dreams, she hid them away; it was only after the hypnotic regression sessions with Dr. Benjamin Simon that she discussed them.

In response to the letter to Major Keyhoe, Walter Webb, a scientific advisor for the National Investigations Committee on Aerial Phenomena (NICAP), visited the Hills. Although he was skeptical about encounters with aliens, he was impressed by the story given by the Hills. After meeting them on October 21, 1961, he wrote a report about their case. In it, he noted:

> It is the opinion of this investigator, after questioning these people for six hours and studying their reactions and personalities during that time, that they were telling the truth, and the incident occurred exactly as reported except for some minor uncertainties and technicalities that must be tolerated in any such observation where human judgment is involved.[4]

A meeting that was to have a great deal of importance for the whole case occurred on November 25, 1961, when two UFO investigators associated with NICAP, Robert Hohmann and C.D. Jackson, interviewed the Hills for 12 hours. Also in attendance was Major James McDonald, an Air Force intelligence officer based at Pease Air Force Base. Some ufologists have suggested dark and sinister meanings to his presence, but he was an old friend of Barney's. Indeed, Betty and Barney socialized with many people who worked at the air base.

During the meeting, investigators tried piecing together the journey. They discovered that the journey was two hours longer than expected. Betty claims that they already knew that they could not account for the whole of their journey and that this meeting merely confirmed that there was a period of missing time.

The Hills spoke about the sighting of the humanoids but not about Betty's dreams. During the interview, they were worried by the idea that they had hallucinated the whole experience. Major McDonald suggested they might consider hypnosis to get to the root of the matter. Since he was unable to recommend any hypnotists, this avenue of investigation was left alone for the time being.

John Fuller gave the impression that Major McDonald was the first person to suggest hypnosis, but this is untrue. John and Anne Spencer in their book *Fifty Years of UFOs* (Boxtree, 1997, 46–49) reveal that Betty actually suggested using hypnosis in her letter to Keyhoe dated September 26, 1961. When Fuller reproduced this letter in *The Interrupted Journey*, he left out just one essential line: "We are considering the possibility of a competent psychiatrist who uses hypnosis." The Spencers thought he delayed the introduction of hypnosis to the story to strengthen its dramatic effect. Another suggestion given at this meeting was to find the exact place where the "men" stopped their car. In early 1962, they felt compelled to visit the mountains in all weathers to try to find it, hoping it would rekindle their memories or give any clues as to what they saw. Hilary Evans noted that the mystery of the abduction location adds a dash of drama to the case and that there was an implication that the aliens had brainwashed them into taking this route. He thought during the confusion caused by the UFO sighting they could have easily strayed onto Route 175 that ran parallel to the main highway.[5]

It is obvious that despite saying that they wanted to forget it, their UFO experience would not leave their minds. Since the incident was still obviously troubling them on March 12, 1962, NICAP suggested that they undergo hypnosis. This time Betty thought the idea of hypnosis was a good idea because "the moment they suggested hypnosis, I thought of my dreams, and this was the first time I began to wonder if they were more than just dreams. Then I really got upset over my dreams. I thought, well now, if I have hypnosis, I'll know one way or the other..."[6]

No hypnosis was carried out on them, but by the summer of 1962, Barney's health dramatically deteriorated. The medication provided by his doctor was of no help, so his doctor sent him to Dr. Duncan Stephens, a psychiatrist who worked in the same building. During these therapy sessions, he spoke about his early childhood and his personal problems. It was when Barney mentioned that they had made repeated visits to the mountains to try to find the location of their UFO encounter that Dr. Stephens thought that he was suffering from some form of amnesia.

After a year with no progress in resolving his anxiety, Dr. Stephens agreed that hypnosis might help both Barney and Betty, so he referred them to psychiatrist and neurologist Dr. Benjamin Simon. John Fuller said when they made their first visit to Dr. Simon on December 14, 1963:

> The reality or non-reality of the dreams was of course foremost in Betty's mind. For nearly two years now, the answer to the question had been gnawing away at her. For Barney, as he had already told Betty, was hoping that for once and all she accept the fact that her experience in regard to an abduction was no more than an intense series of dreams.[7]

This put the emphasis on Betty and the UFO angle rather than on the fact that these sessions were mainly arranged to resolve Barney's psychological and physical problems. Looking back on their first visits to Dr. Simon, Betty said, "I don't know if we even mentioned UFOs. It was to find out why Barney was emotionally upset."[8]

From January 4 to June 27, 1964, they drove once a week to Boston to see Dr. Simon. During these meetings, he hypnotized them separately, and because "reliving" the UFO encounter was so traumatic for them, at the end of their sessions, he would reactivate their amnesia. Reintroducing the amnesia also meant that they could not overtly influence each other's recollection of the events.

All the sessions were recorded on audiotape and these were given to the Hills at the end of the last session. Dr. Simon advised them to listen to the tapes as this might help reduce their trauma.[9]

The Abduction Recalled

Dr. Simon hypnotized Barney first. He took him back to the time when he watched the UFO through binoculars near Indian Head. Barney recalled that the being that seemed to be the leader looked like an evil German Nazi because he was dressed all in black. He even wore a black scarf that was draped over his left shoulder, which sounds like rather unusual garb for an alien. Behind this figure, he saw a more benevolent red-haired, round-faced Irishman. Barney stated, "He's telling me: 'Don't be afraid.... I'm going to be safe.'"[10]

It was when they drove on the secondary road and met the "men" blocking the road that the abduction story and what happened during the missing two hours were revealed. The men told him to close his eyes and he found himself being floated along. He could not feel them holding him, but his feet dragged on the ground.

After going up an incline, he found himself in a pale blue hospital operating room. He found himself lying on a table. There they carried out a physical examination on him that included putting a cup over his groin. When the cup was removed, he got off the table and he was guided back to his car, again with his eyes closed.

He walked, rather than floated, back to the car and he was happy when he opened his eyes to see Betty returning. After two hypnotic regression sessions, Barney began for the first time to have dreams about UFOs. These might have been produced by "real" memories of his encounter, which hypnosis was bringing back to his mind through the backdoor of his subconscious. Alternatively, they could have been further examples of UFO-related fantasies that were not that different from what he "recalled" under hypnosis. Indeed, at his second regression session on February 29, 1964, when recounting being taken from his car by the men, he said, "I feel like I am dreaming."

During Betty's sessions, which began on March 7, 1964, she recalled that when the men approached their car, a kind of drowsiness overcame them. She shouted at Barney to wake up, but he continued to walk away with the men. One of the men, who spoke with a foreign accent, told her not to be afraid. "We are not going to hurt you."

There were already a couple of contradictions in their statements. Firstly, Betty saw Barney walking to the craft while he said he was floated and dragged toward it. Secondly, she said that they spoke to her while Barney said that they used telepathy. He described it as being "as if the words were there, a part of me, and he was outside the actual creation of the words themselves."[11]

In subsequent years, Betty categorically stated, "There was no mental telepathy. They spoke loud and clear and they had a language of their own."[12] Altogether, there were about a dozen aliens, who were approximately five feet, four inches (1.6 meters) tall. These humanoids had no ears but had slit-like mouths, small noses, cat-like eyes that seemed to extend to the side of their heads, and broad foreheads that tapered down to small chins.

Inside the disc-shape craft, Betty was taken to an examination room. They looked at her mouth, eyes, ears and throat, and they took samples of her skin, nails and hair. They unzipped her dress and she was asked to remove it. Needles attached to wires prodded all over her body. When she was asked to roll over, they pierced her navel with a long needle. As the needle was withdrawn, she felt sore, and on asking why they did it, she was told it was a pregnancy test. She replied that it was no pregnancy test she had ever known.

When allowed to put her dress back on, she asked if she could take some proof of this meeting home with her. Finding a book with strange writing in it, the leader alien agreed to let her take it. After asking if she knew anything about the Universe, he showed her a map with dots and lines on it.

Just as she was about to leave the UFO the book was taken away from her. Betty screamed, "You can take the book but you can never make me forget!" As she walked back to the car the leader apologized for frightening them at the beginning of the encounter. In just a few moments, her extreme anger with the aliens turned to joy: "I'm saying to the leader, 'This is the most wonderful experience of my life. I hope you'll come back. I got a lot of friends who would love to meet you.'"[13]

Back at the car, she saw Barney sitting inside it. Although his eyes were open, he seemed to be in a daze. Then the UFO flew away, Barney started the car and Betty was happy. Given that she left the craft happy and that the abduction was nothing like as traumatic as those reported in subsequent years, Betty was asked by Peter Huston why she and Barney had suffered so much anxiety in the aftermath of their encounter. Betty's answer was that the fear of kidnapping and the uncertainty of what was going to happen had really scared them. Their fears and mixed feelings about the experience were the very factors that sent them to seek Dr. Simon's help.

Peter Huston went on to ask hesitantly whether the aliens had a sexual interest in them. Betty was prickly about this issue, as it was something that people kept asking her. Her answer was that they had no such interest. She changed the topic in her reply, but a bit later, he mentioned David Jacobs' claim that they had taken sperm samples from Barney. Betty denied this but pointed out that the type of pregnancy test she had onboard the craft was actually developed in Houston, Texas, in 1970. As for interbreeding with aliens, she thought this was impossible, as they were physically different from us.[14]

Post Abduction

On the evening of the last hypnotic regression session, Barney rang Ben Swett. Way back in

Betty and Barney Hill described the aliens they encountered as humanoid. They were approximately five feet, four inches (1.6 meters) tall, had no ears, slit-like mouths, small noses, cat-like eyes that seemed to extend to the side of their heads, and broad foreheads that tapered down to a small chin (illustration by Richard Svensson).

September 1963, they had spoken to him about hypnosis after he had given a talk on this subject at their local Unitarian church. He had suggested that they consult a more qualified person than himself to carry out hypnosis on them. Now that they had been hypnotized, they asked if they could listen to the tapes with him, as they did not want to hear them on their own. At Swett's home that night they played the tapes. He noted:

> I was skeptical at first, but hearing what was on those tapes, plus the fact they didn't want any publicity, convinced me they were telling the truth. For example, under hypnosis, Barney described seeing the UFO hovering close to the ground near the road. He got out of his car, walked toward it and looked at it through binoculars. Something like a man was looking at him out of a window—right into his eyes—and started putting thoughts in his mind: "He says 'Come a little closer.... Don't be scared' ... uh.... I used to talk to rabbits like that ... when I was hunting them." Just before the point on the tape where Barney started screaming "I've gotta get outta here!" and ran back to his car, the physical Barney jumped up and ran out to our kitchen and vomited in the sink. I thought that would be pretty hard to fake.[15]

They left the tapes with Swett and he spent the next few days listening to them and making copious notes. The Hills were still worried that their abduction experience was nothing more than a fantasy. He met them a few times and offered them the opinion that they had really been taken inside a spacecraft that was carrying out a scientific examination of our planet.

Media Exposure

A Boston newspaper reporter heard about the Hills' abduction at a cocktail party held at Pease Air Force Base. Not long afterward, without consultation with the Hills, the story was splashed across the front pages of the *Boston Herald Traveler* for five days running. On the first day of publication, Betty came home from work to find her home mobbed by the media. Due to the time difference, their story appeared in European newspapers earlier than the United States. The Hills got telephone calls from throughout Europe, and in a panic, Barney rang Ben Swett at 4 a.m. on October 25, 1965, to ask for his help. Barney suspected that someone at NICAP had leaked the story and he was very upset about this. They consulted a lawyer, but he said the story was not libelous so they could do nothing about it.

The interest in their UFO experience became so intense that they agreed to a television interview. This was held at a Unitarian church in Dover, New Hampshire, on November 8, 1965. People packed the small church and formed a line down the street to hear the details of their unusual experience. One person in this mêlée was John Fuller, who asked to speak to the Hills. Thus were sown the seeds for his book on their encounter, *The Interrupted Journey*, and the future course of ufology and the popular conception of alien encounters was to irrevocably change.

2

Mind Games

Flying Saucer Conspiracies

At first, there was a genuine belief that there was something to the flying saucer sightings. Many thought they could be secret Soviet or U.S. aircraft, but as time passed the idea that they were visitors from outer space, exploring our planet before the launch of a fully-fledged invasion, took a grip on the popular imagination.

Given the political context, the Hills could have been embroiled in some form of conspiracy or covert intelligence operation. British ufologist Peter Rogerson pointed out that Betty and Barney's left-wing political activities would have brought them to the attention of the authorities.[1]

We must remember that their experiences took place at the height of the Cold War and that the FBI and CIA and other agencies did monitor groups or people that might be regarded as subversive.

The shadowy presence of the government is often discerned in the reports of the infamous Men-in-Black (MIB) who intimidate UFO witnesses and remove evidence of UFO activities. A neighbor, going to the Hills' house a few weeks after their abduction, saw two such MIB. How the person identified them as MIB was not revealed though it does show that people were on the lookout for such characters.

A more detailed and frightening MIB visitation connected with the Hill case occurred several years later. A single MIB visited Dr. Herbert Hopkins at 8 p.m. on September 11, 1976. A person alleging to be the vice president of the New Jersey UFO Research Organization telephoned him expressing an interest in the case of David Stephens, who Hopkins had recently hypnotized. Almost immediately after Dr. Hopkins agreed to see him, the MIB appeared at his door. He was immaculately dressed in a black suit with a white shirt. Even when he sat down, the crease in his trousers remained perfect. Even stranger, when he removed his hat, Hopkins realized that the man's head was hairless; he did not even have any eyelashes or eyebrows. He had a slit-like mouth, he wore red lipstick, and he spoke perfect English, which was expressionless.

The MIB said, "That's just what I thought" after Hopkins told him about the Stephens investigation. He then accurately guessed the number of coins in Hopkins' pocket and made one disappear. This cheap trickery was followed by a question. Did Hopkins know how Barney Hill died? Hopkins answered that he thought it was of a heart attack (he was wrong but did not know this at the time). The MIB explained that Barney died because he had no heart, just as Hopkins no longer had his coin.

Then came the threats. The MIB told him to destroy all the material he had relating to the Stephens case and to UFOs, otherwise he would end up like Barney Hill.[2] A nephew of Hopkins has revealed that his uncle liked being the center of attention and probably made this story up. He wrote: "My uncle was, unfortunately, a fantasy-prone individual, craved the center of attention and limelight and on a base level he sometimes just made things up—no matter how hyperbolic—to top everybody else. As brilliant as he was in many areas, however, he was unskilled at fiction."[3]

Hopkins' story was possibly inspired by contactee Truman Bethurum, who in the early 1950s had several meetings with a space lady called Aura Rhanes. To demonstrate her power, she asked him to hold a flashlight on his hand. She stared at it and it vanished. Just like Hopkins' MIB, she told Bethurum that this is what would happen to humanity if they were ever attacked.[4]

MIB in general could be used as part of a dirty tricks operation to discredit witnesses and to stop people revealing the "truth" about UFOs and alien operations. Traditionally they go around in gangs of three and drive old yet mint-condition black Cadillacs.

From the very beginning when the term "flying saucers" hit the head-lines, after Kenneth Arnold saw nine UFOs over Mount Rainier, on June 24, 1947, U.S. government agencies took an interest in UFO reports.

While flying from Chehalis to Yakima, Washington, he saw a blinding flash of light. Looking around he saw nine very thin half-Moon shaped objects moving southward from Mount Rainier. They flew in a diagonal formation that stretched about five miles from the first to last craft, and they bobbed about erratically. He estimated that they traveled faster than 1,000 miles per hour as they flew from Mount Rainier to Mount Adams.

At Yakima, he reported his sighting to Al Baxter, the general manager of Central Aircraft. News of his story spread rapidly and when he flew on to Pendleton, Oregon, a group of newspaper reporters were waiting for him. It was here that he described these craft as moving "like a saucer would if you skipped it across the water." Thereby the term flying saucer came from the description of the movement of the craft rather than their appearance.

On July 12, 1947, special agent Lieutenant Frank M. Brown of A-2, Military Intelligence, Fourth Air Force, interviewed Arnold and was very impressed by his truthfulness and character. Later, on July 25, Lieutenant Brown and Captain William Davidson took Arnold and his wife out to dinner. At this meeting, they said they could not explain what he had seen. Explanations from mirages, secret aircraft to the flight of pelicans have all been used to try to explain his sighting but it still remains a mystery.

Within days of the concept of flying saucers getting worldwide publicity, the Maury Island case takes us down the route of conspiracy, sinister plots, MIB, abduction, double bluffs, sabotage, death and assassination. All these elements were to be integrated into mainstream ufology by the 1980s. For this reason alone it is worthy of a detailed re-examination.

At about 2 p.m. on the afternoon of June 21, 1947, Harold A. Dahl, his teenage son Charles and two unnamed crew members were in their boat off Maury Island, Washington, when they observed six large dough-nut-shaped objects high above them. They beached their boat and took several pictures of the craft.

One of the UFOs was wobbling as if it was in trouble. When it dropped to an altitude of about 500 feet, it dumped a large amount of thin white metallic strips resembling aluminum. These were followed by black lumps of hot lava-like material. One lump hit and burned the boy's arm and another killed his dog. It was estimated that an incredible 20 tons of debris was dropped before all six craft departed. Dahl tried radioing for help, but the radio would not work while the UFOs were in the vicinity.

On returning, they gave the dog a burial at sea, and then Dahl showed his skeptical boss, Fred Crisman, samples of the rock as evidence. The photographic evidence did not help as the pictures were ruined by what looked like exposure to X-rays.

The MIB encounter took place at 7 a.m. the next day when a man, about 40 years old, turned up at Dahl's home asking about buying salvaged timber. The man, who was dressed in black, took Dahl in a new 1947 black Buick sedan to breakfast at a smart diner in Tacoma. Here the MIB recounted the full details of Dahl's UFO encounter and went on to warn him to keep quiet; otherwise, something might happen to him or his family. Dahl ignored this advice.

The next day, June 23, 1947, Dahl's boss Fred Lee Crisman visited the scene to see the debris for himself. When a UFO matching those described by Dahl appeared, he grabbed samples of the debris and fled. Crisman gave details of the case to Ray Palmer, who was the publisher of pulp science fiction and horror magazines. Since Kenneth Arnold lived in

Boise, which is not that far from Tacoma, Palmer asked him to investigate the incident. Arnold was not keen on conducting this investigation, but after he gave a lecture at a Boise luncheon club, a member of the audience spoke about the case and said that Harold Dahl was a reliable witness.

Intrigued by this information, Arnold flew to Tacoma on July 29. He checked into room 502 at the Winthrop Hotel. That evening he met Dahl, who warned Arnold that he should not get involved with the case. Unable to put off Arnold, he showed him some of the material dropped by the UFO. It looked like ordinary lava rock and Arnold immediately thought he was being tricked.

The following day Arnold collected Captain E.J. Smith, who had recently seen nine round UFOs over Emmett, Idaho, to help him. On July 31, still feeling out of his depth, Arnold asked the two officers who had originally interviewed him about his own flying saucer sighting to come over. That evening Captain William Davidson and Lieutenant Frank M. Brown came to the hotel where they spoke to Crisman and collected some of the rock samples. Like Arnold, the rocks did not impress them, and at 2 a.m., they decided to return to their base at Hamilton Field, California.

As they were flying back in their B-25, the port engine caught fire. The crew chief and a hitchhiker parachuted to safety before the aircraft crashed at Kelso, killing Davidson and Brown. Later that day Ted Morello spoke to the two survivors of the crash. The hitchhiker, Master Sergeant Elmer Taff, claimed that before they took off he saw a large carton loaded onto the aircraft.

Ufologists tend to think this carton contained the UFO debris. The official explanation was that these were secret files in transit and that was why the military cordoned off the crash site and did not allow any photographs to be taken. The other survivor was flight engineer Woodrew Mathews, who said he saw "something" leave the top of the plane. He assumed it was the parachute of one of the officers, but it was probably the port wing that tore off and slammed into the tail of the aircraft sending it on its fatal descent to the ground.[5]

Only hours before the crash, a mysterious phone caller told the *Tacoma Times* all about Kenneth Arnold's meeting with the two investigators. After the crash and before the details of it were made public, the caller told the newspaper the names of the men who were killed and recalled that the aircraft had been sabotaged or shot down by a 20mm cannon because it was carrying fragments of a flying disc. This seemed to indicate that the caller had bugged Arnold's room, yet after a thorough search, no bug was found.

Was the caller the mysterious MIB who had warned Dahl about dabbling with UFOs? So far, two men and a dog had been killed, and Kenneth Arnold was nearly added to the list. When he took off from Tacoma, his engine failed, and he had to make a crash landing. On checking his aircraft, he found that his fuel valve had been switched off.

Another strange incident occurred not long after the UFO sighting when Dahl's son went missing. He was out of contact for a week until he was found at Lusk, Montana (some accounts say Colorado). He had no memory of how he got there. Perhaps if he was hypnotically regressed, he would have recalled an alien abduction, or was he just being a wayward teenager? Certainly, no one at the time, including Arnold, thought it had anything to do with the UFO sighting.

In her book *MIB: Investigating the Truth Behind the Men in Black Phenomenon*, Jenny Randles was in general favor of the idea that Kenneth Arnold was set up in some sort of elaborate hoax that got out of hand.[6]

Most of the evidence relied on Crisman and Dahl's testimony since the photographs of the craft were lost and samples of rock got spirited away. Palmer was posted some of the rock and these were stolen from his office. A Major George Sander took Arnold's from him. Major Sander, an intelligence commander at McChord Field in Tacoma, visited Captain Smith and Arnold at the Winthrop on August 3. He carefully wrapped every fragment of rock and then drove them to a nearby smelting works where he showed them where he thought they came from.

Out of respect for the two dead officers, Arnold and Smith agreed not to speak about the matter. The samples taken by the officers were presumably destroyed in the air crash, although John Keel stated they threw them away before they got on the plane.

The Federal Bureau of Investigation (FBI) took an interest in this case due to the allegation of sabotage to the B-25 and to discover more details about the flying disc. On August 6 and 7, 1947, an FBI special agent was dispatched to Tacoma to conduct an investigation. He interviewed a newspaper reporter, who was sent by the *Seattle Post Intelligencer* to speak with Howard Dahl about the flying disc story sometime in June 1947. Fred Crisman tipped off the newspaper about this.

In the kitchen of his home, Howard Dahl told the reporter about seeing five or six discs, one of which fluttered to the earth and disintegrated, causing the death of his dog. Dahl spoke in a low voice and was acting suspiciously. His wife appeared and angrily declared that the whole story was a plain fantasy concocted by Dahl, and she made him admit it was a hoax. Given the enraged behavior of the wife, the reporter quickly left. He told the *Seattle Post Intelligencer* that Dahl was a "mental case" and that they should not carry the story.

The agent spoke to Crisman and Dahl, who were evasive and at a loss to explain how the rock fragments became connected with the story of flying discs. After much questioning, they admitted that they had sent Ray Palmer some rock fragments that were found in a gravel pit on Maury Island in early June. It was their contention that Palmer asked if the rocks were connected with flying discs and they told him it was a possibility. They had merely told him what he wanted to hear.[7]

The FBI documents show that the B-25 was not sabotaged. It was their opinion that rather than the hotel being bugged, Crisman had probably been the anonymous caller to the *Tacoma Times*. Although they had no solid evidence, they thought he made the calls to make the story more important, thereby increasing his payment from Palmer.

The files make no mention of the MIB story though they do suggest how it might have originated. Captain Smith told the FBI agent that on the morning of August 2, he, Arnold, Dahl and Crisman had met at a coffee shop near the Winthrop. At the meeting was an unknown man who discussed lumber with Dahl and left after breakfast. To me this sounds like a prototype for the more elaborate MIB story. At the coffee shop Dahl was asked about the photographs of the flying discs, and he said the negatives were in his car's glove box. When he went to get them there was no sign of them anywhere in his car. It was equally frustrating when they went to his boat to visit Maury Island. Here they found no evidence of it having been showered by hot lava rock; furthermore, it would not start, so the trip was abandoned.

As we can see, the story quickly became complex and convoluted and over the years has gained more erroneous and exotic details. Dahl and Crisman are often claimed to be part of the local Coast Guard harbor patrol, when in reality Dahl used his boat to collect unmarked logs to resell and to carry out security patrols for owners of beach cottages. The FBI files noted that Crisman went to work with Dahl as a pilot for his private plane. When investigating Crisman for a job application, the FBI found that he was generally of good character. His faults were that he had a poor credit rating and lacked good judgment. It also mentioned that Dahl was rumored to have dabbled in the black market during World War II and that he stole the idea of running the boat from Crisman. Since it was Crisman who tipped off the press and told Palmer about this case, we can wonder if he did it to set up Dahl as a form of revenge.

Crisman had established a track record for telling tall tales to Palmer's *Amazing Stories* magazine. He wrote to them with a story of one of his wartime experiences to confirm the magazine's ongoing support of Richard Shaver's Hollow Earth theories. This appeared in the letters to the editor section of the June 1946 edition:

Sirs:

I flew my last combat mission on May 26 [1945] when I was shot up over Bassein and ditched my ship in Ramaree Roads off Chedubs Island. I was missing for five days. I requested leave at Kashmere. I and Capt. --- [deleted by request] left Srinagar and went to Rudok then through the Khese pass to the northern foothills of Karakoram. We found what we were searching for.

For heaven's sake, drop the whole thing! You are playing with dynamite. My companion and I fought our way out of a cave with submachine guns. I have two 9 inch scars on my left arm that came from wounds given me in the cave when I was 50 feet from a moving object of some kind and in perfect silence. The muscles were nearly ripped out. How? I don't know. My friend had a hole the size of a dime in his right bicep. It was seared inside. How we don't know. But we both believe we know more about the Shaver Mystery than any other pair.

You can imagine my fright when I picked up my first copy of *Amazing Stories* and see you splashing words about on the subject.

It is often stated that after the air crash Dahl disappeared completely, "as if he had been professionally relocated—a tactic commonly used by intelligence services," according to Jenny Randles.[8] Crisman is thought to have been flown to Alaska in an Army aircraft, which is probably the U.S. equivalent of being sent to Siberia. Reinforcing the idea that this was a government operation, Randles wondered if Brown and Davidson escaped from their B-25 before it crashed. Faking their own deaths to cover their tracks sounds rather extreme even by ufological standards.[9]

To add fuel to the conspiracy theory, Paul Lance, a reporter for the *Tacoma Times*, died of meningitis two weeks after the air crash. He had written about the case for his newspaper and he gave full details of his involvement to the FBI. Years later, Kenneth Arnold claimed, "the cause of his death was not clear … he lay on a slab in the morgue for about 36 hours while the pathologists apparently hemmed and hawed."[10] On the other hand, Lance had been confined to a wheelchair before his death, so it was not perhaps as "sudden" as some reports suggest.[11]

It seems odd that in the FBI file on Crisman the material from Maury Island was described as being rock from a gravel pit. There is even the suggestion that they planned to sell bits of the rock. Yet, in most accounts, the material is described as slag or lava-type rocks. Arnold said he put together some of these pieces and they looked as if they had lined a six-foot diameter tube.[12] In recent years, the fragments have taken on more importance as they provide an alternative and equally sinister explanation for Dahl's UFO encounter.

The answer to this puzzle was all too obvious to controversial ufologist John Keel. The slag was not the remains of a crashed flying saucer or anything connected with extraterrestrial activity. The slag was radioactive waste from the Hanford nuclear processing plant, which was busy manufacturing weapons grade plutonium. To get rid of the huge amounts of radioactive waste it produced as a by-product it resorted to dumping it into the Pacific. Dahl had simply seen a cargo aircraft get into difficulties, causing it to dump its radioactive waste where it could, in this instance Maury Island and Puget Sound.

The aircrew spotted Dahl's boat and took pictures of it. When they got back to Hanford, they alerted the Atomic Energy Commission's own elite force of special agents about the incident. As a means of covering up this highly secret operation, they tracked down Dahl by going through the hospital records where he had taken his son with his burned arm. The next day an agent from the AEC visited Dahl and started this particular MIB rumor.

Keel went on to state that at the time AEC was trying to stop atomic secrets going to the Soviet Union. In the process they tapped phones, bugged hotel rooms and kept track of strangers in the vicinity of atomic plants like Hanford. It was the AEC who had bugged Arnold's room at the Winthrop, and they had employed Crisman to turn the sighting into a flying saucer mystery. They saw this as the best way of covering up their nefarious dumping activities. It was also his contention that Brown and Davidson lost interest in the slag when Crisman mentioned Hanford and his own "vague association" with the AEC.[13]

There are several problems with this solution. First, we have to accept that the crew of a troubled aircraft would have the time to photograph Dahl's boat, with enough detail for the AEC to track him down. How, for instance, would they have known that Dahl's son was injured and that he would go to the local hospital? No bugs were found in the hotel room, and even if it were bugged, why would the AEC telephone the information gained in this way to the local newspaper? Another flaw is why use flying saucers as a method of covering up this incident at a time when such cases were guaranteed to attract front-page headlines?

As proof that radioactive waste had been dumped, Keel noted that the *Tacoma Times* reporter, Paul Lance, visited Maury Island a few weeks after the incident and found piles of slag surrounded by a fence with a sign warning "PROPERTY OF U.S. GOVERNMENT. KEEP OUT." It seems incredible that he made such a visit if he had been confined to a wheelchair and was dead merely two weeks after the affair.

Paul Thompson of *Nebula* magazine agreed with Keel's solution but Jenny Randles dismissed it in one paragraph as unfounded speculation.[14] Even if Keel explained the slag or lava as radioactive waste, we must still ask what happened to the thin white metallic strips resembling aluminum that were initially discharged from the UFO? Arnold and Smith saw that it looked like normal aircraft alloy but they were intrigued by the fact that two pieces had been riveted with a square rather than a round rivet.[15]

Ron Halbritter made the intriguing observation that the debris found at the equally infamous Roswell UFO crash site were also described as resembling thin aluminum material.[16] This occurred only a few days after Dahl's UFO sighting. Initially the USAF declared that they had found the remains of a flying saucer. They quickly retrieved all the material and announced that it was the remains of a conventional weather balloon. The case was largely forgotten or at best dismissed as a footnote in UFO history until the late 1970s. Since then it has encouraged all manner of "eye witnesses" (or friends of friends of eye witnesses) to the debris and talk of dead alien bodies being retrieved and held in storage by the USAF. To some this is the ultimate proof that the U.S. government has concrete evidence of the alien presence; to others it is a myth that has been inflated out of all proportion to the facts.

Rather than a spaceship, some ufologists have claimed that a Japanese FUJI balloon that had been launched during World War II had finally come to earth caused the Roswell crash. Another explanation was that this was a top-secret U.S. balloon. In this context, it is interesting to note that Dahl did not see any propellers or any other type of propulsion system on the UFOs and they did not make any sound. At first, he thought the craft were balloons. They certainly seemed more like balloons than Keel's cargo aircraft.[17]

Captain Edward Ruppelt, the former head of official UFO investigations, in his book *The Report on UFOs*, firmly believed that this was "the dirtiest hoax in the UFO history."[18] Thirty years after the incident, Arnold still wondered who had been hoaxing who.

Even if that was all there was to it, then the Maury Island case would still remain one of the most intriguing chapters in the history of ufology, but it has far more links with current worries about alien activities and their collaboration with secret human organizations. It also extends to links with the Hill case.

If we fast-forward to October 1968, Fred Lee Crisman cropped up again when he was subpoenaed to go before the grand jury in charge of investigating the assassination of John F. Kennedy. District Attorney Jim Garrison's enquiry thought he resembled one of the three tramps arrested near Dealey Plaza, Dallas, Texas, on the day of the assassination. Garrison believed Crisman was a long-standing CIA employee and was involved in a range of dubious activities, including the JFK killing. It was revealed that, between 1947 and 1968, Crisman had an unusual range of occupations: under the name Jon Gold he was a right-wing talk show host for KAYE radio in Puyallup, Washington; he was president of a car lot and several companies that had no offices; he worked in a government project to aid gypsies; he was a bishop in the CIA-linked Universal Life Church; and he worked for Boeing as an industrial psychologist.

At about the time Crisman was subpoenaed, he was arrested for carrying a concealed weapon and drunk driving. John Keel asserts that Crisman had been driving slowly in his brand-new Oldsmobile when he was arrested, indicating that he had upset the police in Tacoma. After he returned to Tacoma in 1966 under the name of Jon Gold, his radio show and his writings attacking local politics had made him many enemies, indeed someone even shot at his car not long before the subpoena. A CIA dossier was circulated, indicating that he was involved in virtually every important political event in the United States including the Watergate fiasco. Keel thinks this dossier was created by Crisman to make his career sound more exciting.[19] Shortly before Crisman died on December 10, 1975, the FBI linked him to stock fraud.

Garrison thought that Crisman was an associate of New Orleans businessman Clay Shaw and that they had conspired to assassinate John F. Kennedy. Crisman and Shaw are alleged to have worked together in connection with the Maury Island case in the *Majestic Documents 1st Annual Report*, point 6 of Annex C, which stated:

> The death of two Air Force counterintelligence officers in the crash of their B-25 aircraft en route to Hamilton AFB, California, after interviewing two auxiliary CG men who reported six UFOs over Maury Island, Washington, in June 1947. CIC agent Crisman had spoken to Kenneth Arnold, who on 26 June 1947, had reported a flight of UFOs over Mt. Rainier, Washington, and filed his report after he had spoken to Captain Davidson and Lieutenant Brown. The material given to Davidson and Brown was believed to come from Maury Island and may be celestial fragments containing metal from a nuclear reactor from a UFO. Fragments were turned over to CIA agent Shaw, and Crisman was ordered to the Alaskan ADC for assignment in Project IVY.[20]

Since the Majestic Documents are of dubious origin, I suspect someone has deliberately produced this to provide the proof that Shaw and Crisman had worked together as CIA agents before they were implicated in the complexities of the Kennedy assassination rumor mill.

Crisman has since been discovered to be a person who had fantastic daydreams AND drew people into his fantasies to make himself look important. He drew people into his many schemes, like Harold Dahl, to gain the fame and attention he craved. The Maury Island incident is his lasting and shameful legacy.

The Kennedy assassination has also become linked with the idea that the U.S. government secretly conspired with the aliens. According to UFO conspiracy theory, the CIA killed President Kennedy because he wanted to share UFO secrets with the Soviet Union.

Kennedy's memorandum on this matter—NSAM No. 271, addressed to the head of NASA—was the last to leave his desk before his fateful trip to Dallas. In further developments, the CIA and the mob killed Marilyn Monroe—on August 5, 1962—because she was talking too freely about UFOs and her affairs with John and Robert Kennedy. Wiretaps on her phone revealed her knowledge of Kennedy's secret trip to a military base where he was shown alien artifacts. It is a fact that, the night before her "murder," she spoke to the TV celebrity columnist Dorothy Kilgallen about the Roswell saucer crash of 1947. To add further weight to the conspiracy Kilgallen subsequently died under mysterious circumstances on November 8, 1965.[21]

There was another equally tenuous link between Shaw and UFOs. In 1945, the German rocket scientist Werner von Braun surrendered to Major Clay Shaw who was working as an agent for Project Paperclip. This project was designed to secure advanced Nazi knowledge, technology and personnel and bring it back to the United States before the Soviets got hold of it. Bavarian intelligence and their sympathizers like Shaw and Crisman infiltrated this CIA project, thereby allowing Werner von Braun and other top Nazi scientists to successfully bring into reality the Apollo Moon landing project under the auspices of NASA.[22]

Some like publisher and ex-crime investigator Anthony Kimery thought the "flying saucers" seen over Maury Island were the outcome of Project Paperclip and that this conspiracy went on to engineer the death of JFK, fake Moon landings and create bogus aliens.[23] For good measure Shaw was said to have died under suspicious circumstances in 1974.

For supporters of such notions, the Hill case fits in neatly with the idea that they were the victims of this conspiracy. They make much of Barney Hill's statement about the "leader" alien he saw through the UFO's window: "He looks like a German Nazi. He's a Nazi...."[24]

The theory was that the Nazi he saw onboard the UFO, and later recalled in such graphic terms under hypnotic regression, was working in league with the grey aliens who carried out the abduction.

Supporters of the idea that the flying saucers are of Nazi origin claim that the Germans established an underground base at Antarctica after World War II. Mattern-Friedrich, in his book *UFOs, Nazi Secret Weapon* (Samisdat, 1975), even stated that Hitler faked his own death and escaped there to continue the war in secret. With or without Hitler, they continued to develop, with the help of the aliens, flying saucers and associated advanced technology.

From here it has been suggested that this alliance has worked with the CIA and the U.S. "military-industrial complex" to create vast underground bases at Dulce (New Mexico); Area 51 (Nevada); Camp Hero (Long Island); and Denver International Airport. Similar bases are reputed to exist in Australia and Europe. "Literally thousands of abductees have been taken to these bases to be 'programmed' and returned to their homes to act as agents of the aliens, or they have been used in hybrid breeding projects or used as slaves inside these multileveled underground bases."[25]

The presence of an alien base in Antarctica was confirmed by the writings of Albert K. Bender. In 1952, he set up the International Flying Saucer Bureau (IFSB) in Bridgeport, Connecticut, and it quickly gained branches throughout the United States and the world. Bender came unstuck in September 1953 when he wrote to a friend to say he had found the "true" answer to the riddle of the flying saucer phenomenon. Not long afterward, he was shocked when three MIB came to his home brandishing the letter. They confirmed that his ideas about the flying saucers were correct and that if the public knew the truth there would be mass hysteria and a breakdown of civilization as we know it. He was told to close down his organization, or else…. The experience was so frightening that he promptly did what he was told. In 1962, when he felt he was safe enough from the menace of the MIB, he wrote *Flying Saucers and the Three Men*. This revealed that the three MIB were tall, dark-skinned and slant-eyed men who turned into serpent-like creatures during his encounter. Later on, they also took him on an astral journey to an underground base in Antarctica. Regarding this trip he wrote: "How much time this floating consumed I do not know, but it seemed like days."

At the base, he saw beautiful female aliens and aliens in the form of men. The purpose of the base was to extract chemicals from seawater to send back to their home planet. They told him that they could detonate all of our atomic weapons if we attacked them. Bender's account is confused and full of the kind of gibberish found in the worst contactee stories.

His MIB are more like ghosts and his experiences following their appearance are nightmares on the edge of reason. Some think he told these wild tales to finally put off or at least appease the demands of the UFO enthusiasts who kept asking him about the MIB. Others think it proves the MIB are not human secret agents but supernatural, or as Keel called them, ultraterrestrial beings who have plagued humanity since time began.

The MIB are just the modern-day manifestation of the Devil or, more prosaically, they are fantasies triggered by watching too many gangster B-movies. Underground UFO bases are not new to ufology, but the concept got an enormous boost on December 29, 1987, when John Lear posted a 4000-word document on the Internet. What is now known as the "Lear Document" claimed that, in 1979, 66 U.S. Special Forces soldiers were killed in a gunfight with alien forces while trying to rescue human workers in an underground alien base near Dulce, New Mexico.

This was partly inspired by the conspiratorial ramblings of Paul Bennewitz.[26] These began in 1980 when Bennewitz attended hypnotic regression sessions with abductee Ms. Myra Hansen, conducted by Dr. Leo Sprinkle. During these sessions, Hansen and her son claimed they saw aliens mutilating animals.

Furthermore, she recalled being flown by a spacecraft to New Mexico, where she was taken inside an underground base. Here she saw human body parts floating in huge tanks. It was Bennewitz's contention that Hansen had been fitted with an alien implant that they might use to control her thoughts and actions. Using his skills as an electronics expert, he attempted to intercept and block the signals he believed were being transmitted to the woman's implant. At one stage, he used metal foil to block the signals, and then he decided to intercept electronic low frequency (ELF) transmissions. He was successful in finding ELF signals but they seem to have been transmitted by the nearby Kirtland Air Force Base in the process of conducting secret experiments as part of the SDI "Star Wars" project.

When the USAF warned him not to continue his work, he was even more convinced that he had intercepted alien signals. Indeed, he contacted anyone who would listen about the UFO threat and he created a computer program to decode the signals. In response, the USAF department of Air Force Office of Special Intelligence (AFOSI) bombarded him with as much disinformation as possible to make him look like a fully certified UFO nut.

Under these pressures, Bennewitz suffered a mental breakdown. Even worse was the revelation that UFO researcher William Moore confessed that he had unwittingly aided the AFOSI by passing on disinformation to Bennewitz.

The disinformation material about alien bases, cattle mutilations, implants and abductions done with the aid and knowledge of the U.S. government also became the subject of Linda Moulton Howe's book *Alien Harvest*, which included a full transcript of Dr. Sprinkle's original hypnotic regression sessions with Hansen.

Howe alleged that documents shown to her later became the evidence used to prove the existence of a secret government project called Majestic 12 (MJ-12).[27] Lear used the same material to claim that trapped workers at the Dulce underground base "had become aware of what was really going on"—that aliens were implanting devices in the brains of abductees, impregnating female abductees, conducting genetic experiments, and, worse, terminating "some people so that they could function as living sources for biological material and substances" and assassinating "individuals who represent a threat to the continuation of their activity."

A witness even came forward to say that he was one of the survivors of the "fire fight" at Dulce. Philip Schneider said he was involved in extending the underground military base at Dulce when the alien base was accidentally revealed. He managed to shoot two aliens before he was shot in the chest by an alien weapon. This emanated from a box attached to the chest of an alien and it gave him a dose of cancer-inducing cobalt radiation. Schneider was the only "talking survivor"; two others were put under close guard. It was his contention that the Eisenhower administration signed a treaty with aliens in 1954 which gave them permission to abduct and implant U.S. citizens. In return, the U.S. government had been given new technologies that enabled them to enslave and dupe the population. Thousands of "black helicopters" and stealth aircraft were used to monitor our activities and AIDS was invented in 1972 through the genetic engineering of human, animal and alien excretions.

In a similar manner, Milton William Cooper used the Lear Document to assert that aliens and a secret government were planning to establish colonies on other planets and that they introduced "deadly microbes to control or slow the growth of the Earth's population. AIDS is only ONE result of these plans." Alien activity has been associated with AIDS, Gulf War Syndrome, Ebola fever and almost every "new" plague. UFO writer David Barclay also promoted the association between aliens and disease. He suggested that the visions of the Virgin Mary seen at Fatima in 1917 were created or manipulated by an alien technology to spread the great influenza pandemic, which claimed 21 million lives throughout Europe from 1918 to 1919.[28]

As Philip Schneider's stories became increasingly outlandish, he feared for his personal safety; "government vans" followed him and several attempts were made to run his car off the road. Eventually, his worst fears were confirmed in January 1996. A friend broke into his apartment in Wilsonville, Oregon, where his dead body had been rotting for several days. At first, it was thought he had died from a stroke, but then an autopsy found that rubber tubing had been wrapped and knotted around his neck.

The official verdict was suicide but his former wife, Cynthia, and several friends could not accept this. He was found with his legs under his bed and his head resting on the seat of his wheelchair—an unusual position for a suicide—and there was blood nearby that did not seem to be Schneider's. His lecture material and UFO writings were missing from the apartment, yet valuables had gone untouched. Prior to his death he had been seen with an unknown blonde woman and, not long after learning about this, Cynthia noticed a blonde woman sitting in a car with a pair of binoculars. She drove off before Cynthia could confront her.[29]

An earlier case, similar to Schneider's, involved Joseph Daniel (Danny) Casolaro. His interest in conspiracy theories began when he discovered that a law enforcement computer program called Promis was stolen and used by the CIA to monitor foreign governments. He soon learned about Area 51 and the secret testing of sophisticated weapons and "flying saucer" technology. He concluded that there was a huge central conspiracy that had tentacles reaching into all areas of national and international affairs; he called it the Octopus.

Casolaro might have been on to something, but on August 10, 1991, he was found with his wrists slashed in a West Virginia hotel room. As with the Schneider case, notes and papers were missing and, just before his death, he had received threatening phone calls. Many thought he was murdered because his wrists had been cut too deeply and savagely for a suicide. Conspiracy mongers found it significant that he was about to meet someone with "proof" of the existence of the Octopus.[30]

In the context of conspiracy and misinformation the meeting between the Hills, Robert E. Hohmann, C.D. Jackson and Major James McDonald on November 25, 1961, becomes even more important. This was when they worked out that the Hills could not account for two hours of their "interrupted journey" and put forward the idea that they should be hypnotized to discover what happened during this period.

Our suspicions are raised by the fact that Hohmann and Jackson were members of the National Investigations Committee on Aerial Phenomena (NICAP). This organization was founded in 1956 to scientifically investigate UFO reports and to encourage the authorities to make public *all* information about the subject. Retired Marine Corps Major Donald Keyhoe was its director from 1957 to 1969. His many articles and books on the topic supported the idea that UFOs are of extraterrestrial origin and that the U.S. government is covering up the truth.

Ironically, because the board of NICAP has consisted of politicians, military officers, professors and former members of the CIA, other ufologists have suspected that the CIA has infiltrated the group as a means of perpetuating the cover up.

Hohmann and Jackson met Donald Keyhoe when they were investigating the work of Nikola Tesla, David Todd and Marconi. They were doing this at the instigation of the Office of the Director of Defense Research and Engineering to see if old research could be of any use for future projects. They looked at the possibility that these scientists had received interplanetary radio communications emanating from Tau Ceti between

1899 and 1924.[31] When they spoke to Keyhoe about their work, he referred them to the Hill case and they wrote to the Hills for permission to interview them.

At the meeting itself, Hohmann and Jackson asked some offbeat questions, which showed that they were either very perplexed about the encounter or they were extremely knowledgeable about it. Since the Hills had taken their short vacation on a whim, the men questioned whether they had actually taken the journey at all. On reflection, even the Hills were surprised at their lack of preparation for such a long journey. Barney had got the idea for the short vacation during his night shift. Straight afterward he got permission for some time off and then went home to prepare for the trip on the same day. They went away with such speed that they only had what cash was on them. Their return home was equally hasty due to storm warnings.

They spoke about LSD and induced trauma, indicating that the men's reasoning was that something along these lines might have made the Hills imagine the whole story.

The men went on to ask if they had any nitrates or nitrate fertilizer in their car. They explained that many encounters are in rural areas and speculated that such materials might influence UFO witnesses in some unexplained manner. The Hills acknowledged that their car's trunk did contain a bag of bone-meal fertilizer. This interest in fertilizer is highlighted by the case of Gary T. Wilcox, who was spreading fertilizer on his dairy farm at Tioga City, New York, on the morning of April 24, 1964, when he came across an egg-shaped metallic object.

At first, he thought this 20-foot-long-by-16-foot-wide object was a wing tank that had fallen from an aircraft. Then he saw two small beings nearby who were carrying trays of soil. One of these aliens told Wilcox that they came from Mars, and he revealed that they grew their food in the atmosphere. Speaking in good English that seemed to come from the alien's body rather than his head, he took a great interest in methods of farming and fertilizers.

When Wilcox went to get a bag of fertilizer to give to the alien, the craft flew away. He left the bag in the field and the next day it was gone. Michael Swords speculated that Hohmann and Jackson thought that a UFO's electromagnetic propulsion system would create nitrates in the nearby environment. It could also have caused the stains on Betty's dress. This certainly makes more sense than Wilcox's story.[32]

In other cases Hohmann and Jackson claimed that UFO witnesses had reported newly purchased items going missing. This might have inspired Betty's story of her earrings going missing after the UFO encounter, as detailed in Chapter 7. John Keel, in his pioneering book *Operation*

Trojan Horse, also noted that contactees often report ordinary objects going missing and then being discovered in an outlandish place.[33]

They also discussed the possibility of life on other planets. So were Hohmann and Jackson simply UFO enthusiasts who were trying to determine the reality of the story? For those of us with suspicious minds, we might conclude that they were trying to manipulate the Hills into doubting their own experiences. The bizarre questions could have been introduced to add an extra level of mystery to the case and destabilize the Hills' grip on reality.

We have already noted that the Hills were friendly with intelligence officer Major McDonald and other Air Force staff at Pease Air Force Base. Some of these friends could have used their relationship to monitor their political activities in a discreet fashion. At the most cynical level, Hohmann and Jackson might have colluded with Major McDonald before the meeting to set up the idea of the missing time and for the major to come up with the idea of using hypnotic regression.

We can also have our suspicions sharpened by the fact that they were studying the work of Nikola Tesla. He has always been a favorite of conspiracy mongers. The most extreme rumor is that Nikola Tesla's death was faked and that he escaped to a Marconi underground base in South America. At this scientific colony, the aliens helped him to carry out the research that was used in the U.S. Navy's Philadelphia Experiment in 1947.[34] Tesla was also credited with trying to develop the radio transmission of electrical energy. Anthony Roberts and Geoff Gilbertson in their book *The Dark Gods* noted that New Zealand researcher Bruce Cathie plotted a UFO grid that included ley lines. When he visited strategic points on this grid, he found secret government establishments bristling with aerials. He was told that these bases were run by a top-secret international group of scientists. Roberts and Gilbertson also alleged that ley line researchers throughout the world have found microwave towers on or near important ley lines. With chilling logic, they wrote, "Microwaves are among the waves most often mentioned in terms of behavior modification!"[35]

This takes us to the thorny topic of the CIA's involvement with mind-control research and experimentation. From the 1950s, they began using mind-altering drugs and technology to control people's actions. Remember Hohmann and Jackson asked about LSD?

The CIA's ongoing MK-Ultra mind-control project has been regarded as responsible for creating alien abduction incidents. Dr. Helmut Lammer in his article "From Alien Abductions Via MK-Ultra to an Implanted Cyber-Situation" argued that implants have been developed by our own governments and have been secretly used on its citizens. One piece of evidence he supplies is this CIA memo:

22 November 1961

MEMORANDUM FOR THE RECORD

SUBJECT: Project MKULTRA, Subproject No. 94

The purpose of this subproject is to provide a continuation of activities in selected species of animals. Miniaturized stimulating electrode implants in specific brain center areas will be utilized.

Initial biological work on techniques and brain locations essential to providing conditioning and control of animals has been completed. The feasibility of remote control of activities in several species of animals has been demonstrated. The present investigations are directed toward improvement of techniques and will provide a precise mapping of the useful brain center in selected species. The ultimate objective of this research is to provide an understanding of the mechanisms involved in the directional control of animals and to provide a system suitable for [deleted word] application.

He regarded it as significant that the Betty and Barney Hill case occurred just at the time when the CIA implant/mind-control experiments were being initiated, though we should bear in mind that the Hills had their experience in September 1961, a month before the memo quoted above. It was Dr. Lammer's view that using hypnosis and hallucinogenic drugs, it is easy to produce alien abduction experiences that hide the implantation of mind-control equipment inside people's brains. Since terrestrial operations of this type push objects of this type up the nasal passage, just as described in alien abduction accounts, he thought it possible that they are in reality the product of CIA "black operation" units.

Covert abductions conducted by the military and aliens are known as MILABS. The proof of this activity comes from reports of human mind-control experiments and the evidence of abductees who say they have seen military officers working with aliens in underground bases or inside flying saucers. As Dr. Lammer acknowledged, even the most open-minded abduction researchers have tended to ignore this evidence.[36]

He wrote about an abductee called Michelle (pseudonym) who had abduction experiences with the classic short, grey, big-headed alien entities since she was eight years old. To retrieve memories of a three-hour time lapse she experienced at Ditch Plains, Montauk, New York, in 1970, she was hypnotically regressed by Dr. Kouguell. She recalled walking with a boyfriend when they were carried into a military jeep by two soldiers.

They were driven through a doorway into a hill. The two soldiers took the boyfriend away while she was taken down an elevator that smelled like a cesspool. Inside a dark room, she was placed on a padded table. From the shadows emerged a six- to seven-foot tall creature which had a tail, yellow glowing eyes and pointed teeth. This reptoid monster raped her on the table then returned to the shadows of the room. Afterward two soldiers dressed her and took her to another room, where she was strapped to a table and examined by people in surgical garments. Following the examination, she was put into an isolation tank where she had hallucinations.

Dr. Lammer thought Michelle could have been drugged and raped by a human and the reptoid was a screen memory of this experience. To support this he referred to Dr. Stanislav Grof's book *Realms of the Human Unconscious: Drug Induced Experiences of LSD Subjects*, which shows that under the influence of LSD, a person can encounter strange entities and lose their sense of time and identity. Losing their identity as a separate person, they can have complete identification with animals or other entities. One of Grof's subjects identified with a large reptile creature, and on opening her eyes, she saw her therapist as a realistic-looking reptile.[37]

To me it sounds like Michelle was recounting a journey into hell. The creature associated with the smell of the sewers is Satan, who has uniformed soldiers and surgeons as his minions. A noteworthy footnote to this case is that many years earlier on September 20, 1957, a radar station at Montauk Point tracked a UFO. The radar indicated that it was traveling westward at a speed of 2,300 mph at an altitude of 50,000 feet. Another radar station at Benton, Pennsylvania, also picked up this object. The possibility that this was a Soviet craft was discussed and ultimately dismissed at a special meeting held by the Intelligence Advisory Committee–Watch Committee the following day. Their only solution was that the mysterious radar returns were caused by equipment error.[38]

The problem with the testimony of abductees like Michelle, or the accounts of people who say they have had illegal brain implants forced upon them by terrestrial surgeons, is that they could be suffering the psychological factors outlined in Chapter 9. Voices in one's head and being forced by God, the Devil or aliens to carry out tasks against one's will are all symptomatic of severe mental illness rather than due to control by an implant. Then again, such a blurring between the two is an excellent cover for agencies who want to simultaneously use and discredit agents under their control.

The inventions of Nikola Tesla were considered instruments of covert control by prominent counterculture figures like Ira Einhorn through to more establishment characters like Lieutenant Colonel Thomas Beardon, USAF (Ret.). In the 1980s, Beardon believed the Soviets were using a Tesla generator to alter the weather in the United States. It was thought that they had created a drought in 1976 that hurt the farming communities of the western states. Reports of power failures in Canada were also ascribed to Soviet experiments with Tesla-inspired equipment back in 1974.

When Einhorn worked for Congressman Charlie Rose, they both had an interest in psychotronic weapons and Tesla's work. In the late

1970s, the congressman had a meeting with an anonymous Canadian who demonstrated a kind of virtual reality helmet to him. One very realistic scenario played out to him through the helmet was that of an alien abduction. There is speculation that this was the work of Dr. Michael Persinger, and some have alleged that he worked for project MK-Ultra and helped create alien abduction screen memories for the CIA.

The conspiracy theorists consider that screen memories of alien abductions are used to hide the fact that the abductees are being used as agents for the CIA. The mind control could even be used to make people carry out assassinations. Adam Gorwrightly's analysis of this subject suggests that it is not just the CIA but also a whole matrix of organizations that could be carrying out these mind-control activities, using different techniques for different purposes.[39]

This also fits with Jacques Vallee's speculation that the whole UFO myth has been carefully manipulated and structured by a secret international group, their intention being to unite humanity against an imagined extraterrestrial threat as a means of preventing us from igniting World War III.[40]

The conspiracy theorists say that with drugs, implants, Tesla technology, microwaves, hypnosis, holographic projections, visits from MIB and the assorted use of disinformation techniques, secret terrestrial organizations and/or alien visitors have manipulated us to believe in alien abductions. As we saw with the attempts to discredit Bennewitz, the disinformation process took on a life of its own that quickly got beyond the control of any individual or organization. The other techniques, if they are being used, are equally crude, and it seems difficult to believe that there has been any single project to dupe the world into believing in, or, for that matter, disbelieving, the reality of alien encounters and abductions by these means.

We should also consider that many people who believe in complex worldwide conspiracies and who think they are being "controlled" by outside forces are mentally ill or indulging in paranoid fantasies. This is especially true if the person thinks that they are the specially chosen focus and victim of these controllers and that virtually everything proves their conspiracy theory.

However, in a world where political "spin," cover-ups and conspiracies really do exist, it is difficult for any of us to really discriminate fact from fiction, especially when we rely so much on electronic media for this information. That is why we do not believe in the Moon landings or that Princess Diana's death was an accident and why we do believe in aliens and satanic abusers.

The complex web of technologies, personalities, organizations, alliances and allegations does make us wonder who or what is really in control of anything, let alone the alien abductions. To believe in grand cosmic alien conspiracies gives us a sense that somebody or something is really in control of our Universe and that it is not subject to human fallibilities.

3

A History
of Abductions

It is often stated that Betty and Barney Hill experienced the first ever abduction by aliens. If this were true, it would support the idea that UFOs arrived in 1947 and gradually escalated their probing of our planet and our bodies in the following years.

If the Hills were the first to be abducted, then they and those who investigated their case had little or no knowledge of abduction by aliens. As this was not an established area of UFO research they could not have been "contaminated" by other abduction reports and any preconceptions associated with them.

The idea of extraterrestrials visiting us in spaceships is relatively new. However, myths, legends, history and folklore indicate that humanity has been subject to abduction by nonhumans throughout history. This seems to show that we have been constantly under surveillance by aliens or that they come to visit us now and again to check up on our evolutionary progress. It would be logical for aliens to visit us in the 1940s due to our development of nuclear weapons that could eliminate all life on this planet.

Classical Greek and Roman texts mention "burning shields" and other wonders in the sky. These visions in the sky were often reported as gods, angels, serpents, dragons, signs and wonders. Over the passage of time, it is even harder to determine if they are misinterpretations of meteors, comets, and meteorological phenomenon or simply fiction for the purpose of entertainment or political satire.[1]

The Bible is said to contain many accounts that refer to meetings with Space People and thereby helped create the religious rules and beliefs that have shaped Western civilization. In Chapter 2 of the Second Book of Kings there is the story of Elijah who saw a fiery chariot that tore asunder. This was followed by a great whirlwind that sent Elijah skyward to heaven.

It is easy to see why he is often cited as one of the first abductees. In the Book of Ezekiel, UFO-type objects are reported on four occasions. The most striking sighting by Ezekiel was of great cloud issuing forth flashes of fire accompanied by stormy winds. Inside this he saw four wheels with eyes, and four sparkling bronze, winged men. Above them was a throne with a man upon it.

Enoch was visited by two tall, strange-looking men who gave secret knowledge about God and took him on a tour of the seven tiers of heaven. Ufologists note that the Second Book of Enoch also said that Enoch thought a few days had passed but when he returned many centuries had passed. This seems to indicate that he really visited other planetary realms rather than tiers of heaven. Although expunged from the Bible by St. Augustine, the Book of Enoch refers to several visitations of aliens or, as people then saw them, angels from heaven. It tells of how the angels lusted after the comely daughters of mankind and took them as their wives. The results of this union were giants who turned against mankind. The corruption and wars of our world caused this injunction from the heavenly creatures: "from henceforth you shall not ascend into heaven unto all eternity, and that judgment has been finally passed upon you."[2]

The Book of Revelation with its apocalyptic visions of doom is often cited by contactees and abductees, and many writers in the 1950s and 1960s noted that the Bible and other ancient texts could have been reporting alien encounters and UFOs rather than religious visions.

These ideas gripped the public imagination with the ancient astronaut theories of Erich von Daniken outlined in his best-selling book *Chariots of the Gods?* At that time, in the late 1960s, the Apollo astronauts were preparing for our own Moon landing, which made his reinterpretation of the Bible perfect sense at the height of the secular space race.[3]

In the Middle Ages, a country or region beyond the clouds called Magonia was believed to be the home of flying ships seen in our skies. Since the publication of Jacques Vallee's influential book *Passport to Magonia*, ufologists have used the term Magonia to highlight the historical and cultural context of UFO sightings.[4] This concept was explored by contributors to the *Merseyside UFO Bulletin* (*MUFOB*) to the extent that it was renamed *Magonia* by its editor John Rimmer.

Using references from the Psalms, Genesis and Isaiah, Christians argued that Earth was flat and that the firmament was a solid roof that stretched over us. Above this roof was a huge water tank from which the angels regulated the fall of rain. It was thought that if you sailed too far you would end up sailing in the ocean above us. If you could enter heaven above us by such means, then it made sense that you could also stumble into an opening into the underground chambers of hell. The fear

Erich von Daniken in 2016. He was the best-known researcher, but not the first, to put forward the theory that ancient astronauts visited us in the past. His 1968 book *Chariots of the Gods?* gripped the public imagination at a time when the Apollo missions were launching men to the Moon and nothing seemed impossible (photograph by the author).

of a great opening into hell, located in the Atlantic Ocean far away from Europe, made it difficult for explorers to recruit crews to explore such regions.

In the 20th century, Charles Hoy Fort reintroduced these ideas with his suggestion that there is a Sargasso Sea moving about above us. Such a sea would account for the hundreds of reports of falls of fish, frogs and other animate and inanimate matter that he collected from his extensive search through newspapers and scientific journals.

The ancient ships of the sky that regularly sent their anchors down to Earth had a strong connection with the famous airship scare of 1896–1897 that tore through the United States. The vast majority of the sightings were of lights or objects in the sky that witnesses thought were a fantastic new airship soaring through the air with its proud inventor at its helm. Here again there were reports of unknown aerial craft dropping anchor. At the end of March 1897, a farmer named Robert Hibbard, who lived near Sioux City, Iowa, had his clothing hooked by an airship's anchor. After he was dragged along the ground for several feet, he escaped when he grabbed a sapling. The anchor flew away with a portion of his trousers as he fell to the ground.[5]

Another anchor turns up in the *Daily Post* (Houston, Texas) of April 28, 1897, which is chillingly like those reported in the Middle Ages:

> Merkel, Texas, April 26–Some parties returning from church last night noticed a heavy object dragging along with a rope attached. They followed it until in crossing the railroad it caught on a rail. On looking up they saw what they supposed was the airship. It was not near enough to get an idea of the dimensions. A light could be seen protruding from several windows; one bright light in front, like the headlight of a locomotive. After some 10 minutes, a man was seen descending the rope; he came near enough to be plainly seen. He wore a light-blue sailor suit, was small in size. He stopped when he discovered parties at the anchor and cut the rope below him and sailed off in a northeast direction. The anchor is now on exhibition at the blacksmith shop of Elliott and Miller and is attracting the attention of hundreds of people.[6]

The Daily Chronicle (Muskegon, Michigan) of April 30, 1897, reported that on the previous evening at 11:30 p.m. an airship visited the town of Holton:

> It came from the north and descended until it was about 200 feet from the ground, directly over the bridge. It was lighted with electricity and loaded with revelers who were making a good deal of noise.
>
> The music was entrancing; the like of which never was heard in this place. It wasn't long before everybody was on the street to look and listen, many in their nightclothes. Not a few thought the Judgment Day had come. It was 300 feet long, tail about forty feet. Its breadth and depth was about ninety feet. It stayed fifty-five minutes. Its tail commenced whirling and it moved off toward Fremont. But just as it began to move, a grappling hook was let down and caught one of our most truthful citizens who was instantly hoisted on board and carried away. The truthful citizen came back on the 11.30 train from White Cloud and has been talking ever since about aerial navigation.

The glib references to the "truthful citizen" indicate that this story is one of the many tall stories the newspapers used to poke fun at the sightings of the airship. True or not, it is interesting that this airship was associated with unknown music, Judgment Day, bright electric light and abduction by means of an anchor.

Over the years several authors have considered the stories of ships in the sky dropping anchor. They are particularly impressed by the Merkel, Texas, case and its close similarity to the accounts in the ancient texts like the *Otia Imperialia*. Abductee Whitley Strieber mentioned these historical cases, adding that the kobold dwarfs who were said to haunt medieval German mines also wore dark blue outfits like the sailor in the Merkel report. Strieber himself had seen small beings with similar outfits and wondered if this was a uniform alien beings used at nighttime.[7]

The research of Robert Neely deflated these intriguing musings by noting that by the end of April 1897 an article entitled "A Sea Above the Clouds" appeared in large and small newspapers throughout the country. This recounted stories from the 13th century *Otia Imperialia* of anchor dropping sky ships that carried sailors through the heavens. As far as Neeley could tell this article first appeared in the *Nebraska State Journal* of March 6, 1897.[8] It is noteworthy that no witnesses in Merkel were actually named or interviewed by the newspapers. Therefore, in all probability an enterprising journalist adapted or invented the Merkel story.

A large object with a light was seen by hundreds of people flying over Sacramento on the night of November 17, 1896. It helped start the great U.S. airship scare featuring more reports of mysterious flying objects and alien visitors. Illustrations like this from the November 22, 1896, *San Francisco Call* typically showed the airship with powerful lights and propellers (author's collection).

The same article could also have been the source for Hibbard's story of being dragged by an anchor near Sioux City. Daniel Cohen in his book *The Great Airship Mystery* thought it was an obvious tall tale told in a serious manner.[9]

John Keel in his seminal *UFOs: Operation Trojan Horse* suggested that we dismiss these stories as "poppycock" or we have to accept them as true. If we take the latter option, Keel wondered, why would spaceships need or use primitive anchors.[10] Perhaps they are just poppycock, especially when we look at the famous Hamilton calf-napping case.

On April 19, the airship pilots fished for a two-year-old heifer at the Le Roy, Kansas, farm of Alexander Hamilton.

The craft was seen at 10:30 p.m. by Hamilton, his son and Gid Heslip. As it slowly descended, they could see it was a 300-foot-long cigar-shaped vessel with a carriage underneath it. The carriage appeared to be made of narrow transparent strips alternating with strips of dark reddish material. A "great turbine wheel" underneath the carriage seemed to be its means of propulsion in the air.

Inside they could see "six of the strangest beings I ever saw. They were jabbering together but we could not understand a word they said," according to Hamilton's sworn affidavit. Going to a nearby heifer that was tangled in a fence they found "some material" in a slipknot around its neck leading up to the airship. Once the men freed the heifer from the wire fence the airship slowly ascended, taking the beast with it. The next day Link Thomas found the hide, legs and head of the heifer on his farm located four miles west of Le Roy.[11]

Cohen showed that the Hamilton story was declared a hoax in 1943 long before ufologists were even aware of it. The editor of *The Farmer's Advocate* admitted that he and Hamilton had concocted the whole thing.[12]

The diligent research of Thomas Bullard revealed that the *Atchison County Mail* published as early as May 7, 1897, a letter from Hamilton confessing that his story was a hoax, explaining, "whenever I get a chance to help Kansas in any way I always do it..."[13] In the 1960s the original news reports were rediscovered by ufologists and repeated in countless UFO books. It was not until 1976 that anyone explored the possibility that it was a hoax. It was found that in his local community Hamilton was known for his whopping stories. He and his friends had a weekly liars club where they tried to top each other's tall stories, and the calf-napping tale was their most famous achievement. Jerome Clark published these findings in *Fate* magazine, but the Hamilton calfnapping is still repeated in many UFO books as a fact.[14]

The Hamilton calf-napping incident sounds reasonable compared to other stories that circulated in the newspapers of the period, which were also backed by the testimony of "reliable and respectable" witnesses. Some people claimed to meet the pilots of the airships as they restocked their craft or made repairs. Some, like the contactees of the 1950s, got invited onboard the aerial vessel where they were shown its technological marvels.

Judge Lawrence A. Byrne was surveying land on McKinney bayou when he came across a landed airship. It was manned by three men who spoke in a foreign language and looked like "Japs." Seeing his astonishment, they beckoned him to the craft and showed him around.

Apparently it was built of aluminum, and they pumped gas into a tank to raise it and pumped it out to lower it. It is noteworthy that when Judge Byrne first made this sighting on April 23, 1897, he described it as being "anchored to the ground." This might indicate that he actually saw an anchor keeping it from flying off or he was speaking in general terms. Jerome Clark, Loren Coleman and John Keel have indicated the similarity between the oriental features of these men and those of the Hill case.[15]

Another encounter concerned W.H. Hopkins, who worked as an agent for the Hartford Steam Boiler Inspection and Insurance Company, St. Louis. His employer, C.C. Gardner, confirmed that Hopkins was a reliable person who did not court notoriety. His wife added that he was a member of the Maple Avenue Methodist Evangelical Church and that before he went away on business he made fun of the airship stories. Given his sober character what can we make of his letter written on April 16, 1897? "I was wandering through hills east of Springfield, Missouri, and coming to the brow of a hill overlooking a small clearing in the valley a short distance below me I saw a sight that rooted me to the spot..."

He was amazed to see the outline of a craft just like one published in the *St. Louis Post-Dispatch* of a few days earlier. The vessel was about 20 feet long and eight feet in diameter. The craft was resting on four legs and it had one vertical propeller at the stern and horizontal propellers at the bow and stern, which were all about six feet in diameter. His letter continued:

> Near the vessel was the most beautiful being I ever beheld. She was under medium size but of the most exquisite form and features such as would put to shame the forms as sculptured by the ancient Greeks. She was dressed in nature's garb and her golden hair, wavy and glossy, hung to her waist, unconfined except by a band of glistening jewels that bound it back from her forehead.... She was plucking the little flowers that were just blossoming ... with exclamations of delight in a language I could not understand. Her voice was like low, silvery bells and her laughter rang out like their chimes. In one hand she carried a fan of curious design that she fanned herself vigorously with, though to me the air was not warm and I wore an overcoat.
>
> In the shade of the vessel lay a man (also naked) of noble proportions and majestic countenance. His hair of dark auburn fell to his shoulders in wavy masses and his full

beard... reached to his breast. He also was fanning himself with a curious fan as if the heat oppressed him...

After gazing for a while I moved forward and the woman, hearing the rustle of the leaves, looked around. A moment she stood looking at me with wonder and astonishment in her beautiful blue eyes, then with a shriek of fear she rushed to the man who sprang to his feet, threw his arm around her and glared at me in a threatening manner.

I stopped and taking my handkerchief from my pocket waved it in the air. A few minutes we stood. I then spoke some words of apology for intruding but he seemed not to understand and replied in a threatening tone and words which I could not make out. I tried by signs to make him understand and finally he left her ... and came toward me. I extended my hand. He looked at it a moment, astonishment in his dark-brown eyes, and finally he extended his own and touched mine. I took his and carried it to my lips.

I tried by signs to make them understand I meant no harm. Finally his face lighted up with pleasure and he turned and spoke to the woman. She came hesitatingly forward, her form undulating with exquisite grace. I took her hand and kissed it fervently. The color rose to her cheeks and she drew it hastily away.

I asked them by signs where they came from but it was difficult to make them understand. Finally they seemed to do so and smiling, they gazed upwards for a moment, as if looking for some particular point, and then pointed upwards, pronouncing a word which, to my imagination, sounded like Mars.

I pointed to the ship and expressed my wonder in my countenance. He took me by the hand and led me toward it. In the side was a small door. I looked in. There was a luxurious couch covered with robes of the most beautiful stuff and texture such as I had never seen before. From the ceiling was suspended a curious ball from which extended a strip of metal which he struck to make it vibrate. Instantly the ball was illuminated with a soft white light which lit up the whole interior. It was most beautifully decorated...

At the stern was another large ball of metal, supported in a strong framework, and connected to the shaft of the propeller at the stern was a similar mechanism attached to each propeller and smaller balls attached to a point of metal that extended from each side of the vessel and from the prow. And connected to each ball was a thin strip of metal similar to the one attached to the lamp. He struck each one and when they vibrated the balls commenced to revolve with intense rapidity and did not cease till he stopped them with a kind of brake. As they revolved intense lights, stronger than any arc light I ever saw, shone out from the points at the sides and at the prow, but they were different colors. The one at the prow was an intense white light. On one side was green and on the other red.

The two had been examining me with the greatest curiosity in the meantime. They felt of my clothing, looked at my grey hair with surprise and examined my watch with the greatest wonder. Signs are a poor medium to exchange ideas and therefore we could express but little.

I pointed to the balls attached to the propellers. He gave each of the strips of metal a rap, those attached to the propellers under the vessel first. The balls began to revolve rapidly and I felt the vessel begin to rise.... I sprang out and none too soon, for the vessel rose as lightly as a bird and shot away like an arrow.... The two stood laughing and waving their hands to me, she a vision of loveliness and he of manly vigor.[16]

This bears comparison with modern-day contactee stories rather than abduction accounts. The occupants are beautiful flower-picking innocents who have descended from a celestial heaven. They are like Greek gods, or Adam and Eve who have drifted in from the Martian equivalent of the Garden of Eden. Their craft is luxuriously appointed but the revolving ball propulsion system seems inadequate for aerial flight or the challenge of propelling it between Mars and Earth. Like the stories of the contactees this is an eloquent mixture of science fiction and religious imagery, with a big dose of imagination. My alarm bells ring by the way the newspaper goes out of its way to say that W.H. Hopkins is a very reliable witness.

I'm also suspicious about the way gentlemen like Hopkins and Judge Lawrence A. Byrne just happen to see these craft as they wander about the countryside incognito. Neely regarded the Hopkins story as a real incident though cautioned that it sounded a bit too good to be true, and he considered the Judge Byrne report as probably true even if his explanation of its propulsion system sounded implausible.[17]

Mars was also said to have been the home planet of an alien whose craft crashed into a windmill at Aurora, Texas, on April 17, 1897. The pilot and his craft were badly mangled, leaving tons of aluminum and silver wreckage. Papers containing indecipherable hieroglyphics were found on the body of the alien. In the 1960s, when the case was reinvestigated, it was discovered that there had never been a windmill at this location. In the 1970s several eyewitnesses to the crash were located at a nursing home, where they claimed that they never saw the airship crash and that the newspapers had made up their stories. This was almost certainly a hoax, yet this has not stopped UFO researchers from searching for the Martian's grave and fragments of his spaceship. This indicates that ufological "holy grails," such as Roswell, are by no means a new phenomenon.[18]

Talk of extraterrestrial airships was usually done in a tongue-in-cheek manner, as most of the airships were mainly regarded as the work of inventors or pranksters. Nonetheless, Mars was seriously considered as the possible home of intelligent beings. This idea was given more credence by the charts made by Italian astronomer Giovanni Schiaparelli during the oppositions of Mars in 1877, 1879 and 1881. He termed long dark lines he saw on the surface of Mars *canali*, meaning channels, but when translated into English they were erroneously called canals. He abandoned his observations in 1890 due to failing eyesight, but other astronomers confirmed the existence of the Martian markings. After studying occult phenomena in Japan, Percival Lowell returned to the United States in 1893 to set up an observatory at Flagstaff, Arizona. In 1895 he claimed in his book

Mars that this planet is inhabited by intelligent beings who are three times larger than humans. In 1906 he detailed further evidence for this theory in *Mars and Its Canals.*

Considering that Mars is older than Earth, he postulated that Martian life was superior to our own and that the canals were evidence that they were still in existence.

Today, we know his ideas are wrong. Psychoanalyst Charles Hofling asserted that Lowell's observations were illusory; however, his rigorous use of logic to interpret his data was due to an *idée fixe* rather than delusions. Considering which came first, the *idée fixe* or illusory observations, Hofling favored the former as he thinks Lowell already knew what he would see. Significantly, when he used more powerful telescopes the canals were less visible. After getting disappointing results for observations made on a superior 24-inch telescope in Mexico, Lowell was diagnosed with neurasthenia, from which he did not fully recover until 1901 when an opposition of Mars was approaching. This signified that Lowell's belief in the canals and Martian life had a great psychological importance to him and his mental health.

Studying his biographical details Hofling regarded Lowell's Martian observations and theories the product of unresolved unconscious forces.[19]

Another story that has excited the imagination of writers on sociology, the paranormal and UFOs is that of a mysterious "mad gasser" who plagued Mattoon, Illinois, in 1944. This visitor was humorously linked to the sighting of a fireball that zoomed low over the Midwestern states on the night of August 8, 1944. In *The Fortean Society Magazine,* editor Tiffany Thayer speculated that the "man" had come from the celestial realms and was searching for spare parts to fix his space vessel that was seen coming to Earth on the 8th.[20]

The idea that the Mattoon gasser was an alien was given more serious consideration by J. Vyner in an early edition of *Flying Saucer Review.* He linked him with the appearances of a figure called Spring Heeled Jack who haunted London from November 1837 to February 1838 and has made other brief appearances in Britain since then. Jack was described as a tall, thin, cloaked man who had claw-like hands and cropped ears. He carried a lantern and had a penchant for belching flames into the faces of young women. Under the cloak, he had a tight-fitting, metallic-looking outfit and he wore a metal helmet. He escaped capture by leaping prodigious distances. He became the subject of songs, Penny Dreadful stories, plays and all manner of rumors.[21] Vyner compared him to a flier lost behind enemy lines who seemed to be searching for someone or some place before he could return home. He lyrically wrote about the reappearance of Jack at Mattoon:

For nearly a month Jack flitted through bedrooms of Mattoon with the energy of Groucho Marx. Then, as suddenly as he had come, he disappeared in a night of strange and wide-spread hysteria. Such phenomena, indeed, as have been associated with intense magnetic disturbance—or with saucer landings.[22]

The facts of the matter certainly indicate that the prowler had plenty of energy. The first case at Mattoon to be reported to the police was on September 1. Mrs. Kearney and her young daughter retired to bed at 11 p.m. when she noticed a sickly odor in the room. This quickly dried their throats, burned their lips and caused Mrs. Kearney to lose sensation in her legs. The police were unable to find anything or anyone to explain the incident when they visited the home that night. Mr. Kearney got a glimpse of the prowler on returning home at 12:30 a.m. He described him as "tall, dressed in black cloth, and [wearing] a tight fitting cap." He ran after him but the prowler was too quick for him to catch.

The next night the *Mattoon Daily Journal-Gazette* covered the story with the headline "Anesthetic Prowler on Loose." Following that story, several people reported similar symptoms that were reportedly caused by this gas or odor, although they saw no sign of the perpetrator.

By September 6, police and bands of armed men were on the lookout for the gasser. Despite their vigilance, he struck seven residences and a prowler was seen in connection with two of these instances. He was described as being tall and thin.

Frances Smith and her sister were the only victims on September 7 when gas was pumped into their room accompanied by a buzzing sound. Their arms and legs felt paralyzed by what they described as a blue vapor.

A cloud of gas appeared outside the home of C.W. Driskell on DeWitt Avenue on September 8. About 70 people, including two Chicago newspaper reporters, smelled the gas and suffered nausea, dry throats and unsteadiness. Later, at a house on the western edge of Mattoon, five people woke up at the same time with the same symptoms.

Four more attacks were made on September 9, including a return to the home of Frances Smith. One of the victims, Mrs. Fitzpatrick, was taken to the town's Memorial Hospital where she was diagnosed with acute anxiety. On the next night, the same doctor gave the same diagnosis to a woman who had caused a stampede at the local theater after screaming about being attacked. By now the police, who had come under severe criticism from the local newspaper, were keen to put an end to the affair. Chief of Police Cole now made it clear that if anyone reported smelling gas, they were to be examined by a doctor or put in prison for the night.

This had the desired effect of deterring any more reports to the police, save one from Bertha Bence. On the night of September 11, she awoke suffering from the usual effects of the gas. When her two sons ran outside, they saw a short, dark figure running away from the scene. Near their mother's bedroom window footprints were discovered, apparently made by a woman's high-heeled working- style shoes.

The most fanciful reports came from the owner of the Lincoln Inn, Mrs. Edna James. On September 7, she went to her kitchen, where she saw a grunting, hairy, ape-like man. He had long arms, stooped shoulders and warts on his face. Using a spray gun, he gassed her, causing her to collapse while he made his escape.

On September 9, Mrs. James, who regarded herself as psychic, saw the gasser again in her motel lobby. Although there were several people in the lobby, she was the only one who actually saw the gasser. He promptly disappeared when he realized that he was visible to her.

Chief of Police Cole on September 11 declared that hysteria was to blame for most of the reports. Wind blowing carbon tetrachloride produced at the Atlas Imperial Diesel Engine Co. plant was his explanation for the odor. The manager of the plant replied that this was impossible, and it would not explain how the wind selected one or two bedrooms rather than whole areas of the town. However unsatisfactory, the menace of the mad gasser went away.

Altogether 29 people, mainly women, claimed the mysterious gasser attacked them, dating from August 31 to September 12, in 25 separate incidents. They all experienced after-effects from the sweet-smelling gas, which included vomiting, palpitations, nausea, a burning or dry mouth, and unsteadiness or even paralysis of the limbs. After investigating these reports, Donald Johnson from the University of Illinois agreed with Cole that they were caused by mass hysteria. He thought that the media coverage of the affair had caused people to redefine otherwise "mundane" strange smells or anxiety attacks as the work of the gasser.[23]

On reviewing Johnson's report, Willy Smith concluded that this was not a clear-cut case of mass hysteria. Smith favored two other theories. One was that it began with cases of gas leaks that were linked with a prowler; the other was that there was a real gasser on the loose. Whatever the reason, the reports were hyped by an over-enthusiastic reporter and the situation got out of control, making the allegation of hysteria convenient for all parties.[24]

Another hypothesis is that the U.S. military secretly conducted chemical warfare experiments in the town. In his book *The Mad Gasser of Mattoon: Dispelling the Hysteria*, Scott Maruna revealed that Farley Llewellyn was the gasser. He was a loner who had majored in chemistry at the University of Illinois. On returning home to Mattoon, he built his own chemistry laboratory. When he was in his 30s, he drank heavily, and the townsfolk attributed his increasingly odd behavior to his homosexuality.

Maruna thought Llewellyn began the gassings, but when the police started watching him, his two sisters, Florence and Katherine, continued the gassings to deflect suspicion away from him. It is significant that they fit the description of the prowler given by Bertha Bence's sons, and their involvement explains the footprints outside her window. It might also explain the sighting of a hairy ape-man by Mrs. James, as the two sisters were heavy set and not too careful about their hygiene. The attacks stopped because the Llewellyns probably ran out of the gas and because Farley was put into a mental institution on September 11.[25]

I doubt that this prosaic explanation will meet everyone's approval, though it does seem to fit the facts better than an extraterrestrial on the loose. Like the Spring Heeled Jack sightings and alien abductions, the Mattoon gasser had a predilection for visiting ladies at night and was associated with buzzing sounds, paralysis and the unleashing of psychic visions and hysteria.

In the 20th century, sightings of UFO-like objects went through several transitions. In 1909, there were airship scares similar to the 1896–97 U.S. scare in Britain, New Zealand and the United States. Another airship scare struck Britain from the end of 1912 to 1913. There were other aerial scares in South Africa during 1914, Canada from 1914 to 1916, the United States in 1916 and Britain throughout World War I. Except for the U.S. scare in 1909 that overlapped into 1910, they were all associated with the fear of invasion from the powerful German air force.[26]

In the 1930s, mystery aircraft were seen in Scandinavia, Britain and the United States. Approximately a thousand Scandinavian sightings involved a gray-colored aircraft that used a powerful searchlight. It has been considered that they were operated by smugglers or were secret training flights by the German Luftwaffe.

Los Angeles had a war scare in February 1942 when there were sightings of Japanese submarines and unidentified aircraft, and in 1944 to 1945 glowing lights, globes and disks were seen by Allied bomber crews over Europe and Japan that they nicknamed "foo fighters."

After World War II, in 1946, there were 1,600 reports of ghost rockets seen over Sweden. These "rockets" were often described as being cigar-shaped; at night they gave off luminous flames like rockets. One of these rockets was seen to crash into Lake Kolmjarv, though an extensive search failed to find anything of the object.

Swedish, British and U.S. intelligence agencies investigated these sightings but could find no proof that any rockets had been fired at Sweden.[27]

Much of the early history of ufology might have been lost to us entirely if it was not for the research of Charles Hoy Fort (1874–1932). His years of diligent noting of these mysteries created a body of work that was not very popular at the time, but it has had a long-lasting and insidious impact on science fiction, ufology and paranormal literature. He often speculated about the possibility that we were the property of extraterrestrials. In his book *Lo!* Fort mused: "It may be that if beings from somewhere else would seize inhabitants of this earth, wantonly, or as a matter of scientific research, the preference would be ... remote from observations by other humans of this earth."

From this, we can say that he anticipated the abduction phenomenon of today. His far-ranging writings on odd events and his amusing, tongue-in-cheek explanations for them brought him in the literary circle of Theodore Dreiser, Ben Hecht, Booth Tarkington and Alexander Woolcott. His writings also had a more direct bearing on the science fiction tales of Edmund Hamilton and Eric Frank Russell.

In September 1937, writer Tiffany Thayer began publishing *The Fortean Society Magazine*, which had an erratic publishing schedule. Thayer was not so keen on aerial mysteries or talk of alien invaders, as he preferred to regard Fortean phenomena as an opportunity to question the rigidity of scientific theories and explanations.[28] Nonetheless, he did publish an article by Norman Markham about mystery aircraft over Europe and phantom parachutes seen over New Jersey. This appeared in the December 1941 edition, but it did not make much of an impression as the more momentous bombing of Pearl Harbor eclipsed such fanciful sightings.

Markham felt the Fortean Society should concentrate on the correlation of the orbit of Venus in relation to Earth and maritime disappearances, fearing that we were in as much danger from Venusians as the Japanese. Thayer was not convinced.[29]

R. DeWitt Miller also used the works of Fort for a regular column in *Coronet* magazine during the 1940s, and in 1943, a short-lived group called the Society for the Investigation of Unusual Phenomena was formed. It was in this period that *The Fortean Society Magazine* was retitled *Doubt*.

Raymond Alfred Palmer (1910–1977) is often credited as the inventor or father of ufology, though he owes a great debt to Charles Fort, who more rightly established the foundations of this subject. As the editor of the *Amazing Stories* science fiction magazine, Palmer promoted the writings of Richard Shaver (1908–1975) as fact from 1944 to 1948. These stories claimed that two groups of aliens lived beneath the earth. The Dero (detrimental or deranged robots) were dangerous to humanity, while the Tero (terrestrial or integrative robots) tried to protect us. They were descendants of aliens who populated the legendary continents of Lemuria, Mu and Atlantis, magical places that were often referred to by the occultists of the period and contactees in the 1950s. When solar radiation caused the Deros and Teros to die off they were forced to return to their home planet or seek refuge underground.[30]

The Deros used machines to make us hallucinate, go crazy or die. Their operations helped crucify Jesus, controlled Hitler, and made Lee Harvey Oswald assassinate John F. Kennedy. For good measure, they had machines to help them perform acts of sexual debauchery. Many readers confirmed the existence of these beings and the stories boosted the circulation of the magazine.

Almost as a primer for the coming of the flying saucers, Palmer wrote in the July 1946 edition of *Amazing Stories*, "If you don't think space ships visit the earth regularly ... then the files of Charles Fort ... are something you should see. And if you think responsible parties in world governments are ignorant of the fact of space ships visiting earth, you just don't think the way we do." The concept of aliens from outer space as fact combined with them being kept secret from us by governments is not much different from the same firmly held ideas today. The June 1947 edition of *Amazing Stories* contained another editorial by Palmer peppered with references to the UFO-type reports from the works of Fort as well an article by Vincent Gaddis about mystery aircraft of the 1930s and 1940s.[31]

As we saw about the Maury Island case, Palmer bankrolled Kenneth Arnold to investigate it for the first edition of his *Fate* magazine published in 1948. From then onward, he continued to publish a range of occult and UFO magazines along with books under the Amherst Press imprint. By the end of the 1950s, he favored the view that UFOs came from the Hollow Earth rather than from outer space, and by the mid–1960s, he boasted that he had started the whole flying saucer bandwagon as a joke.

Occultist Dr. Meade Layne established the Borderland Sciences Research Association (BSRF) in 1945 and produced its *Round Robin* newsletter. It established two groups in Los Angeles and San Diego. They took an active interest in psychic research, astral travel, Fortean phenomena and UFOs, and they went on to publish several books on these topics, including *Native American Myths & Mysteries*, written by Vincent Gaddis, in 1991.

The many interconnections between these publications and groups are highlighted by the career of Vincent Gaddis (1913–1997). He became acquainted with the works of Charles Fort when they were serialized in the *Astounding Stories* science fiction pulp magazine in October 1933. He went on to write about Fortean phenomena for Palmer's *Amazing Stories*, and under numerous pseudonyms for *Fate*, he was also a member of the Fortean Society and a contributor to *Doubt*.[32]

As Palmer's *Amazing Stories* was delighting in weird subterranean alien stories, the publication of the Fortean Society, *Doubt*, under the editorship of Tiffany Thayer had drifted away from cosmic musings. He did publish reports of the ghost rocket sightings in Sweden during 1946 though he thought they were concocted by the U.S. Office of Strategic Services to convince the public that the Soviets were capable of sending rockets with atomic warheads to the United States.

When the flood of flying saucer sightings spread throughout the United States in June and July of 1947, after Kenneth Arnold's famous observation of flying saucers on June 24, even Thayer had to go with the flow. His June/July edition of *Doubt* was filled with a long list of UFO reports and his comments on them. The UFO genie was now free from the cultic precincts of the pulp science fiction magazines, the Fortean Society, and the Borderland Sciences Research Association, which had kept the flickering spirit of Fort's work alive for so long.

4

Contactees
and Space People

I have a soft spot for the so-called contactees who thrived in the 1950s. Generally speaking, the contactees are different from the abductees because they were invited, rather than forced, to go onboard a flying saucer.

The occupants of these craft were tall, humanoid, long-haired and basically elegant Nordic-types. They looked like perfectly formed and attractive examples of the male or female gender. However, in a period when men did not grow their hair long, some contactees found their aliens disconcertingly androgynous in appearance. The aliens would show the contactees around their flying saucer, discuss religion and philosophy, and even take them on rides to planets in our Solar System. Mars or Venus, as we know now, are inhospitable, indeed, downright deadly to us, yet in those heady days, the contactees were always visiting them without the need for a space suit or even as much as a flu shot.

Compared to the encounters reported by abductees, who are physically and mentally subdued by their captors, the contactees met their visitors in a normal fashion. Indeed, the Space People looked so similar to us that they even met contactees in diners or coffee bars without raising suspicion. The contactees often kept in contact with the aliens through ham radio messages, telephone conversations, séances, automatic writing, trances, dreams and telepathy. Abductees sometimes used these techniques, but the more stringent abduction researchers frowned on them.

When I first took an interest in the subject, in the early 1970s, I read a couple of old UFO books that soberly looked at sightings reported by pilots, military personnel and other "reliable" people. Those books speculated that extraterrestrials might be visiting us, and they tried to present the evidence in a scientific manner.

When I got my hands on my first contactee book, it was a completely new experience. It was full of contacts with aliens, trips into space, and revelations about the philosophy and intentions of the Space People. Stripped of science and circumspect theorizing, I got the full-on alien encounter experience. They were enjoyable adventure fantasies with a sprinkling of dodgy photographs and pseudo-science to prove that this was not fiction but FACT in capital letters. To add further credibility to their yarns, the contactees often provided themselves with fancy titles and qualifications.

Contactees were the charismatic, self-promoting and self-proclaimed heroes of a new era for humanity. They were riding shoulder to shoulder with the beautiful Space People into the starlit future, where there would be harmony, peace and love. For them there were no anal probes or painful implants. They were equals with these highly evolved beings who promised a heaven on Earth.

If we believed the contactees and their friends from outer space, we would no longer need to worry about atomic warfare, pollution, over-population, natural disasters, famine, disease, pain or even death itself.

The promises were great, but were the contactees just exploiting our personal and universal anxieties for their own private gain? Many UFO researchers and organizations would not touch such cases with a Venusian flabbergasser. As Jacques Vallee put it, "No serious investigator has ever been worried by the claims of the 'contactees.'"[1] Later in the same book, Vallee condemned the contactees for their childish stories that were just "little space operas."[2] Such language did not upset the contactees, as they did not seek others to investigate or examine their claims. They preferred to appear on radio shows, give lectures and pass on the knowledge of the Space People through newspapers, magazines and books. Some would establish their own cults or cult-like organizations with fanatical followers ready to do the bidding of the contactee.

For the sake of clarity, it makes life simple to say that there was a great divide between the believers of the contactees and the "scientific" ufologists. Yet there have been many credible and scientific ufologists who have believed the contactees, and some out-right nutters, who have regarded themselves as "scientific" and rational investigators. We can point to the fact that what became the world's most respected UFO magazine, *Flying Saucer Review* (*FSR*), began in 1954 by publishing articles by contactees and was willing to consider evidence for their claims. This led to a small argument between Jacques Vallee and *FSR*'s editor, Waveney Girvan. The latter thought that Vallee should have included the Venusian aliens as reported by contactees in his classification of Type 1 events.[3] In response, Vallee argued that his survey of Type 1 events only included reports of UFO landings that were consistent and "are simple and very clear."[4]

Belief in them took a battering when the space missions conducted by the United States and the USSR in the 1960s showed that Venus and Mars were nothing like the planets described by the contactees. This should have totally finished off any interest in contactees, but by the late 1960s, there was renewed interest in the possibility that UFOs were from other dimensions or they were some form of psychic or elemental force. John Keel spoke of his own network of "silent contactees" who did not publicize or brag about their dealings with the Space People. In the 1970s, Jacques Vallee amended his view of contactees and began to see them and their attendant cults as part of a social phenomenon that could have important consequences for all of us.[5]

Vallee made the distinction between direct and indirect contactees. The former have a physical encounter with a UFO and have a special relationship with the alien intelligence. Indirect contactees have communications with an alien intelligence (e.g., via automatic writing or trance mediumship) and have a special relationship with it, but they do not have a physical encounter.[6]

As we have already noted in Chapter 3, the airship wave of 1896–97 contains many newspaper reports that sound like the contactee stories of the 1950s. Most of these are what Vallee would categorize as involving direct contactees. While the phantom airships were whizzing about in the skies, there was considerable interest in contacting the dead through séances, automatic writing and other forms of mediumship.

The medium Hélène Smith (the pseudonym for Catherine Elise Muller) who lived in Geneva, Switzerland, had several communications with Mars in the 1890s and she can be described as being an indirect contactee.

Professor Flournoy's book *From India to the Planet Mars* provided a detailed look at Smith's life and psychic career.[7] From an early age, she had visions of objects and color landscapes. When she was 10 years old, a person wearing a long robe with a white cross on their chest suddenly appeared in order to rescue her from a dog. From then on whenever she felt in danger, this phantom of "Leopold" would come to her rescue. In her childhood, she wondered if she was a changeling and not really the daughter of her parents, and as a teenager a bright light threw her against a wall. By the turn of the century she no longer visited Mars but she did visit Uranus and Ultra-Martian worlds with the help of two Martian guides.[8] From 1903 her visions changed from astronomical adventures to being religious in nature that included a vision of Christ.[9]

Smith's childhood paranormal and visionary experiences are very common in the UFO literature. Contactees *and* abductees often report such occurrences, which tend to haunt and puzzle them throughout their lives.

The first contactee story after Arnold's flying saucer sighting in 1947 seems to have occurred only a few months later. When driving down a back road, Simon Estes Thompson saw a UFO. The naked pilots of this craft invited him onboard and explained that they came from Venus. The aliens spoke about vegetarianism and reincarnation. This seems to anticipate many of the contactee themes of the next decade, and the naked aliens remind us of those seen by W.H. Hopkins during the U.S. airship wave of 1896–97. Even the encounter down a side road brings to mind the Hill case. What undermines Thompson's story is that it was published in the April 1 edition of the *Centralia Daily Chronicle* newspaper. Despite the possibility of it being an April Fool's Day hoax, Kenneth Arnold thought Thompson was being truthful when he interviewed him.

George Adamski became the best-known contactee of the 1950s, and he leaves a shadow over our subject to this day. Adamski was a self-proclaimed professor who gave the impression that he was an astronomer at Mount Palomar observatory. In reality, his only connection with Mount Palomar was that he worked at a nearby hamburger stand. What he lacked in academic qualifications and status, he made up for in his powers of invention and conviction.

Adamski's involvement with the occult can be traced back to the 1930s. It was in this period that Guy Ballard's I AM movement was formed. Ballard (a.k.a. Godfré Ray King) said he had met beings called Lemurians who flew in "aerial boats" and lived under Mount Shasta, California. The mountain was said to hide a beautiful city and caves lined with gold saved from Atlantis. Tall, robed figures, weird events and strange visions were and are seen in the area. Ballard's meetings with the "Ascended Masters" included the spirit of Count de Saint-Germain. These Masters told Ballard that they needed people to spread their philosophy to humanity and needed "messengers." With his wife Edna, he published books about the Masters under the Saint Germain Press imprint. In his book *Unveiled Mysteries* (1934) he told of his induction into the Brotherhood of Mt. Shasta, a branch of the Great White Lodge. In a sequel, *The Magic Presence*, he claimed that the Masters had a radio transmitter underneath Colorado that they used to contact other planets and cities. In 1939, he and his wife were charged with mail fraud. Their conviction was overturned, but it was the effective end of the I AM movement. Their teachings, however, were taken up and carried on by other organizations.

The I AM movement had its roots in the occult teachings of Helene Petrova Blavatsky (1831–1891), who founded the Theosophical Society. One of her followers, Charles Leadbeater, claimed that the highest spirit masters in the Great White Brotherhood are "the Lords of the Flame" who live on Venus. This planet is on a higher evolutionary plane than our own, and these Lords are intent on guiding us to this higher level. Madame Blavatsky had childhood visions and became a medium.

She claimed to have encountered a secret brotherhood of Himalayan "Masters." These beings have aided the evolution of humanity, and the Theosophical Society promoted the idea that there were seven "root" races. As the fifth root race we would evolve to the sixth level when we return to Lemuria, where the third race of giant, telepathic ape beings originally lived. If we avoid the fate of the fourth race of Atlanteans, who killed themselves off through the use of black magic, we would move to Mercury as part of our evolution to the seventh race root.

This concept of different subhuman and superior races helped give credence to white supremacist and Nazi ideas. Madame Blavatsky is said to have communed with adepts inside a mountain at Karli, India. There were a great number of myths of "gods" living inside mountains or in caves, and occult organizations had tried to contact and serve these beings. The Nazis searched for openings to the underworld in Tibet. Like the Nazis, Madame Blavatsky used the symbol of the swastika, which originally represented the wheel of life.[10]

Annie Besant, who took over the running of the Theosophical Society, believed that a new Lemuria would be created from the spiritually enlightened people of Southern California and that a version of humanity would live on Mercury in the far-off future.

Timothy Good's appraisal of Adamski indicated that, like the abductees of today, he had childhood contacts with the aliens and that he spent six years under their tuition in Tibet. In a footnote, Good remembered reading a Rosicrucian book of the 1930s, which described tall, strange people, garbed in long robes, who lived inside Mount Shasta. People living nearby also reported seeing airships in the area at the turn of the century. Good wondered if these strange people and their airships had visited the young Adamski. Unknown to Good, this book is probably *Lemuria: The Lost Continent of the Pacific*, published by the founder of the Rosicrucians in 1931.

This work was inspired by Frederick S. Oliver's book *A Dweller on Two Planets*. Through channeled communications with a reincarnated being from Atlantis, between 1884 and 1886, Oliver discovered that Mount Shasta hides a subterranean world. For good measure, he also had an astral trip to Venus to gain the secrets of the Universe.[11]

Whether or not these aliens darted around Mount Shasta or visited Adamski, they had an influence on the "Hollow Earth" stories of Richard Shaver, as publicized in Ray Palmer's *Amazing Stories* science fiction magazine, and on the contactee beliefs of the 1950s. Shaver's direct influence can be seen in a short book titled *A Spacewoman Speaks* by Rolf Telano (a.k.a. Ralph Holland). This told of extraterrestrials called the Borealis, who can live up to a thousand years through constantly reincarnating themselves. Thousands of years ago, they came to Earth and specially bred people in underground bases called Edens. Through this breeding program, they created the human race, known as the Adam. Like the Dero, some Adams rebelled and remained underground, where they could indulge in their nasty vices, and became what we now call devils. The book also provided information about alien gods, monsters, Atlantis and Lemuria. These revelations were disclosed to Holland in 1954 and published by contactee Daniel Fry's Understanding Publishing Company in 1960.

Returning on a more sinister note to the I AM movement, it had followers who were also members of the fascist Silver Shirt movement.[12] Adamski is said to have had connections with William Dudley Pelley before World War II. Pelley, the leader of the Silver Shirts, was sentenced in 1942 to eight years' internment for sedition. In 1950, he wrote a book, *Star Guests*, which was based on automatic writing. His racist views were prompted in his own *Valor* magazine, and he ran an occult group called Soulcraft. Contactee George Hunt Williamson (a.k.a. Michel d'Obrenovic) worked for Pelley's Soulcraft Publications and went on to describe his own communications with aliens via Ouija boards in his book *Other Tongues, Other Flesh*.[13]

Adamski authored his first book in 1936. Titled *Wisdom of the Masters of the Far East*, it became a cause of controversy and dissent among his followers in the 1960s, when it was discovered that his Science of Life Study Course was no more than a reworking of his *Wisdom* book. He simply replaced the "Masters" of the Royal Order of Tibet with the "Space Brothers."[14] It was

"Better not touch the hull, pal; it's still hot," said an alien voice when contactee Daniel Fry (shown here ca. 1955) came across a remote-controlled flying saucer at White Sands Proving Grounds, New Mexico, on July 4, 1950. He went on to claim that the aliens came from Lemuria thousands of years ago (Archives for the Unexplained).

during the 1930s that he founded and ran the Royal Order of Tibet and its monastery at Laguna Beach, California. To make ends meet, he toured the country giving lectures and talks on universal laws and astronomy.[15] Ray Stanford, who published contactee books and had his own contacts in the mid–1950s, claimed that Adamski admitted that the Order of Tibet was a front for an extensive bootlegging operation during Prohibition. When Roosevelt abolished Prohibition, he resorted to "all this saucer crap."[16]

Shortly before the age of flying saucers was officially introduced, Mark Probert and a friend saw a winged bat-like craft on October 9, 1946. It was high above San Diego, and it inspired him to obtain more information about it from a "clairaudient source." He was told it came from a planet west of the Moon, showing that they knew nothing about celestial navigation. More tellingly, Probert found out that;

> the strange machine is called the Kareeta, or Corrida ... it is attracted at this time because the Earth is emitting a column of light which makes it easier of approach. The machine is powered by people possessing a very advanced knowledge of anti-gravity forces. It has 10,000 parts, a small but very powerful motor operating by electricity, and moving wings, and an outer structure of light balsam wood, coated with an alloy. The people are non-aggressive and have been trying to contact Earth for many years. They have very light bodies. They fear to land, but would be willing to meet a committee of scientists at an isolated spot, or on a mountain top.[17]

This landing on a mountaintop *and* a meeting with scientists anticipated the very plot of Spielberg's *Close Encounters of the Third Kind* by nearly three decades. The description of how the spacecraft worked was as detailed and nonsensical as those given to other contactees in the 1950s and during the 1896–97 airship wave. Like future contactees, Probert was aware that the space beings were intelligent, technically advanced (despite their weakness for balsam wood) and fearful of humanity and that they have visited us for "many years."

Probert kept in contact with aliens and dead Earth people through deep trance mediumship. He thought that they all lived at a high vibrationary level. Besides the aliens, he also communicated with the famous inventor Thomas Edison, who lived on what Probert called the etheric plane or dimension.

The Inner Circle Teachers of Light website tells us that Probert channeled information from the Yuga civilization from 1948 to 1968. This civilization was destroyed thousands of years ago and still lies beneath the Himalayan Mountains. Yada di Shi'te, the leader of this civilization that existed for 1,024 years, and other "Inner Circle Teachers of Light" gave him a vast range of information about ancient history, space beings and religion. He was informed that the story of Jesus was symbolic and that we have to wake up from our superstitions to acknowledge our "divine heritage." When we die, we live on the same etheric plane as the Space People, but they could not release this information until people got used to the concept of flying saucers.

Dr. Meade Layne published these messages in his Borderland Sciences Research Association (BSRF) *Round Robin* newsletter. Desmond Leslie mentioned Dr. Layne and his theory that Venusian life existed at a "higher octave" in the first edition of *Flying Saucers Have Landed*, but he dropped him in later additions, presumably due to the mediumistic source of his ideas.[18]

BSRF member Trevor James (a.k.a. Trevor James Constable) championed the idea that there is an invisible world composed of ether. This theory proposed that invisible creatures and craft piloted by Etherean beings fly in our atmosphere and are only occasionally recognized as UFOs. He used infrared film to capture images of these craft in the 1950s and 1960s.[19] Another member of the BSRF was Ralph Holland, whose first book, *The Flying Saucers*, was published by this group in 1952. Information on UFOs came to him by telepathic communication from Borealis, whom we have already noted starred in *A Spacewoman Speaks*.[20]

An engineer called Frederick G. Hehr of Santa Monica, California, corresponded with UFO writer Harold Wilkins from 1952 to 1953. In one of his letters, he provided Wilkins with some prophecies:

> I was told in 1903 that a third world war may wipe out our civilization, and that an older race on Venus is taking measures to re-establish a new and better order in the shortest possible time. The saucers have been taken out of storage, and are now being tested, in order to train crews, in their handling. When the atomic bombs begin to fall, these extra-terrestrial aeroforms may be used to salvage what is good in our civilization, either persons or things. The target date for the start of the third war will probably be in 1960, the re-establishment of peace in 1965. In between, there may be little active war, but five years of chaos and total anarchy.[21]

One wonders how in 1903 anyone could imagine three world wars in the space of 60 years. And where were these saucers being stored? Without any other evidence, this was just a rumor and as substantial as the predicted third world war. The message that the saucers were operated by Venusians, to save us from our atomic bombs, was very much of the 1950s.

If you mix Probert's "Kareeta" and Hehr's Venusian saucer ideas you get the building blocks for George Adamski's contactee stories. Just like Probert, Adamski also saw a UFO in 1946 before Kenneth Arnold's johnny-come-lately flying saucers of 1947. However, Adamski's most important encounter came on November 20, 1952, in the California desert. He was with a gaggle of his supporters, Mrs. Lucy McGinnis, Mr. and Mrs. A Bailey, Dr. and Mrs. G.H. Williamson, and Mrs. Alice K. Wells, when they all spotted a UFO mothership. Adamski felt compelled to walk toward it on his own.

Out in the desert he saw a scout ship fly down from the mothership and land nearby. Outside this scout ship he met a space being called Orthon from the planet Venus. He described him as being a five-foot, six-inch-tall humanoid with long blond hair and gray eyes. He wore a one-piece ski suit that had no visible buttons, zippers or fastenings.

Through a telepathic "conversion," Orthon warned him about the dangers of atomic testing. He explained that most aliens in the galaxy are humanoid and that their magnetically-controlled flying saucers had a worrying design flaw that made them crash on Earth (Orthon must have been thinking of Roswell).

When the scout ship flew away, Adamski found imprints from Orthon's boots in the desert sand. George Williamson had some Plaster of Paris conveniently on hand and made a cast of these imprints. They show a multitude of hieroglyphics and what look like swastikas.

Worldwide fame came in 1953 with the publication of his book *Flying Saucers Have Landed*, which he co-authored with Desmond Leslie. The journalist Frank Edwards was very skeptical when it came to Adamski, even though he was generally sympathetic to the subject of UFOs. He alleged that *Flying Saucers Have Landed* was based on an earlier work of fiction by Adamski titled *An Imaginary Trip to the Moon, Venus, and Mars* (1949). A lady writer, Clara John, saw its poten-

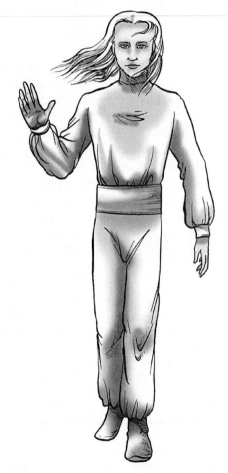

Contactee George Adamski met Orthon, an alien from the planet Venus, on November 20, 1952. The blond-haired being warned Adamski telepathically about the dangers of atomic testing (illustration by Richard Svensson).

tial and helped him to rewrite it while Adamski obtained photographs of the scout ships. Edwards said that he rejected the manuscript, and after years of searching he found that the photographs were of the top of a 1937 vacuum cleaner.[22]

Ray Palmer, the editor of *Amazing Stories*, said that he saw a version of Adamski's manuscript in 1946. When he read *Flying Saucers Have Landed* he realized it was the same story but with a Venusian visiting in a flying saucer, not Jesus Christ in a spaceship as in the original.[23] Adamski's contact with the Space People continued and he recounted these experiences in another book, *Inside the Space Ships*. This was ghost written by Charlotte Blodget. Again, this seems to have been based on a work of fiction by Adamski, ghost written by Lucy McGinnis, titled *Pioneers of Space: A Trip to the Moon, Mars and Venus* (Leonard-Freefield, 1949). Timothy Good noted that there are several striking similarities between both books, and he could only ponder that Adamski originally used a fictional format because people would not believe it as nonfiction. Since the aliens did not have names, Charlotte Blodget made them up in order to make Adamski's stories easier to read. We can blame her for the creation of Orthon, Ilmuth, Kalna and Firkon.[24]

Adamski came to the attention of the Federal Bureau of Investigation (FBI) as early as September 1950. An informant told them that, in a discussion with Adamski at the Palomar Gardens Café, he stated that the U.S. government was in contact with the Space People. What Adamski called the U.S. "Military Government" kept these communications secret because the aliens probably had a Communist government. He went on to predict that San Diego would be bombed within the year and that Russia would peacefully rule the world for 1,000 years.

For good measure, he said that a corrupt form of government ran the United States and its capitalists were enslaving the poor. Such subversive talk made the FBI understandably consider him a "security matter." He crossed swords with the FBI in March 1953 when at a public lecture he alleged that his talk was cleared by the FBI and Air Force Intelligence. The FBI persuaded him to sign a document to say that he did not have their clearance. Ever the opportunist, he doctored this official document to prove to people that he was cleared by these agencies. In December 1953, an FBI agent was sent to retrieve the document from Adamski and to read him the riot act "in no uncertain terms."[25]

Evidence that the U.S. government knew about, and even had contact themselves with Adamski's friendly Space Brothers, came in the form of a letter in December 1957. It was sent by R.E. Straith of the Cultural Exchange Committee and was written on U.S. State Department stationery.

The letter stated: "The Department has on file a great deal of confirmatory evidence bearing out your own claims…. While certainly the Department cannot publicly confirm your experiences, it can, I believe, with propriety, encourage your work."

This was obviously fantastic news for Adamski and his followers, but they hit a brick wall when they tried to contact the Cultural Exchange Committee or R.E. Straith. This only encouraged them to believe that the department was so secret that its existence could not be admitted. In the 1980s, Jim Moseley, the editor of *Saucer News*, finally admitted that he and ufologist Gray Barker had produced the letter to hoax Adamski.[26]

In 1959, the FBI received another complaint from a member of the public who wrote to say that they were worried that Adamski was spreading Soviet propaganda. This was because he was saying the Space People had abolished money, private property, individual governments, schools and churches. If attacked, he advocated that we should lay down our arms and that the Space People advised us to get rid of our nuclear weapons.[27] As the FBI files show, Adamski had in the post-war years become a sympathizer of Communism and the Soviet Union, which is very different from his right-wing associations in the 1930s. It is hard to define with any certainty whether he was genuinely committed to any of these political viewpoints or just liked to be outspoken and opposite to prevailing attitudes and beliefs.

The day after Adamski's death on April 24, 1965, he returned to Earth in a flying saucer. Arthur Bryant said he saw this craft land near Scoriton, Devon, England. There were three humanoids altogether; the one who was presumed to be a reincarnation of Adamski called himself "Yamski." In an American accent, he said he came from Venus and mentioned "Des Les," which was interpreted as a reference to Desmond Leslie. Eileen Buckle, who was a regular contributor *to Flying Saucer Review*, wrote a book about this case, *The Scoriton Mystery*, which was immediately discredited as a hoax by her collaborator, Norman Oliver. I must confess that as a teenager I was totally engrossed by Buckle's book. It probably made an impact on me because it showed that alien activity could occur anywhere, including your own backyard.[28]

Adamski's stories of trips to the Moon and Venus with the Space Brothers, and his photographic evidence of their scout ships, inspired fanatical followers who believed every word he said. There have always been a number of "scientific" ufologists who have taken Adamski's claims seriously even if they dismissed those of other contactees. Even today, he still has supporters and believers. In comparison, contemporary contactees like Daniel Fry, Truman Bethurum, Howard Menger, Orfeo Angelucci,

George Adamski (shown here in Denmark, March 3, 1965), gained fame with the publication of his book *Flying Saucers Have Landed* in 1953 co-authored with Desmond Leslie. He regularly had encounters with aliens and rode in their flying saucer. The man at right is unidentified (Archives for the Unexplained).

George Van Tassel, Aladino Felix (a.k.a. Dino Kraspedon) and Gabriel Green are just footnotes in the history of ufology.

Cults

All the contactees seem to think peace will come to Earth if we win the right to join some fancifully titled galactic federation. We could only do this if we give up our war-like behavior and stop polluting our planet. As we have seen, many of the contactees of the 1950s emerged from or were associated with right-wing groups.

The coming of the flying saucers gave them the chance to rebrand their views in an extraterrestrial package. Contactee messages sometimes had anti–Semitic components to them. They wanted to do away with international monetary systems because they distrusted the elite groups and "Jewish" bankers that they believed secretly ruled the world. The good Space People tended to be Aryan types who were intellectually, spiritually and physically superior, while the evil aliens tended to be small, ugly and deformed.

Most of the encounters are with beings who spout the same religious or mystical philosophies that the contactee already agreed with. The contactees often met Biblical figures, especially Jesus, and they usually put forward warnings of apocalyptic doom. Old-hat religion, just like old-hat fascism, was rebranded by the contactees for the Space Age.

From a cynical perspective, contactees blatantly exploited the belief in space visitors for their own aims. They were simply conmen, hoaxers, tricksters and opportunists. By spinning a few yarns, they could easily achieve fame and fortune. In some cases, they might have started by reporting a simple UFO sighting, and then they were inspired to report ever more complex encounters and past experiences. Their stories thereby took on a life of their own, and the contactee might even have come to believe their own fantasies.

Conspiracy theorists regard contactees as victims of trickery or duplicity by the CIA or other groups for their own nefarious purposes. Ufologists have suggested that contactees like Adamski were set up by the U.S. government. According to Leon Davidson, the testing of secret U.S. aircraft caused many UFO sightings in 1947 onward. To deflect the USSR from gaining knowledge of these experimental flights, the CIA sponsored NICAP and contactee clubs to sow confusion and disinformation.

The experiences of Adamski and other contactees were elaborate hoaxes created by the CIA as part of this plan. Jacques Vallee noted that Adamski seemed to own a passport with special privileges (a waiver for excess baggage to Venus, no doubt) and his co-author Desmond Leslie had been a British intelligence officer. Leonard Stringfield in a similar vein thought that contactees were government plants to discredit serious UFO research. The flaw with this argument is that Adamski's and most other contactees' aliens extolled ideologies that challenged Western democracy.

Contactees have also been subject to covert studies by academics. The most famous case involved Marian Keech (pseudonym). The messages to Keech from the planet Clarion obtained via automatic writing contained the usual mixture of cosmic philosophy and warnings of imminent doom. One of her contacts was called Sananda, who was a reincarnation of Jesus, and for up to 14 hours a day she would receive messages from "The Guardians," as she called these Space People.

In 1954, her warnings of devastating floods and geological changes throughout the United States were published in her local newspapers, and she held out the promise that her followers would be saved by the flying saucers. Sociologists at the University of Minnesota monitored and joined her group to see how the group acted and responded to the predicted day of doom.

When the predicted floods did not come, the sociologists were surprised to find the group was not despondent; instead, they were encouraged by the fact that their efforts had saved the world. Besides the dodgy ethics, we can see how easy it would be to infiltrate or even manipulate such groups. Fears of infiltration of all types made contactee groups suspicious of newcomers, and some had "inner circles" that have had higher levels of knowledge than the normal membership.[29]

Another alternative is that the contactees were duped by their own subconscious mind. Most of us only know Uri Geller for his ability to bend spoons with his mind and as a friend of Michael Jackson, but back in the early 1970s, he had numerous communications with a cosmic intelligence called SPECTRA. Under hypnotic regression, he recalled seeing a light in the sky above his garden in Tel Aviv, when he was three years old. A faceless shining figure appeared before him. It sent a ray of light at him that made him pass out. Significantly, this took place on Christmas Day, December 25, 1949. The implication is that he was "born" like Jesus on this day to serve humanity. SPECTRA admitted that on this day they had programmed Uri so that we could be prepared for a mass landing of flying saucers. Geller and Dr. Andrijia Puharich continued to receive communications from SPECTRA through automatic writing and messages left on a tape recorder. Jacques Vallee was surprised that they took the rambling pseudoscientific messages seriously, and he noted that they reflected many of the ideas held by Geller and Dr. Puharich. Indeed, they even confused astronomical units of time with units of space in just the same way Uri Geller did.[30]

In my own investigation of cases involving contact using automatic writing or telepathic communications, the philosophy espoused by the aliens was virtually indistinguishable from that of the contactee. Their messages relate as much to their own personal experiences as they did to the universal themes of love and peace or warnings of planetary doom. Norman Harrison (pseudonym), for example, was a very depressed person who had premonitions of disasters and a coming Judgment Day. He started writing a stream of consciousness novel with a guerrilla leader as the hero. The main drive of the story, which begins with an atomic explosion, is about this man being threatened and sadistically tortured by technocratic police authorities. He admitted to me that the hero represented his own feelings of being an outsider from established authority and society.[31]

There is also the possibility that contactees intuitively tell their followers and readers what they want to hear. In this manner, the communications reflect the ideology and interests of a group rather than an individual. Messages received through mental impressions, automatic writing and séances can be neatly explained as the outpourings of the unconscious mind of the contactee. This does not easily explain encounters where the contactee says he has actually met the Space People and ridden in their spaceships. In some cases, these could be attributable to hallucinations or other visionary experiences. George Adamski admitted that he was an expert at hypnotizing himself and other people, and that he could easily put himself into a trance. He added that he did not use these methods to contact the Space People, though even some of his supporters suspected he might have resorted to such techniques.[32]

Another possibility is that the contactees really are in contact with alien beings or intelligences. The simplest thing is to say they have actually ridden in "nuts and bolts" spacecraft and that their superior technology seems like occult magic to us. Since there is little physical evidence for their literal reality, ufologists have resorted to more sophisticated theories to explain these contacts. In John Keel's view, contactees have minds that are open to manipulation from "super-high-frequency radiations." This would explain why certain people are targeted by strange visions and communications from childhood onward. Their paranormal experiences and perception of streams of telepathic communications can literally make them insane if they cannot understand where they are coming from. These dark forces used MIB and hallucinations to totally devastate the minds of contactees. Keel acknowledged that Dr. Meade Layne knew about this "contactee syndrome" as early as 1955 when he considered:

> It is possible that some persons may be less affected by supersonic frequencies than others; this may account for the selection of certain persons by the Etherians [his name for Space People—N.W.]. It is also possible that some such persons are now showing signs of amnesia and other physical and mental deterioration.[33]

Such attributes could be applied to today's abductees who have certainly suffered from amnesia and much psychological torment. The main characteristics of the direct contactees can be summarized as follows:

1. The contactee is male.
2. The contactee meets space beings and rides in their flying saucers to other planets.
3. Their meetings with the aliens are voluntary. The contactee might be compelled to seek or initiate alien contact.
4. Meetings and contact are frequent.
5. The description of the aliens, flying saucers and the alien planets are nonsensical and pseudoscientific.
6. The contactee is chosen (often in childhood) and is regarded as special.
7. The contactee might have an alien origin or believe they were an alien in a previous life.

8. Followers spread the messages received by the contactee.
9. The messages from the aliens tend to reflect the ideas of the contactee.
10. The messages contain predictions of doom and the aliens offer salvation.
11. The messages can be inherently totalitarian and/or anti-democratic.
12. Belief in the contactees' messages is usually based on faith rather than on evidence.

Indirect contactees are more likely to be women like Hélène Smith and Marian Keech. They do not satisfy points one and two above, but the other points do apply.

In summary, we can say that contactees are simply outright fraudsters who have no bearing on alien abductions except to say they use the belief in UFOs to further their own ends. Alternatively, they are victims of manipulation by terrestrial groups or extraterrestrial intelligences. On the other hand, they are deluded by a combination of psychological and sociological factors, and in extreme cases they are suffering from schizophrenia or similar psychopathology.

5

Alien Intercourse

Besides the trips to the planets and cosmic philosophy, all the contactee stories indicate a sexual attraction between the contactee and the Space People. For example, Howard Menger from childhood met beautiful space women in the woods near his home in New Jersey. The power of their attraction is certainly underlined by Menger's description of meeting a space woman when he was 10 years old:

> There, sitting on a rock by the brook, was the most exquisite woman my young eyes had ever beheld! The warm sunlight caught the highlights of her long golden hair ... the curves of her lovely body were delicately contoured.... She spoke my name and I trembled with joy.[1]

The space women said they would always keep an eye on him, and from 1946 onward they regularly visited him. In return for cutting their hair and buying them clothes, he was given a ride to the Moon.

Unlike the Apollo astronauts of the 1960s and 1970s, he found the Moon had a breathable atmosphere and plenty of vegetation. To prove his point he brought back some highly nutritive lunar potatoes. Menger gave the potatoes to the government, which has kept their superior qualities a closely guarded secret. He also took a trip to Venus, which was, you guessed it, a veritable paradise. He was encouraged to become a vegetarian, and he was told that in a past life he was a citizen of Saturn. In that life he had been in love with a Venusian called Marla (a.k.a. Connie Weber). As luck would have it, she was also now an Earth person, living in New Jersey. They eventually fulfilled their alien destiny by getting married in 1958.

After this romantic interlude, Menger's story ended on a flat note. On the *Long John Nebel* radio show several years later, he could only say that he might have had these encounters and experiences. Hilary Evans noted that this was a very rare example of a contactee undermining and denying their original story.[2]

When Truman Bethurum went inside a landed UFO, he had his first encounter with what he called the "queen of women," Captain Aura

Rhanes: "That is where my eyes bulged again. I stood before their captain, a beautiful woman.... Her smooth skin was a beautiful olive and roses, and her brown-eyed flashing smile seemed to make her complexion more glowing."[3]

Most of these stories involve stereotypically beautiful Space Women who would not look out of place on the cover of a science fiction magazine or film poster of the period. The Space People, male and female, were beautiful, intelligent, peaceful and caring. The space women were sexually attractive. The contactee rarely had intercourse with them except in cases like that of Menger, who married an Earth woman who was a reportedly reincarnated alien.

The rather innocent and coy encounters of the contactees contrast sharply with the modern-day abduction stories we will look at later in this chapter. This difference might be artificial due to the fact that the contactees and their followers were unwilling to go into intimate detail. Laura Mundo, for instance, claimed that two young women in Australia met George Adamski's friendly alien, Orthon. They went to his house where they did the "sexual bidding" for 32 men. Adamski regarded this as some

Connie and Howard Menger (pictured here January 28, 1992) were contactees in the 1950s. Howard claimed to have met beautiful space women since childhood and Connie was a Venusian in a past life. They married in 1958 (photograph by Clas Svahn, Archives for the Unexplained).

kind of psychic or astral encounter, which he considered dangerous. It was his contention that the most highly evolved aliens did not use telepathy because of recent atomic bomb testing, sunspots and other disturbances that were upsetting the astral plane. Later, Adamski met Orthon in San Francisco, and Orthon informed Adamski that he had met the two Australian girls and that the sexual encounter was a physical event. At Orthon's suggestion, one of the women was invited to the United States and lived at Adamski's place.

Ray Stanford said at a UFO convention in 1977 that years previously, when Adamski lived at Palomar Gardens, his female followers had sex with Space Men. Adamski would have intercourse with any woman who was "left over." These followers offered sex to Stanford, who was only 14 years old at the time. Even Mundo, who organized public meetings and lectures for Adamski, confessed that he made sexual advances toward her in public places on several occasions.

It would be easy to discount Mundo's revelations as malicious, but she herself offered several reasons for the behavior of Orthon and Adamski. The two Australian women could have been Space Women posing as humans. Apparently, the men and women who say they have had intercourse with aliens are themselves Space People. Mundo went on to make the point that aliens do not use contraceptives as they mate "in line with nature," so their planets are never overpopulated. Having no monetary system, they can also have large families without any financial strain. Therefore, we have to take into account the aliens' different sexual behavior and cannot judge it by our own Earthly standards. As for Adamski, he acted in a lewd manner to put off the people who saw the messenger rather than the message. Mundo felt that this was true because Adamski never made advances to her in private.[4]

Nonetheless, for cynics it is easy to see that predatory contactees could easily use their power over their followers to obtain sex, financial gain and other forms of control for their own gratification. It could be that these contactees come within the orbit of evil Space People, who encourage such activities, or it could be that the contactee is merely exploiting the gullibility of UFO believers.

So far it would be easy to think that the contactee phenomenon is purely male dominated, but there have been a few female contactees who had equally amazing encounters. The most outstanding is Elizabeth Klarer, who fell in love with an alien called Akon in 1956. He took her back to his home planet, Meton, where he explained, "Only a few are chosen for breeding purposes from beyond this Solar System to infuse new blood into our ancient race."

Klarer wrote, "I surrendered in ecstasy to the magic of his lovemaking." Her union with this alien scientist produced a highly intelligent son, whom they called Ayling. He remained at his celestial home, while Klarer returned to South Africa where she died in 1994.[5]

These outrageous claims of the contactees help to explain the dearth of abduction cases before the late 1960s. UFO researchers would not consider any case that involved the sighting of alien beings or trips inside their flying saucer. Any indication that a witness was exhibiting contactee behavior, such as having frequent meetings with aliens and messages containing cosmic philosophy, would tend to scare away any self-respecting UFO researcher.

John Keel alleged that the National Investigations Committee on Aerial Phenomena (NICAP) was so keen to suppress such cases that they hid a report on the Betty and Barney Hill encounter. According to him, it was only the work of John Fuller that accidentally brought their story to our attention.[6] Keel was probably referring to Walter Webb's report on the case, which he produced in October 1961. Given the details of the Hills' case, we can understand the reservations a conservative organization like NICAP would have about publicizing it, and we have to be aware that there was a long period between the UFO encounter and the hypnotic regression sessions that revealed the abduction in detail. Another factor is that the Hills in 1961 were still trying to come to terms with their sighting and the puzzling period of "missing time," and they did not want any publicity.[7]

Earlier in 1961, NICAP had been involved in the case of Joe Simonton, who had encountered a UFO containing three five-foot-tall dark-skinned aliens. They offered him a jug, which Simonton filled with water and gave back to them. In return for this service, they gave him some small cookies that they were baking inside their craft. NICAP investigators said they were not going to analyze the cookies as they had more important cases to study, and Simonton told the press, "if it happened again, I don't think I'd tell anybody about it."[8] This brush with publicity surrounding an alien encounter could easily have confirmed NICAP's opinion that these cases tarnished their scientific study of UFO reports.

While the ufologists haggled and argued, people reported sightings of alien encounters to newspapers and magazines that were not always so fussy about whether it was a contactee story or not. The contactees and their organizations also published their own newsletters and spread contact stories to anyone who would listen. Even in the early days of ufology, some "serious" writers were already willing to consider cases of human disappearances in the context of flying saucers.

In 1954, Harold Wilkins considered the possibility of abduction in his book *Flying Saucers on the Attack* (a.k.a. *Flying Saucers from the Moon* in Britain): "One wonders how many cases of mysterious disappearances of men and women in 1948–52 might be explained as TAKEN ABOARD A FLYING SAUCER IN A LONELY PLACE."[9]

His thundering use of capital letters showed what a shocking possibility this might be. His next book on the subject, *Flying Saucers Uncensored*, considered the disappearance of two contactees, Karl Hunrath and Wilbur Wilkinson, as the result of alien abduction.[10]

So ufologists and writers like Harold Wilkins were willing to consider an alien contact story if it came from "respectable" witnesses or sources that did not blatantly promote cosmic philosophy. The investigator, "serious" or not, would also be more likely to investigate a case if it fitted in with their own preconceptions and theories. A truism then and now.

Implants, doorway amnesia and paralysis featured in an improbable story given by John Robinson on the *Long John Nebel* radio show in March 1957. He said that once he had a neighbor, Steve Brodie, who told of meeting two strange figures in 1938. They pointed a rod-like device at Brodie that paralyzed him and burned his partner, who was prospecting with him. Brodie lost consciousness when a set of earphones was put on him.

He woke up to find himself with other prisoners in a cave. He thought this cave/prison was run by Richard Shaver's infamous Dero. The earphones were readjusted on his head, and when he became fully conscious again, he found himself in Manhattan, two years later. As evidence of his story, Brodie said he had small scars behind his ears. The experience also made him become a vegetarian, which is not an uncommon feature of contactee and abduction stories.[11]

It would be safe to say that there was a constant dribble of contact stories circulating within ufology and mainstream media that hinted at the abduction experiences of today.

In 1978, Rich Reynolds had a couple of telephone conversations with Bosco Nedelcovic. He was a Department of Defense translator who said that from 1956 to 1963 he worked for the Agency for International Development (AID) in South America. He claimed that the CIA ran Operation Mirage, which used the methods outlined in Chapter 2 and ufologists in their pay to simulate UFO events. While based in Sao Paulo, he was sent by military helicopter, crewed by U.S. Navy men, on a psychological testing operation. Using the Brazilian/American air base at Serro do Espinhaco, they made reconnaissance flights over several days. One night, using heat-seeking equipment, they hovered over a man in a field. After spraying a drug called Lorazepam on the man, they landed and dragged him to their helicopter. When he was taken into the helicopter, he was groggy and he banged his jaw on the ramp of the craft. Bosco remained outside the helicopter with two other AID members and the three crew members, while a doctor, a U.S. Navy man, and a Brazilian navy officer attended the man.

After two hours, at 3 a.m., the man, who was still unconscious, was taken out of the helicopter and placed next to his tractor. This episode obviously related to the abduction of Antonio Villas Boas.

Generally speaking, Bosco said that the CIA "terminated" ufologists who threatened national security, that ufologist Dr. Hynek attended CIA briefings, and that the Hill and the Hickson/Parker, Pascagoula, Mississippi, abduction cases were created by the CIA using holographic equipment.

Reynolds was rightly skeptical about several elements of Bosco's testimony. A person with a good reading of the literature could easily have invented this participation in these experiments, and the hitting of Villas Boas' jaw on the helicopter ramp fits a little too neatly with his account of having a blood sample taken from his chin. When Reynolds tried contacting him again, he had no success, so Bosco might have been a hoaxer or really who he said he was. If the latter is true, it still does not mean what he said was correct, as he could have been spreading disinformation in an attempt to discredit leading ufologists (like Hynek) and to scare people away from ufology, lest they get "terminated."[12]

It was claimed that Bosco was recruited in 1964 by Marion Pettie, the founder of a group called the Finders, to infiltrate the Institute for Policy Studies. The Finders was formed in the 1940s by Pettie as an open house to members of the counterintelligence services and in the 1950s to beatniks and fellow travelers. In the late 1990s, they were headquartered in Culpepper, Virginia, where you could drive to them, appropriately enough, on state route 666 from Washington, D.C. The Finders have been regarded as a CIA front and several of its members have been linked to the CIA. It has been claimed that they kidnap and torture young children in the United States using trained sexual degenerates. The children were also said to have been initiated into bloody, orgiastic satanic rituals involving the murder of animals and other children. Pettie has brushed aside these allegations, saying that the Finders was just a name for a scene—a setting for people to hangout. There was no group or constitution as such, but because Pettie was interested in the CIA and other counterculture happenings, the Finders have been the target of rumors, half-truths and guilt-by-association.

This gives additional confirmation that Bosco really was connected with the CIA, even if it was only on an informal basis, but it does not give any further proof of whether his claims were true or not.

By the late 1970s and 1980s, the concept of alien breeding gained prominence with the rise of abduction reports and investigations. Within abduction research circles, it became a given that women were routinely abducted, impregnated and then re-abducted a few weeks later for the extraction of the hybrid fetus. These activities explained the short-lived pregnancies experienced by female abductees. Either male abductees had intercourse with an alien woman, or their sperm was extracted by mechanical means. In the case of Villas Boas, the aliens collected his sperm by both methods.

Screwed by the Aliens, **a 2018 book edited by Timothy Green Beckley and Sean Casteel, highlighted the continued belief that aliens caused "false" pregnancies and were intent on creating a hybrid super race (courtesy Timothy Green Beckley).**

In this chapter we have looked at how some contactees were in a position to gain sexual favors from their followers and the fact that there was a sexual component to their relationships with the Space People. Abduction cases were largely ignored by ufologists until about 1965, when the Villas Boas and Hill cases were published and widely disseminated. Abductions became a legitimate part of UFO research, but the contactee material continued to be derided and dismissed. Since then men and women have claimed to have been abducted, taken inside a flying saucer, and then coerced or forced into having sexual intercourse with aliens. Like the contactees, these abductees are often told that they are special and that the aliens are conducting some form of human/alien breeding program.

John Keel felt that the roots of the hybrid breeding concept came from the contactees themselves. Many of them were orphans, who were told that they had a mixed alien/human parentage. The object of the program was to populate the whole planet with hybrids. In his egotistical fashion, Keel thought that the aliens were trying a little too hard to convince *him* of the reality of this project. He saw through it as a modern-day version of the biblical stories of sons of God consorting with the daughters of men. As soon as these skeptical thoughts came to him his "pregnant contactees suddenly became unpregnant."[13]

By the 1980s, it had become common for male abductees to report being stimulated to produce sperm that was collected by the aliens, which was also a feature of the Villas Boas and Hill cases that were not made public until decades later. Meanwhile, the rumors and the few reports of women being raped by aliens in the 1960s changed to numerous accounts of female abductees suffering from phantom pregnancies. The contactee and abduction reports have featured intercourse with humanoid and Nordic-type aliens, but in recent years, sex with reptoids has been increasingly reported.

Today abductions often include paranormal elements taking place inside the abductee's own bedroom and might not even include a UFO sighting or abduction into a spaceship. Unlike the contactee stories and the early abduction reports, the experience of alien encounters and intercourse has become exceedingly traumatic for abductees.

6

Ufological Origins

The late John Mack, like many UFO abduction researchers, was of the opinion that the Betty and Barney Hill case began the modern history of abductions. It is considered that cases prior to the Hills', like those of Antonio Villas Boas, do not fit the pattern of the modern abduction phenomenon, or what is known as the classic abduction scenario (CAS).

Such a view is short sighted because there is an abundant amount of abduction-type cases that were not fully investigated or were simply ignored from 1947 onward. What the Hill case did was open up the possibility that normal people—not the self-publicizing contactees—were being abducted. More important, the technique of hypnotic regression was regarded as *the* means for discovering the full truth about alien encounters.

The Hill case gained worldwide publicity because it happened to an honest, educated, married American couple who had undergone extensive investigation. The Villas Boas case certainly had an equal impact on ufology but it only involved a single witness, who at the time was considered uneducated. Because he lived in Brazil it was not so easy to wheel him onto U.S. radio and TV talk shows, plus his story was far more sexually explicit than the Hill case. Villas Boas's report is better than the Hills' in the sense that he was able to recall his experience without the use of hypnotic regression and that it was documented in detail by the most respected ufologists in Brazil.

Two important cases like these seemed like a genuine break-through toward solving the riddle of the flying saucer visitations. It was even better that they had a good number of similarities. Charles Bowen noted that both encounters described:

1. aliens with thin lips, large heads that thinned down to the chin, and eyes that slanted outward; and
2. writing that featured lines and dots.

Charles Bowen thought that the chances of the Hills knowing about the Villas Boas case were "millions to one against."[1] These odds are reduced when we look at how Villas Boas' story was published and circulated. First of all, Villas Boas was interviewed four months after his encounter by journalist Joao Martins and Dr. Olavo Fontes but they thought his story was too "wild" to publish. Dr. Fontes filed his detailed report in the hope that some similar report might come along to confirm Villas Boas' story. The case was re-investigated by Dr. Walter Buhler three years later, and he published his findings in the April–June 1962 edition of his UFO society's publication, *SBESDV Bulletin*. A copy was sent to Waveney Girvan, the editor of *Flying Saucer Review* (*FSR*), in 1962, but he also found it too "wild" to publish. The story was finally published by *FSR* under the editorship of Charles Bowen in 1964 and 1965.[2]

In 1965, Walter Webb wrote to *FSR* hinting that he knew of a case very much like that of Villas Boas. He was referring to the Betty and Barney Hill incident, which, like the Villas Boas story, was finally becoming public. Peter Rogerson disputes this by observing that Dr. Fontes sent a copy of his report to Coral and Jim Lorenzen of APRO in 1958, and they did not publish it until it was released elsewhere in the 1960s. In the same year, Fontes also wrote about the Villas Boas report and his tentative skepticism of these types of cases to Alexander Mebane.[3]

In addition, one of the investigators of the Hill case, Walter Webb, had an interest in Brazilian car-stop reports and he could have learned of the Villas Boas case through conversation with other ufologists or through the *SBESDV Bulletin* report in early 1962. Therefore, it is possible that Webb spoke about the Villas Boas report and cases like it to the Hills and thereby helped shape what they "remembered" about their abduction.

Peter Rogerson pointed out that Villas Boas' encounter had similarities to other UFO stories of that time.[4] The female alien's eyes, high cheekbones and pointed chin are reminiscent of George Adamski's description of Orthon's features. Villas Boas' aliens wore red reflective badges and tight-fitting coverall uniforms and thick-soled "tennis" shoes. Dr. Fontes showed Villas Boas sketches of Orthon who wore loose-fitting trousers and a different type of shoe. This reveals that Villas Boas was exposed to UFO pictures and information that a hoaxer would use to validate their story, or it could unconsciously persuade a witness to integrate this information into their own account.[5]

There was not a flood of abduction cases after the publication of *The Interrupted Journey* but a few did start being reported and investigated. Dr. Leo Sprinkle, a psychologist at the University of Wyoming, was one of the first experts to regularly use hypnotic regression to investigate abductions.

One of his first cases involved 22-year-old Sergeant Herbert Schirmer of Ashland, Nebraska. He was on patrol at 2:30 a.m. when he saw some lights ahead of him. Thinking they were the lights of a truck, he flashed his headlights at them. This caused the row of lights to fly away at a fast speed. Returning to his station, he found a mark below his left ear and he suffered from a bad headache. He recorded in his logbook: "Saw a FLYING SAUCER at the junction of highways 6 and 63. Believe it or not!"

When his report was investigated, 20 minutes remained unaccounted for. To discover what happened to Schirmer on that morning of December 3, 1967, Sprinkle hypnotically regressed him. Under hypnosis, Schirmer recalled driving down a dirt road to follow the football-shaped object. He was compelled to drive toward the craft. He could not pull out his revolver or turn the car around; neither could he get any help as his radio stopped working. His car engine also stopped and aliens from the UFO that had now landed came toward him and shot a green gas at his car. At his car window, the humanoid aliens asked, "Are you the watchman over this place?"

He was taken inside the craft, which was full of computers and control panels. Through telepathy, they said that they had bases in the United States and that they came from a nearby galaxy. To power their craft they took water from reservoirs and used the principles of reverse electromagnetism. Pointing to the view of the surrounding landscape seen through a large window, one of the aliens told Schirmer, "Watchman, some day you will see the Universe" and said they would return two more times. The aliens, who wore one-piece outfits emblazoned with a winged serpent, said that he would forget what occurred to him.

As Jacques Vallee observed, the UFO occupants mixed garbled half-truths and falsehoods, as if they were deliberately trying to trick us.[6] By these means, skeptics could scoff at the patent absurdities of such stories while believers followed ever-more convoluted and bizarre lines of enquiry. This was aptly put by one of Schirmer's aliens when he said, "You will not speak wisely about this night."

At the risk of not speaking wisely, it is noteworthy that the circumstances of Schirmer's encounter were much like those of the Hills.' The compulsion to drive off the main road, the inability to escape, the entry to a landed craft, the telepathic communication, and missing time are consistent with the Hill story. Vallee added that the painful welt under Schirmer's ear and his perception of a buzzing in his head after the encounter have been reported in other UFO incidents. He speculated that the aliens in such circumstances might be using some form of beam to put the UFO witness into an altered state of consciousness.[7] The green-colored gas sent toward his car reminds us of the "smoke" Villas Boas re-

Computer expert Jacques Vallee (pictured here in 2015) wrote the influential book *Passport to Magonia* (1975), which showed that alien visitations have occurred throughout human history and are part of our social and cultural fabric (author's collection).

ported during his experience, but Schirmer was not medically examined or used as breeding stock. More prosaically, Peter Rogerson argued that Schirmer was not completely satisfied with Sprinkle's work, and in June 1968 he was regressed by Loring Williams who uncovered the ever-more exotic details of his case. Rogerson indicated that most of the elements of his story seemed as if they had been cherry-picked from the UFO litera- ture. Schirmer now came to think that the aliens were conducting some type of breeding program, and he joined the contactee lecture circuit.[8]

The Pascagoula, Mississippi, abduction of 1973 is intriguing because it involved two abductees. While fishing on the evening of October 11, Charles Hickson and Calvin Parker heard a buzzing sound and saw a fish-shaped UFO land nearby. As three short, humanoid aliens with gray wrinkled skin floated out of the craft, Parker fainted and Hickson became paralyzed and felt weightless. Hickson recalled being floated by the aliens to a brightly lit room inside the UFO. An eye-like device moved backward and forward over him as he lay floating in a reclining position. Inside this room, there was no sign of Parker. After about 15 to 40 minutes he was left alone for a few minutes then he was floated back with Parker to the riverbank by the aliens.[9] The aliens returned to their ship, which seemed to rapidly disappear rather than fly away.

When the anglers reported their encounter to the local sheriff that evening, they were visibly shaken. When they were left in a bugged room, it was obvious that they were traumatized. Parker resorted to praying. Hickson passed a long lie detector test that indicated that something traumatic did happen to them. Furthermore, he suffered nightmares and psychic experiences resulting from this encounter. Parker did not fare so well; he had a nervous breakdown and was hospitalized for treatment.

The humanoids seen by Hickson had two claw-like fingers at the end of each arm, and unlike today's greys, they had small, slit-like eyes and conical ears and noses. Their legs remained straight and together. He got the impression that they were creatures or robots. The door that allowed entry to their craft disappeared when it closed, a characteristic of the doors inside the UFO that intrigued Villas Boas. Hickson also said that the intensely lit interior of the UFO did not come from any apparent light source—a feature of many contact cases. When the craft first appeared, it made a buzzing sound, which is reminiscent of the Hill case.

There were other UFO sightings in the area on the night of the anglers' abduction, but investigators found it odd that no one driving over the nearby Highway 90 bridge or the bridge's attendant saw anything. In addition, security cameras used to scan the Pascagoula River recorded nothing out of the ordinary. UFO skeptic James Oberg has also devalued the worth of the lie detector test as a press agent Hickson employed after his encounter organized it.[10] Philip Klass added that the operator of the test was not fully qualified and it was his opinion that the case was a hoax.[11]

Like the contactees, Hickson claimed he was one of 12 chosen people on Earth who were being used to liaise between the aliens and humanity. It was his opinion that we needed the help of the aliens to prevent us from total destruction and that he planned to spread this message through lectures, books and films.[12] A few months earlier Hickson had filed for bankruptcy and it was thought that he had a financial motive for exploiting the encounter.

Jerome Clark and Loren Coleman speculated that the men had fallen asleep and dreamed the whole encounter. They offer the theory that the dominant Hickson telepathically transferred his dream to Parker.[13] Rather than telepathy, it could be argued that they had discussed their "experience" before seeing the sheriff and that Parker went along with whatever was said by Hickson. Since Parker fainted and could not recall anything about the abduction means that we have to rely on Hickson's testimony anyway. The main question is what triggered this dream that caused so much trauma? And, if it was a dream, why did it include features of other "real" abductions?

Martin Kottmeyer is able to answer that last question by discussing the possibility that Hickson read the 1968 paperback *UFOs Over the Americas*.[14] It has a chapter about a man called C. A.V. who encountered five-foot, nine-inch-tall mummy-like aliens in Peru. They glided along the ground and had claw-like hands. The chapter about them is titled "The Flesh Crawlers," which is recalled in Hickson's statement "My flesh crawls when I think about those three things that appeared through the opening [of the craft]."[15] Elsewhere in the book a fish-shaped UFO, an examination by an eye-like device, the Hills' medical examination, and the shock induced by UFOs are discussed. Reinforcing Jerome Clark and Loren Coleman's idea that the encounter was a dream, Kottmeyer states: "The blending and distortion of the elements of these cases is identical to the way dreams remix and composite recent memories to come up with a dramatic experience." The C. A.V. case was also considered to have been a dream or hallucination brought on by the family and business pressures he was under at the time.[16] Steve Sessions adds that the claw-handed aliens are reminiscent of the mutant beings in *This Island Earth,* and that the night before the abduction, ABC's Movie of the Week was *Don't Be Afraid of the Dark,* a thriller about creatures abducting a housewife.[17]

Charles Hickson with co-author William Mendez gave his side of the story in *UFO Contact at Pascagoula* way back in 1983 (reprinted by Flying Disk Press in 2017). In 2018 Calvin Parker finally decided to write his own book to get the real story out there. *Pascagoula—The Closest Encounter: My Story* tells us much about Parker's life in his own words and it has transcriptions of the "secret" tape recording by the police, diagrams, handwritten notes, photographs and numerous magazine and press clippings.

Previously, he claimed he fainted when the UFO appeared so as to avoid media attention, but here Parker tells of seeing the three gray-wrinkled-skin creatures floating toward them. One of the creatures grabbed him with its crab-like hands and injected him with something that made him feel relaxed and weightless. Inside the craft a small entity with big brown eyes telepathically told him not to be afraid and he was inspected by a couple of alien devices. Then he was returned to where he was originally captured by one of the faceless entities.

Another highlight of the book is the transcript of a hypnotic regression session with Calvin conducted by Budd Hopkins on March 14, 1993. It took him back to the fateful night of the encounter, and he recalled an entity inside the craft cutting his hand and injecting him. He hated this "female" being as she caused him to have a burning pain and pumped out all his blood. Reading her thoughts, he thought she wanted to kill him.

How much this regression session, the passage of time and Charles Hickson's repeated telling of the story has influenced his recollection of the event is hard to tell. Whatever happened, this book does show how the incident changed his life and still had an impact on him 45 years later.[18]

A Research Trip (1981) by Stefanos Panagiotakis showed that even eight years after the event interest in the story had not waned and most people were happy to help him in his research. Stefanos took at face value that the two men had an encounter with a spaceship and were examined by mummy-like aliens. He compared himself to the aliens who also traveled to this port from a foreign place.

Hickson was able to reassure Stefanos that there is no hell and we all reincarnate to reach a higher level of perfection. Hickson claimed he has lived five times before and we should believe "in the Supreme Being which is God."

Apparently God revealed to Hickson that he sent these beings from another world to visit him. He is a chosen person and he will make a big announcement on national television when the time is right. Hickson added that the world had to change or it would be in danger of being destroyed. This had happened in the past but this time the beings from another world would come to save us.

Whatever happened to Hickson and Parker it had a shattering effect on their lives and it had a ripple effect on the world. Hickson never did give us the big reveal, but that's ufology for you![19]

On October 25, 1974, Carl Higdon went hunting for elk in the northern area of Medicine Bow National Park in Wyoming. As he shot at an elk, the bullet from his rifle moved in slow motion before dropping in the snow. It seemed like time stood still. As he felt a tingling sensation, he turned to see a six-foot-tall humanoid looking at him. This being had small eyes, no chin or eyebrows, long arms with rod-like hands, bowlegs, and it wore a black one-piece suit. After asking if he was hungry and giving him some pills, which Higdon swallowed, the being pointed at him. The next thing he knew he was inside a transparent, cube-shape craft. Inside the craft, there were two aliens and five elk. They told him they were traveling 163,000 light years to their home planet. After a helmet with wires attached to it was strapped on Higdon's head, he saw a bright sun and tall "space-needle"-type buildings. This made him assume that they had arrived at their home planet, but the helmet could easily have been some form of viewer or virtual reality device. Their sun was so bright that it hurt his eyes, and because of this, they decided to return him. Two and a half hours after firing his rifle, Higdon found himself back in the park. Using his CB radio, he called for help. When the sheriff picked him up at midnight, Higdon was cold, disorientated and in a state of panic. His truck was found stuck in a mud hole three miles away.

As confirmation of his story several people had seen strange lights in the area at the time he was abducted. Blood tests at a local hospital showed he had a rich supply of vitamins in his system. This indicated that the pills given to him had been some form of food pellets or supplements. It was claimed that his old TB scars had disappeared from his lungs, but I cannot think why anyone would have X-rayed his chest. Under hypnotic regression by Dr. Leo Sprinkle, Higdon recalled seeing other humans on the spaceship. The main purpose for their visits to Earth was to hunt for food, and they had returned him because they discovered he had had a vasectomy and was therefore useless for their breeding program. It strikes me that Higdon could have been concussed or at least traumatized after crashing his truck in the mud hole and that his mind created the alien contact to deal with this frightening situation.[20]

The broadcast of *The UFO Incident*, a faithful TV movie adaptation of *The Interrupted Journey*, in October 1975 preceded a new crop of abduction reports. The most prominent example happened in the Sitgreave-Apache National Forest in Arizona on November 5.

A group of woodcutters saw a UFO over some trees as they were driving home in their pickup truck. They stopped to get a better view of the UFO and, ignoring warnings from his friends, Travis Walton walked toward it. The domed object made a beeping sound, then a louder rumbling noise as it spun on its vertical axis. As he went to return to the truck, a green/blue light struck Walton and sent him flying to the ground. This scared his friends so much that they drove off in a panic. When they recovered their composure, they returned to the site, but Walton was no longer there.

A full-scale search failed to find him but he reappeared on November 11 in a telephone booth 12 miles away from where the encounter took place. He was in a confused state but tests showed only some dehydration and no malnutrition.

Under hypnotic regression, he recalled waking in a hot and damp room. He was lying on a table with some type of apparatus on his chest, as if a medical examination or operation had been performed on him. Three beings five feet in height with large heads and large brown eyes, but having no other prominent facial features, watched over him. They wore brown overalls and reminded him of human fetuses. Shocked by their appearance, he tried attacking them but they wisely left the room. Looking outside the room, he saw a corridor that curved to the left and right. In a blind panic, he ran down the corridor and entered a circular room containing a dentist-type chair and a view of the stars through a transparent wall.

When he moved a lever and pressed some buttons on the chair's armrests the view of the stars outside changed, implying that this equipment operated the craft. A humanoid wearing a blue outfit and a helmet led Walton to a large hanger which contained several disk-shape craft. Walton went into one of these craft and found three humans who wore blue outfits. The last thing he remembered was an oxygen mask being put on his face. The next moment he found himself on a road watching the craft flying away, leaving a wave of heat in its wake.

Several disputed lie detector tests were conducted with the woodcutters and Walton that left skeptics and believers unsatisfied with the results. In addition, his conscious recall of the events and recall under hypnosis only covers about one hour of the five days he was abducted. Investigators have put forward the idea that this was a hoax created by the woodcutters because they were behind on a contract with the U.S. Forest Service. On October 20, 1975, Mike Rogers, the head of the woodcutting team, wrote to the USFS saying he was determined to finish the work by the deadline of November 10, 1975. Significantly, he wrote the letter on the same day as the NBC broadcast of *The UFO Incident*, which could have sparked the idea of a hoax to terminate the contract and yet still receive payment for his crew. Against this theory, some wonder how all the men were able to tell a consistent story without at least one of them giving it away. In answer to this, they were threatened with prosecution if it was a hoax, so they had an incentive to keep to the same story.

Besides the financial aspects, it was noted that the Walton family had a long-running interest in UFOs and that when Travis disappeared his family showed little stress or concern about his whereabouts. Dr. James Harder, the Director of Investigations for APRO investigated this case, and he was involved with hypnotically regressing other abductees of this period.

On November 25, 1978, Pam Owens, a 19-year-old American, had been visiting friends in Trier, West Germany, when she saw a large oval-shaped craft in the sky. She watched it for a few minutes with her husband and their 20-month-old son, and then they continued on their car journey.

When they arrived at their destination, they realized that their trip had taken an hour and a half long longer than it should have, and neither Pam nor her husband could account for the missing period of time. On returning to the United States, they contacted a UFO group which advised her to undergo hypnosis.

Under hypnotic regression, Pam recalled that during the missing period of time she drove off the main road and parked in a clearing. They all got out of the car. Surprisingly they did not feel afraid. Pam held her son Brian, and then the next moment she was inside the flying saucer. A yellowish-white light showed that she was in a small room. As she lay paralyzed on a table, Pam cried out for her child and husband. A flat-sounding voice reassured her of their safety and this helped her to calm down. Then, she said,

> suddenly two strange creatures moved into my line of vision. They looked almost like mummies. They had very tiny noses and just straight lines for mouths. One started talking to me, telling me everything would be O.K. His mouth didn't move—it was like he was talking through his eyes.

They pulled up her shirt to expose her five-months-pregnant stomach. As their hands touched her she felt dizzy and sick. Despite her cries of "My baby" and "Oh God" they carried on examining the position of her baby. That was bad enough, but she got really scared when they produced a six-inch-long silver needle. They plunged it just below her navel and the pain was so bad she felt like being sick. The next thing she knew she was on the ground watching the flying saucer flying away into the sky. A strange pimple was found where the needle was inserted, but there were no other adverse effects. Four months after the encounter she gave birth to a healthy baby girl.[21]

Pam's encounter has several parallels to the Hill story. There are the elements of missing time, driving from a main road to a clearing for the abduction itself, the medical examination and the insertion of a needle. The "mummy" aliens sound different from the Hill story, though the tiny noses and straight lines for mouths resemble the Hill descriptions. Most of all, the talking through the eyes recollection is something straight out of Barney Hill's account of his abduction. Significantly, Pam's husband was not hypnotically regressed and there is no mention of what he thought about the whole affair.

The experience of Sandra Larson has echoes of Pam's and Carl Higdon's experiences. Larson was driving with a friend from Fargo to Bismarck, North Dakota, in August 1979 when they experienced a period of missing time. Under hypnotic regression by Dr. Leo Sprinkle, Larson recalled encountering a six-foot-tall, mummy-like entity that had metal arms. The main difference here is that during her abduction, the aliens took out her brain and reconnected it back inside her skull slightly differently.

In 1977, MUFON investigators, headed by Raymond Fowler, investigated the claims of Betty Andreasson. She and her family, especially her daughter Becky, had mental flashbacks of an odd UFO sighting on the evening of January 25, 1967. A strange light and strange creatures were seen outside the kitchen window of their home in South Ashburnham, Massachusetts, but they could not remember much more. Under hypnosis, Betty recalled that after the light appeared her seven children and parents went into suspended animation. Only Betty remained conscious and uninfluenced by this paralysis. Then four entities in dark blue uniforms literally walked through the kitchen door. They had wraparound eyes with "mongoloid" faces, gray skin and virtually no mouths or noses. The slightly taller leader, who was about four feet tall, was called Quazgaa. He seemed to communicate with her through mental impressions. They gave her a blue book that contained glowing pages with Egyptian- looking writing; in exchange, she gave them a copy of the Bible. Quazgaa ran his hand over it and made thicker copies of it that he passed to his fellow aliens.

Standing behind Quazgaa, she was floated through her kitchen door to a waiting spacecraft. Inside she was put under a cleansing device and instructed to put on a white garment. In a brightly lit, domed examination room, she was floated onto a table where a needle was inserted into her left nostril. When the needle was withdrawn, it had a small ball-like object on the end. Another needle was inserted into her navel. Her terror at recalling this examination is such that Fowler writes, "I suddenly felt like shouting out in protest at what we were allowing this poor woman to relive." Elsewhere, he writes of the terror on Betty's face, and we have to wonder if hypnotic regression is more harmful for the abductee than half-forgotten nightmares or flashbacks.[22]

After the examination, she was floated into a chair-like immersion tank filled with gray liquid. It was speculated that this chair protected her from the acceleration forces inside the ship as it traveled at high speed through space. On landing, she was taken through tunnels and passed through a mirror into a world that had a red atmosphere and square buildings which had headless lemur-like creatures crawling over them. Passing into a green colored environment, she was floated over a pyramid and she saw a city with tall domed buildings with bridges in the air "like science fiction." Passing through clear crystals, she saw a huge bird. There was intense heat and fire, and then the bird was nothing more than gray ashes. From the ashes came a worm. A loud voice said to her, "You have seen, and you have heard. Do you understand?" A Christian fundamentalist, she asked if she was talking to God or the Lord Jesus. The voice told her that she was chosen and implied that it was God. On being returned home, via the spacecraft, she was told that she would forget the experience until the appointed time. The next thing she knew it was the next morning. This is only a brief outline of Betty Andreasson's original contact recollection' since then her contacts have filled three more books by Fowler.

Going back to Hickson's Pascagoula encounter and the C.A.V. cases, Martin Kottmeyer argues that they probably influenced the Larson case. He suggests that since APRO investigators made the connection between Hickson's aliens and the mummies seen by C.A.V. they might have inadvertently primed Larson to recall similar details before they conducted her hypnosis sessions. The Larson case also has many comparisons with Betty Andreasson's case:

missing time;
nasal implants;
floating and traveling through walls;
viewing desert landscapes scattered with buildings;
travel through tunnels;
placement inside "transport bubbles"; and
showering to remove alien contamination.

In 1981, Budd Hopkins' book *Missing Time* contains the details of seven cases of abduction obtained from hypnotic regression sessions.[23] Strikingly, three of these people had abductions in 1950 and were born in 1943; furthermore, it was not until they had hypnotic regression that any of them knew about this. He brought to life the concept that the aliens can disguise themselves as animals or birds. One of the abductees, Barry Maddock, saw a large-eyed gray owl that led him into a huge chamber where it transformed into a bird of paradise. Another of the abductees even encountered a talking deer. Maddock's vision is comparable to Betty Andreasson's "phoenix" though Hopkins explained these visions as "screen memories" that hide or disguise the aliens so that we can cope with such experiences. His theory that abductees are being selected and used for an alien hybrid breeding program was now taken seriously. Rather than being rare events, Hopkins suggested that thousands of normal people have been abducted but most do not realize it.

Hopkins' ideas made an even bigger impact with his 1987 book *Intruders*. It centers on the story of Debbie Jordan Kauble and her family who resided in Indianapolis (to protect her identity the book gave her the pseudonym Kathie Davis and the location was called "Copley Woods"). They were subjected to alien visitations that started in 1966, returned in the late 1970s, and then persisted from 1983 to late 1986. Hypnotic regression sessions tell us that Debbie at the age of seven wandered off to a strange playroom where a boy cut her leg. He then turned into a large-headed grey alien. Other abductees, including Betty Andreasson in 1987, and investigator Raymond Fowler a year later found scars on their legs. Hopkins regarded them as the result of cell sampling by the aliens. During her pregnancy with her son Robbie, Debbie was abducted and subjected to probes being inserted into her nostrils. On another occasion she had something inserted in her ear. The aliens also took an interest in her son Tommy who was visited by grey aliens at night and subjected to the insertion of a nasal implant. Later on, in September 1986, Robbie had a severe nosebleed that indicated that he had also had a similar implant. Without

American ufologist and artist Budd Hopkins (shown here November 11, 2009) discovered that after seeing a UFO, witnesses often could not account for a missing period of time, ranging from minutes to hours. Under hypnosis they invariably recounted an abduction experience that occurred during this "missing time" (photography by Erik Östling, Archives for the Unexplained).

the need for hypnosis, she was able to remember being abducted in April 1986. Onboard the alien spaceship, she was shown a hybrid baby. They wanted her to hold it to show how people love their children. In subsequent abductions, by other people, this need for hybrid babies to have human contact to enable them to prosper is repeated. In a book Debbie wrote, she told of further paranormal experiences, illnesses and mood swings that have plagued her life.[24]

Intruders helped establish most of the main elements of the abduction experience as we know them today. In the same year, horror writer Whitley Strieber's striking account of his alien experiences in *Communion* put the subject firmly in the mainstream of public consciousness. He tells of being floated from outside his cabin in upstate New York on December 26, 1985, by alien visitors. He found himself in a smelly, circular room where he was subjected to several medical procedures, including a needle being jabbed behind his right ear and a probe inserted into his rectum.

Not knowing what the memory of this encounter meant, he was referred by Budd Hopkins to psychiatrist Dr. Donald Klein.

Hypnotic regression conducted by Dr. Klein uncovered many more encounters with these alien visitors that had occurred throughout Strieber's life. Regressed to October 4, 1985, when a loud bang was heard and a blue light was seen at his cabin, he recalled encountering a goblin in his bedroom. The goblin struck him on the head with a wand. This caused him to see terrifying pictures of the world exploding, then he had images of his son lying dead in a park and his father choking to death. On the same night, his son said he had a realistic dream about being taken outside to the porch by beings that looked like little doctors. Others in the cabin at the time either only saw the light or heard the bang.

On going back to December 26, he related being dragged from his bedroom to the woods by blue-uniformed aliens. He was sent upward several hundred feet in the air and found himself with a female alien who pushed a penis-like device up his rectum. She helpfully tells him he is the chosen one. She tried seducing him, but her yellow, leathery skin and insect-like mouth put him off. His next memory was finding himself naked in his living room. These and other half-memories, periods of missing time and anxieties about aliens, including a belief that an implant had been inserted into his brain via his nose, turned him into a nervous wreck. As a means of coming to terms with these experiences, he wrote a book called *Body Terror*. Talking in a deep voice in her sleep, his wife warned him to retitle it *Communion* so he would not frighten away potential readers. Hopkins felt that it was too much like his previous fictional horror stories and got him to tone it down so that people would be more accepting of it. From there *Communion* sold millions of copies, and no one could avoid the staring image of what is now a stereotypical grey.

If *Communion* was the only book that Strieber wrote on these experiences, then we could agree with skeptics that this was a piece of fiction to exploit the UFO believers. However, Strieber has written several more books on his encounters and it is obvious he is grappling to understand and explain the nature of his and other people's alien encounters.[25]

The Abduction Experience

The powerful combination of *Intruders* and *Communion* for good or bad set the standard for abduction experiences. As might be expected there is no such thing as an "average" abduction experience, but we can outline their structure and format as reported in the UFO literature.

First, there is what I will call the trigger-event that causes the abductee to report it to the media and to UFO investigators. This usually takes place when the abductee is alone in their bed at night or when driving late at night on deserted highways.

The trigger for someone to discover they have been abducted does not have to be an actual UFO or alien encounter. A series of strange nightmares or some other traumatic experience might make someone think that they have been abducted. Reading about the subject or seeing a film or documentary about UFOs can also trigger a memory of an encounter. Visual images of aliens seem to be particularly potent. The illustration of the alien head on the cover of Whitley Strieber's book *Communion* has triggered many such memories.[26]

All these instances indicate that abductees have no control over how and when they are contacted, but there are cases of people making deliberate contact on their own initiative. This might be done through meditation, trance or even drug-induced states.

Bedroom encounters usually involve the person waking suddenly. They hear a buzzing or whizzing sound, and they are paralyzed so they cannot get out of bed. At this moment, they might see a strange figure or figures at the bottom of their bed. They are usually described as being human-like with large heads, and they wear one-piece silvery outfits.

For abductees taken from their cars or from outdoors, they usually see a light in the sky that comes toward them. They might then go through a fog or mist. Car engines and their associated electrical systems and radio equipment have also been known to cut out or act erratically in the presence of a UFO. It is assumed that UFOs create an electromagnetic effect that stops cars that get within their range, but studies of this effect have proved inconclusive.

Everything in the area might seem to be silent and strange, as if time or space has become distorted. This change has been termed the "Oz Factor" by Jenny Randles. She thought witnesses entered an altered state of conscious at this stage. She explained this in relation to the sighting of a large disc-shaped UFO by two fishermen:

> The witnesses said that they were not afraid; indeed, they were strangely calm and subdued. They felt themselves isolated in time and space, as if removed temporarily from the real world and melded with the UFO above them; only they and it existed.[27]

Minutes or hours later the person will "wake" and discover that they cannot remember anything during this missing time period. Motorists who experience this will suddenly find themselves miles down the road without knowing how they got there.

Entering the Alien World

The trigger event causes the abductee to discover why they cannot remember a period of missing time after witnessing a UFO, or they might want to know why they feel traumatized by "alien" nightmares. I will detail the full extent of post-abduction experiences later in this chapter. It is usually when a UFO investigator hypnotically regresses a witness that we learn about the person's abduction experience.

In his 1987 study of 270 abduction cases, folklorist Dr. Thomas Bullard identified six major elements of abduction accounts:

1. Capture
2. Examination
3. Conference
4. Tour
5. Otherworldly Journeys
6. Theophany.[28]

It is worthwhile to use these points to gain an understanding of what might occur during an abduction. First, capture involves the abductee being floated up to a flying saucer or simply walking up a stairway that extends from the craft. Much to the disbelief of more hard-headed ufologists, many abductees have reported being floated through solid walls or windows on their journey to a saucer hovering over their home or car. Often people do not remember how they got inside the flying saucer; this has been labeled "doorway amnesia."

Inside, the craft is a clean, sterile environment with no windows, but light emanates from no apparent source. The abductee is taken down a curved white or gray metallic corridor, which eventually takes them to the center of the craft. This seems to be a medical center. Working in a business-like manner with great efficiency, the aliens strip the abductee and place them on an examination table where they are medically examined. Some people have even reported being put inside a machine; others have been put in a tank that is filled with fluid like Betty Andreasson.

Generally, spindly "grey" aliens are regarded as the main abductors of human beings, but this is not always the case and they can be seen with other types of aliens. Humans in military uniforms have also been seen helping the alien examiners. The aliens who conduct the examinations tend to be taller than the ones who bring the abductee to the examination table, and they wear close-fitting outfits, sometimes featuring a cowl or hood. Like surgeons, some wear boots and surgical masks.

The aliens use strange-looking surgical equipment to scan the subject and to probe their body. Needles are inserted in their abdomen. There is usually an intense interest in the person's genitalia, and blood, sperm, or ovum samples might be extracted. Parts of the body, such as eyes or whole brains, have been removed and then returned without any damage. Others have reported having a tube placed up their rectum and waste sucked out of them.

They are also likely to place small implants in the brain via the nose, or behind the ear, or in other parts of the body. The spine or other parts of the body might be pierced with a needle to extract or inject fluids.

There are many cases of people being raped or forcibly seduced by the aliens. To encourage sexual intercourse the aliens may disguise themselves as celebrities, religious figures or even appear in the guise of an abductee's dead spouse.

Female abductees who have been raped by aliens and become pregnant suddenly "lose" the fetus; later they are abducted and shown their "lost" hybrid baby. Other abductees have seen on flying saucers or in what they believe to be underground bases on Earth nurseries containing such babies and human bodies in liquid-filled containers. There have been accounts of abductees seeing other humans on the ship being mutilated, flayed, dismembered, drained of blood and stacked in a heap. They are threatened that if they do not cooperate, they will end up like these people.

The procedures are conducted on the abductee while they are in a conscious yet paralyzed or sedated state. More than one type of alien might be present during the examination, and they often induce great fear, pain and humiliation.

Conference with the alien captors is usually limited. The aliens do not ask permission to operate on their victim and there is usually no explanation for their activities. Rather than by verbal means, the aliens tend to communicate telepathically with the abductee. If other human abductees are present, they seem to be in a trance, and it is impossible to talk to them or make any other form of contact with them. When the aliens communicate with each other, it is either in an unknown language or in a manner that is inaudible to the abductee.

Abductees are sometimes given a tour of the ship. They might be shown films or slide shows presented on TV monitors. There is an attempt to train abductees in the use of alien technology or they are lectured on how this alien technology works. They might also see the ship's control room, which contains maps of star systems showing where the aliens come from. According to David Jacobs, none of the 50 abduction cases he investigated contained any reports of seeing the living quarters of the alien craft.

Some abductees are taken on what Bullard calls "otherworldly journeys" to the home planet of the aliens, or they get a short ride round the Solar System. Contactees of the 1950s were most likely to report such trips, usually with detailed descriptions of alien civilizations on Mars and Venus. Since our own space probes have proved that life of this type does not exist in our Solar System, supporters of the contactees contend that they must have traveled in a different dimension or astral plane.

After this, the abductee receives important information about the future of our planet and our species. They are warned that we will be destroyed and that only the chosen will be saved and taken to another planet. The aliens are regarded either as our spiritual benefactors or as minions of the Devil. After an abduction experience, the abductee will want to spread the word that they have come to save us or to destroy us. This could be because there are evil and good aliens carrying out these abductions or it could be that they act the same toward everyone. In the latter case, it is how the abductee responds to them that conditions whether they are perceived as good or evil. Ufologists have noted that the biases of the investigator seems to have a bearing here, as some investigators seem to only see abductees who have negative and painful experiences and others only see abductees who have been spiritually uplifted by their experience.

Finally, the abductee returns to full consciousness several miles from where they were taken if the incident involved a car, or they are dumped several yards away from where they were originally taken. Others wake up in their bed and wonder if the abduction was a dream. Jacobs notes that abductees wake up to find themselves in odd positions or their clothing rearranged. They find unusual stains in the bed and feel they have not had a proper sleep.[29]

Abductees have a screen memory planted in their subconscious mind to hide their abduction experience. The screen memory takes the form of seeing owls, wolves, eagles, raccoons, mythical birds like the Phoenix, angels or devils, yet the memory of the abduction is never totally erased and most of it can be retrieved through hypnotic regression.[30]

Post-Abduction Experiences

After what I have called the trigger event, the person can suffer a multitude of physical and psychological signs that indicate that they have been abducted, including the following.

1. Amnesia or "missing time" after seeing a UFO.
2. Nightmares, insomnia, and fear of the dark and enclosed spaces.
3. Scars, scoop marks, bruises, punctures on the person's body

without any immediate explanation for them. The abductee might have frequent nose bleeds and feel that they have an unusual growth or implant inside them.

4. Deteriorating health. Serious illness sometimes leading to death can occur in the months after an abduction. Terminal brain tumors can appear after abductions. Female abductees can develop serious gynecological problems.

5. Changes in behavior. These can be for good or bad. Abductees might become born-again Christians or become more spiritual and relaxed in general. They might become vegetarian and take up animal rights or become involved in charitable works.

6. Conversely, they can take to drug, food and alcohol abuse. Their behavior can become excessive and erratic. They get obsessive about their abduction experience and its implications. They lose any meaningful relationship with their partner, family and friends. They cannot deal with normal life and can become suicidal.

7. The abductee might become psychic and/or be plagued by paranormal apparitions or poltergeists.

One or a combination of these indicators will cause the person to seek help that will uncover their abduction experience. Hypnotic regression is used to recall this information, but sometimes this is not necessary and it is spontaneously recalled.

When recalling their abduction experience the person often remembers that they have been in contact with aliens since childhood. It is only after the trigger event that they realize why they have had certain phobias or strange screen memories.

Several of these indicators have been used by investigators to determine whether people have been abducted or not. There is an online survey (www.abduct.com/survey.htm) that asks 28 questions of this nature. If one gets a high score, one could well be an abductee. I should add that I scored three points, so it seems the aliens have left me alone—so far.

Ufologists have also come to think that abductees are chosen rather than randomly snatched. This is indicated by the fact that whole generations of families have been plagued or blessed by alien abduction experiences.

Discussion

UFO researcher and historian David Jacobs' survey of 60 abductees involving 300 abduction experiences published in his book *Secret Life* in

1992 and Harvard professor of psychiatry John E. Mack's case histories of 12 abductees in his 1994 book *Abduction* set the seal on the subject. They gave powerful support to Hopkins' view that thousands of U.S. citizens are being abducted and confirmed that the abductions followed a stereotypical pattern.

John Rimmer agreed that "there is strong 'family resemblance' between a great many cases and many uncanny details [are] repeated in case after case."[31] Bullard's study equally conveyed the impression that abductions fit a highly structured format that suggests that they are the product of real experiences rather than rumor or fantasy.

As we have seen through the work of Kottmeyer, each abduction case seems to gain details from previous cases and other cultural images and sources, which would explain the consistency of abduction details.

Wittingly or not abductees and researchers have picked up on these details and helped feed and sustain the alien abduction mythology. It is noteworthy that many of the prominent abduction cases like the Travis Walton case have been championed by the tabloid newspaper *The National Enquirer.* In 1975, after the broadcast of *The UFO Incident* movie, it offered a million dollars for hard evidence of extraterrestrial contact and $10,000 for the best story. This appeal encouraged Betty Andreasson to report her UFO experiences, though she was ignored. There has been a financial incentive for reporting such experiences, and the media has helped promote the work of abductionists because of its popularity.

The framework of abductions can be explained by the fact that Bullard takes his data from UFO literature rather than from case files or other documents. Most abduction accounts place the often jumbled and confusing information gained over months or years into a structured form that fits a theoretical and/or chronological structure. Furthermore, many of the prime U.S. abductions have been investigated and publicized by a relatively small group of individuals and organizations who are likely to take an interest in cases that conform to their preconceptions.

From the contactee cases and the Villas Boas and Hill episodes, there has been a steady escalation of abductions and they have come to feature increasingly more fantastic and exotic elements. This again could be the result of media coverage that has become more frequent and detailed.

What intrigued Rimmer was that abductions broadly agree on details like examination rooms that are brightly illuminated with light from no visible source, nasal and navel implants, and the seamless outfits of the entities. On the other hand, there is no agreement about the origin of the aliens, and abductees keep adding new components and making refinements to the "classic" abduction scenario. For example, in the Betty Andreasson case, she suddenly reported the image of the Phoenix and the attendant mystical experience that shocked the UFO investigators, who were surprised by these religious overtones. They could accept the detailed descriptions of the entities, their equipment and technology, even that she was floated through a solid door, but they had to question whether the Phoenix was as real as the other events.[32]

The classic elements of abductions unravel when we look further at neglected cases from the past and at cases that have come to light in recent years that are literally unbelievable by any normal standards of judgment.

In 1974, an extraterrestrial called Antron came into Lydia Stalnaker's life. One evening as she was driving home, near Jacksonville, she saw what she thought was an aircraft crashing. Going to see what had happened to this huge object that had gone behind some pine trees, she blacked out. The next thing she knew she was back inside her car driving along the road again. The next day she was violently ill, and then she suddenly recovered and found that she had psychic powers. Another side effect was terrible nightmares about an operating theater. They were so bad that she sought the help of Dr. James Harder (who was involved in the Betty and Barney Hill case). A series of hypnotic regression sessions indicated that she had her first encounter with a UFO when she was nine years old.

During 26 hypnotic regression sessions conducted by Dr. Evelyn Brunson, Stalnaker recalled her 1974 encounter. Inside a flying saucer, she was put on a table head to head with another woman. They were linked by a device that covered part of their heads and then spun around. This procedure brought Antron within her body.

Antron came from a green planet in another galaxy that had two suns. Antron was female, thousands of years old, and she lived inside a glass tube onboard the spaceship that operated near Earth. Many other aliens on this ship communicated with each other telepathically.

It took Stalnaker several years to come to terms with the union with Antron. The alien had a powerful personality that made Stalnaker retreat into a corner of her mind to avoid her control. Eventually, she came to regard the aliens as her friends and missed them if they did not keep in contact.[33]

Stalnaker's encounter takes us a step closer to the contactee claims that they are reborn incarnations of aliens or emissaries of the space people in human form. The belief that we might be so-called Star People gained considerable popularity in the 1970s. When Francie Steiger had a dream about two men who told her, "Now is the time," she regarded this as a message to reveal that she was a Star Person. Apparently, there are thousands of Star People on our planet and many of them do not even know it.

Star People, according to Steiger, have more sensitivity to sound, light, electricity and electromagnetic fields. They are subject to chronic sinus trouble, subnormal blood pressure, sleeping problems and lower body temperature, and they are more likely to have a rare blood group. A Star Person has psychic abilities and an extra vertebra.[34]

All the aspects of the Star People phenomenon seem to have been absorbed into the abduction mythology. The signs of being a Star Person are now the signs that you have been abducted. To be fair, this is probably because the terminology has changed, but the experience of discovering or realizing you are an alien from outer space has not.

Ironically, Budd Hopkins, the very person who helped establish the concept of abduction has published ever-more fantastic accounts that even his followers find hard to accept at face value, and he has thereby eroded the validity of his original concepts.

The doubts set in with the publication of *Witnessed*.[35] It claims that in the early morning of November 30, 1989, Linda Napolitano (referred to as Cortile in the earliest reports) was floated through her closed Manhattan apartment window. Once she was inside a hovering spaceship, the craft plunged into the Hudson River. She was given a visual display about ecological matters and returned home.

The vision of Napolitano floating in a blue-white light was allegedly witnessed by the secretary-general of the United Nations, Javier Perez de Cuelar, and his two security guards. It seems that they were abducted at the same time. One of the guards and Napolitano had met as imaginary playmates during previously shared abductions many years earlier.

Napolitano reported her abduction on the same day, and it was under hypnotic regression that the details of it were revealed. In February 1991, the two guards, calling themselves Richard and Dan, began writing to Hopkins revealing that they and their V.I.P. witnessed the event. Richard and Dan began visiting Napolitano at her apartment. At first, they went on a friendly basis, and then in April 1991, they kidnapped her in a black Mercedes and interrogated her about her abduction for hours as they drove through the streets of New York. A few months later, in October, Dan threatened her with a gun and made sexual advances to her. At Christmas, he wrote a long letter saying he hated her and thought she was the spawn of hybrid breeding. His claim "The staff here usually keeps me pretty much sedated" implied that he was safely ensconced in some kind of mental institution.[36]

A letter from Janet Kimble (pseudonym) confirmed that she and other drivers on Brooklyn Bridge saw four people being floated into a brightly lit object on the morning in question. There was screaming and panic, and, oddly enough, she thought a film was being made of *Snow White and the Seven Dwarfs*. Napolitano also claimed that Perez de Cuelar had written to Hopkins telling him to stop looking for the "third man" (presumably he meant himself) as it would upset world peace.

Ufologist George Hansen made the sensible suggestion that if this was true, then the activities of Richard and Dan should be reported to the police or other authorities. This caused a firestorm of criticism from supporters of Hopkins. Hansen and his associates also showed that Hopkins had done little work to confirm Napolitano's assertions. Furthermore, Hopkins only ever met Napolitano face to face; all the other evidence came from correspondents who were reluctant to meet him.[37]

Since Hopkins and Jacobs were convinced of the literal truth that "nuts and bolts" spacecraft are coming to abduct us, how did they account for stories full of magical happenings? Jacobs acknowledged that when he started hypnotically regressing abductees, they recounted wild and impossible events. He regarded these factors as the result of false memories and dreams that filled the vacuum of the "legitimate memories." Through continued work, he felt he was able to distinguish between the false and truthful memories, and after two and half years of work, he was able to fit them into a three-tiered matrix. His abduction matrix consisted of physical, mental and reproductive procedures that the aliens carried out on regular, less frequent and irregular bases. Regular procedures are "primary experiences" that are carried out on the majority of abductees. Less frequent procedures are "secondary experiences" that do not occur in every encounter by an individual who is abducted on several occasions or by abductees as a whole. Irregular procedures are "ancillary experiences"—sometimes of a specialized sexual nature—that are a rarer form of secondary experiences.[38]

Jacobs was selective about the people he regressed and used in his abduction studies. Reminiscent of the contactee George Adamski, Jacobs was dismissive of alien contact that involved the use of automatic writing, mediumship and other psychic means that became popularly known as channelling.[39] Jacobs determined whether an abductee was genuine or not by using a set of 25 questions and interviewing them to get a "feel" for their character.[40]

Like Bullard's narrative structure for abduction accounts, Jacobs' matrix did not distinguish between fact and fiction. A fictitious abduction story would neatly fit into his ever-evolving matrix. The skill of the investigator was the main factor in separating real and imaginary abductee stories.

The abduction scenario is heavily influenced by U.S. periodicals, websites and books, yet it does show other national and/or cultural biases. Jenny Randles noted that when she conducted a study of 19 British abduction cases between 1979 and 1986, none of them involved the stereotypical greys. Instead, British abductees saw monsters, robots or Nordic-type human entities.[41]

When John Mack first looked at cases referred to him in 1990 by Hopkins, Jacobs, Leo Sprinkle and John Carpenter, he could not explain them within terms of psychiatry or the Western scientific framework. Unlike Jacobs, he did not think that we should try to discriminate between real and false abduction memories. His criteria for studying a case was whether the abductee felt that what they experienced was real and that they were sincerely communicating these experiences.[42]

Hopkins' philosophy is equally open-ended in that he asserts that we should never pre-judge and that genuine skeptics should accept the impossibility of anything.[43] This contrasts with Charles Fort's philosophy that "we accept nothing."

The different approaches to the subject are due to the role of the researcher. Members of UFO organizations are likely to be more interested in collecting evidence about people's experiences, while counselors or therapists are more interested in helping people come to terms with the traumas associated with abduction experiences. Whether a researcher is connected to a UFO organization or is a therapist, they should consider the interests of the abductee first and foremost, which are often at odds with proving the literal existence of alien contacts. This also means that since abductees are regarded as victims that need protection, any criticism or questioning of their accounts is met with great hostility.

7

Alien Appearances and Evidence

The image of the abducting aliens is generally that of the greys. They have large heads with big, almond-shape eyes, and they have short, feeble, spindly bodies. The prevalence of the greys in witness testimony and of the other types of aliens associated with flying saucers helps us determine whether they are more than just the product of our imagination. Finding patterns in their appearances and behavior, however, is not as convincing as physical or any other supporting evidence for abduction stories.

Here we will look at the variety of alien appearances. Then we will consider the various pieces of evidence that have been put forward to indicate that the Hill abduction actually took place, and we will consider other forms of evidence that have been examined to prove the reality of abductions in general.

Alien Appearances

The term "alien" can be used to describe anything from a two-foot-tall hairy dwarf with a laser gun to a shambling nine-foot-tall robot with flashing lights. From the very start of the flying saucer craze in the late 1940s, aliens were jokingly referred to as Little Green Men.

Betty Hill described the aliens in her dreams about her encounter as five feet to five feet, four inches in height. They had dark hair and eyes, gray skin, large chests and long noses like Jimmy Durante.[1] Under hypnosis Barney said they wore outfits like Navy pea jackets. He was most struck by their eyes, which came toward his face telling him to close his own eyes. He also thought the beings outside the craft had spindly legs whereas those inside did not. It is significant that consciously and under hypnosis the Hills referred to the aliens they saw as "men."[2]

When the British ufologist Peter Hough surveyed the various descriptions of aliens, he despairingly observed,

> There is an almost total lack of consistency in reports of alleged contact. Occupants are variously described as tall, small, thin, fat, human-like, grotesque, saintly, covered in fur, hairless, with long arms, short arms, hands, claws, large heads, headless, friendly, indifferent, aggressive, appear "solid," able to pass through walls, levitate...[3]

John Mack noted that the United States has the greatest number of abductions followed by England and Brazil. He thought this might be because abduction experiences in other countries are put into a supernatural or religious framework and are not thought to be associated with flying saucers. His research also indicated that abductees in the rest of the world see a wider range of alien beings than U.S. abductees. In the United States, the so-called greys are most likely to be seen, but even there, all manner of different aliens have been reported.

Other ufologists assert that there are hundreds of different types and claim that they come from a vast range of different star systems. The Burlington UFO and Paranormal Research and Education website features 67 different alien descriptions and races, and that does not include various sub-categories.[4] The variety of alien descriptions could be due to the fact that no witness description is ever exactly the same as another person's description of real objects, let alone aliens in stressful conditions.[5]

Patrick Huyghe tackled this issue by classifying four broad types of aliens: humanoid, animalian, robotic and exotic ghostly entities.[6]

Hilary Evans defined four categories of aliens:

1. Those that look indistinguishable from any Earthly human being.
2. Human-like aliens that have a few differences. They might have fewer fingers or toes than us or none at all. They might lack reproductive organs.
3. Humanoids who have large heads and wrap-around eyes like the greys.
4. Bear or monkey-like beings that display intelligence but rarely interact with witnesses.[7]

He stated, "Almost without exception, UFO-related entities are bi-pedal, and have heads, trunk and limbs disposed much as ours are; their faces have much the same features, disposed in much the same configuration—single eyes and no mouths, though occasionally reported are rare."[8]

Certainly, the majority of reports do not contain as many exotic looking aliens as you might imagine. Most aliens would fit one of the following categories, more specific than Evans' outline of alien types.

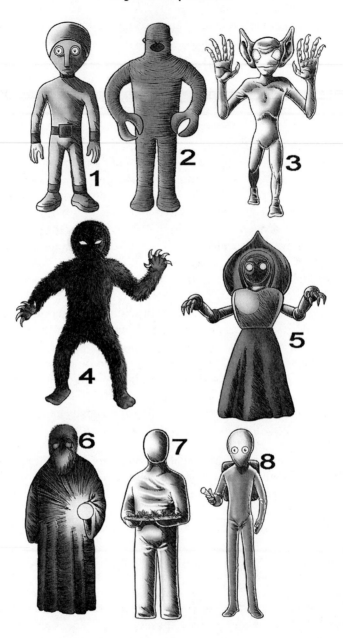

The wide variety of alien entities seen throughout the world. 1: Villa Santina, Italy, 1947. 2: Pascagoula, Florida, 1973. 3: Kelly-Hopkinsville, Kentucky, 1955. 4: "Hombrecitos," Venezuela, 1954. 5: Flatwoods, West Virginia, 1952. 6: Pournoy-la-Chetive, France, 1954. 7: Newark Valley, New York, 1964. 8: São Paulo, Brazil, 1947 (illustrations by Richard Svensson).

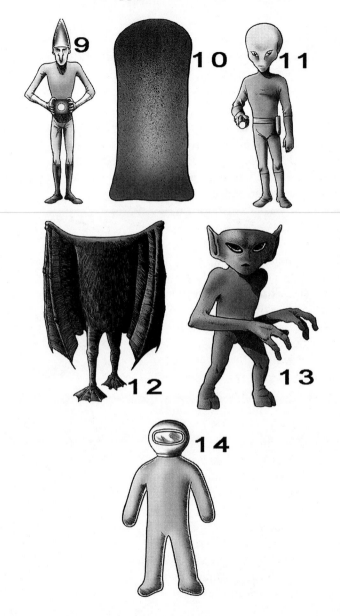

Celebrated American astronomer Carl Sagan observed, "Far from being global, the alien abduction stories are disappointingly local. They hardly transcend American culture." These illustrations show the range of aliens reported before the "grey" stereotype established itself. 9: Imjärvi, Finland, 1970. 10: Domsten, Sweden 1958. 11: Valensole, France, 1965. 12: Kent, England, 1965. 13: Ilkley Moor, Yorkshire, England, 1987. 14: Kinnula, Finland, 1971 (illustrations by Richard Svensson).

Humanoid

Contactees like George Adamski reported meeting fair-skinned aliens who had long blond hair and seemed androgynous. Other than their long hair, they did not look out of the ordinary in 1950s America.

Besides these spiritual Nordic/Aryan-types, human-looking aliens are often described as looking foreign or Oriental. In 1952, contactee Truman Bethurum met Aura Rhanes, the lady captain of a flying saucer, whom he described in these glowing terms: "Her skin was dark olive and her brown eyes, lighting up when she smiled, seemed to make her complexion glow even more.... Her short black hair was brushed into an upward curl at the ends."[9]

It is noteworthy that during the 1896–97 U.S. phantom airship scare, the pilots of these craft were described as dark-skinned, slant-eyed and Oriental-looking gentlemen or women. It has been speculated by skeptics that these "foreign" attributes have evolved to create the small, dark-skinned greys that have almond-shaped eyes that slant upward and wrap around their head in an exaggerated fashion.

Humanoids can also be related to the mysterious Men in Black who force UFO witnesses to not publicize or report their experiences. They have been described like the pilots of the airships and flying saucers as dark-skinned and/or slant-eyed. Humanoids generally wear close-fitting silver suits or uniforms which appear to be seamless with no visible buttons or zips.

A fearsome-looking small alien illustrated by British contactee Norman Harrison. Harrison's depiction suggests a family connection with the Mekon aliens who were the archenemy of space hero Dan Dare in the *Eagle* comic during the 1950s (author's collection).

Greys

The greys are now the "classic" shape of the alien. They have large, bald heads and large eyes that seem to stare right into the soul of the observer. The eyes are the most prominent and literally hypnotic aspect of their faces. They have small, slit-like nostrils and thin lips, and they do not seem to have any ears.

Some aliens have wrinkled skin from beneath their eyes to their neck. Some have long necks, whereas others do not have necks at all. Their arms and legs are long and spindly, and their body is small. Greys can be short or tall.

Although greys became the most dominant type of alien by the 1980s, there are several earlier accounts of them. For example, in July 1974, an anonymous witness driving near Warneton, Belgium, saw a UFO land in a nearby field. His car's engine and electrical system stopped working. and he was forced to watch, no doubt with some degree of horror, "two entities ... walking slowly and stiffly towards the witness. Both were about 4 feet tall, with greyish skin, round eyes, a rudimentary nose, and a slit-like, lipless mouth. They wore helmets and metallic grey coverall-type uniforms."[10]

The ever-industrious Martin Kottmeyer, in a survey of UFO literature, found descriptions of large-headed small beings with skin color ranging from black, white, transparent, brown, tan, pink, orange, yellow, green, blue to purple. This variation has been explained as being due to different alien metabolisms and their ability to change color. Kottmeyer suggested that we need a better name for the greys, but I think it is too late now. Their name has stuck, whatever they really look like.[11]

Dwarfs

Small, hairy humanoids who act aggressively seem to be most common in South America but have been reported elsewhere. Small entities of a general humanoid appearance are not uncommon and are the main reason for comparison with the creatures of traditional folklore.

Giants

There were several reports of very tall beings seen with their craft during the U.S. airship wave of 1896–97, and in South America aliens over six feet tall have been nearly as common as sightings of dwarfs.

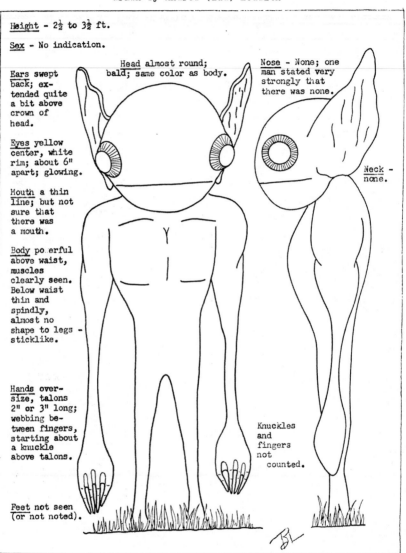

"Little Man" as described by
Elmer Sutton, J.C. Sutton and O.P. Baker
drawn by Andrew (Bud) Ledwith

Height - 2½ to 3½ ft.

Sex - No indication.

Head almost round; bald; same color as body.

Nose - None; one man stated very strongly that there was none.

Ears swept back; extended quite a bit above crown of head.

Eyes yellow center, white rim; about 6" apart; glowing.

Mouth a thin line; but not sure that there was a mouth.

Body powerful above waist, muscles clearly seen. Below waist thin and spindly, almost no shape to legs - sticklike.

Neck - none.

Hands oversize, talons 2" or 3" long; webbing between fingers, starting about a knuckle above talons.

Knuckles and fingers not counted.

Feet not seen (or not noted).

A gang of small, goblin-like aliens attacked the farmhouse of Elmer Sutton and Billy Ray Taylor near Kelly and Hopkinsville, Kentucky, for several hours on August 21, 1955. It helped promote the idea that aliens are "little green men" (illustration by Philip Mantle).

Reptoids

Reptoids have hairless, scaly skin and vertical irises. In the minds of abductees, they are regarded as the descendants of the dinosaurs that roamed on Earth millions of years ago. I know of at least one witness who has even seen a green and red colored baby dinosaur walking outside a grounded flying saucer.[12]

Insectoids

As early as 1950, Dr. Gerald Kuiper, a professor of astronomy at the University of Chicago, claimed that it was possible flying saucers contained either intellectual insects or incredible vegetable creatures. Several abductees have reported seeing grasshopper-like entities.[13]

The most common insect type reported since 1986 is the praying mantis. This could be attributed to the influence of Whitley Strieber, who in a hypnotic regression session on March 14, 1986, recalled seeing, in his grandmother's home back in 1967, a "big bug." He went on to say, "It looks exactly like a bug. A praying mantis is what it looks like. Only it's so big. How can it be so big?"[14]

Even if the aliens do not look like insects, some witnesses report that they seem to act as if they are under instruction or control, like worker ants or bees.

Brains

Brains or blob-like beings have been seen inside UFOs, but these are fairly rare. Robert Dickhoff many years ago put forward the idea that flying saucers serve a Super-Brain that was created by biological brain engineering with "more or less of an atrophied, limp, and useless body, with hands resembling flippers and feet dangling uselessly, beside the shriveled remainder of what would substitute for the body of this God-Brain-Head."[15]

Robots and Androids

Robots are sometimes seen in association with UFOs or aiding other types of aliens. Most do not seem much more sophisticated than those depicted in 1950s B movies. These robots might really be alien humanoids inside suits to adapt to our atmosphere or some humanoids might really be androids—robots made to look like humans. John Keel noted that many Men in Black (MIB) who visit UFO witnesses to stop them making their stories public act in an odd manner. The MIB don't seem to know a lot about normal social interaction and act in a robotic fashion.

It does seem logical that aliens would use technology and genetic modification to explore our planet. Jason Gammon, who is one of the few to discuss the possibility that aliens might be cyborgs, told me:

> I feel that we need to look to our own future, specifically referencing the subject of transhumanism/posthumanism, in order to understand what form any visitors may take. We simply would not be visited by beings "just like us" but with better technology.
>
> Instead, we would be dealing with cyborgs, advanced A.I., machines to which minds have been uploaded into, and genetically engineered organisms. Any advanced civilization in the Universe capable of visiting earth would have gone through its own version of the technological singularity. The result would be these types of beings, far removed from their organically evolved predecessors. These are the forms any visitor to Earth would take and these are the forms the human species will eventually become, assuming we survive the transition.[16]

Ghosts

Aliens have been seen gliding rather than walking and have appeared translucent or ghostly. In these cases, they do not seem to be solid biological beings.

Winged Entities

Creatures with wings have often been associated with UFOs or have been regarded as aliens. The most famous example is the Mothman, who was seen in West Virginia from 1966 to 1967. His body was featherless and gray-colored, and although he had a 10-foot wingspan, he never seemed to flap his wings when he flew. He was seen taking off vertically and had a penchant for scaring women and chasing cars. He had glowing red eyes.

An angelic being with piercing blue eyes told Whitley Strieber that he should not eat sweets. Strieber was also told that in three months' time, he would take a journey that would lead to life or death. This prophesy came true four months later.[17]

Bigfoot and Out-of-Place Animals

Sightings of Bigfoot or creatures like the Surrey Puma in Britain have been reported during flurries of UFO activity. Some witnesses have seen these creatures leave or return to landed UFO craft. In Pennsylvania in the summer of 1973, a strange creature was seen on 118 separate occasions. It kept to woodland areas and was associated with local UFO sightings. The creature or group of creatures was described as "hairy, ape-like beings with glowing eyes and apparent ears, large noses, fang-like teeth, and the long arms of an ape."[18]

These could be cases of aliens shape-shifting or examples of screen memories used by the aliens to create a psychological smokescreen.

Shape-Shifters

Witnesses have seen animals change into aliens or vice versa. Some ufologists say the aliens can take on any shape or form. The most common form of shape-shifting alien seems to be the Reptoid species. Many witnesses have also claimed that they have actually turned into an alien or seen other people turn into aliens.

John Mack recounted the case of 34-year-old Joe, who claimed he had weird dreams and alien experiences from childhood onward. As an adolescent, he recalled looking in a mirror when he suddenly saw an alien looking at him. It had green or gray warty and bumpy skin with a small round head on a thin neck.

Under hypnosis, he told of his struggle being human and alien. In his abduction memories, he recalled that he had an alien identity, "Orion." In this humanoid manifestation, he was nearly eight feet tall, but he thought he could shorten himself if he wanted to. In this state, he had sexual intercourse with an alien woman called Adriana.[19]

David Icke believes that lizard-like and Reptoid aliens are controlling our world. When he visited the United States in 1998, he met several people who said they had seen people turn into reptilian aliens and then returned to their usual form. He quotes from a book by Cathy O'Brien and Mark Phillips, *Trance Formation of America*, in which Cathy claimed to have seen none other than President George Bush looking at a book about aliens before he transformed into a reptile himself. Icke also suggests that the British royal family are really alien reptiles. His views are at the extreme edge of ufology, but in general, most abduction researchers accept the possibility of shape-shifting aliens.[20]

Invisibles

While attending a Wicca circle sanctuary weekend held near Madison, Wisconsin, in 1987, Whitley Strieber and three other people heard footsteps. They called out a greeting to the person. There was no reply, and the footsteps seemed to walk through underbrush and toward the edge of a cliff. No sound or sign of anyone falling down the cliff was evident, though there had been UFO sightings earlier that evening.[21]

Footsteps created by an invisible walker were commonly heard by sky watchers who visited Warminster, UK, during the height of its UFO flap in the 1960s.

Alien Round Up

If we accept that the aliens can change color, shape-shift and become invisible, any attempt at classifying the appearance of aliens is doomed to considerable confusion and failure!

Reading Jacobs' *Secret Life*, I was struck by the unrealistic, cartoon-like nature of the aliens reported by abductees. They are not seen to eat or drink; they do not have teeth, stomachs or any variation in weight or body mass. Their skin is smooth without hair, spots or blemishes. They do not seem to breathe. Their faces do not have unique features to distinguish one from another. They do not have fingerprints and often have only three fingers with no opposing thumb. Even though the aliens have a predilection for sexual intercourse with abductees, they do not show any genitalia and are often regarded as androgynous or sexless. Given that their behavior is businesslike, and inside their craft no living or recreational facilities are ever seen, they seem more like blank automated machines rather than living entities.[22]

Alien Evidence and the Hills

Their UFO Sighting

Determining whether the Hills actually saw something inexplicable in the sky in the first place would add a lot of credence to their abduction story. If they had only seen a planet or aircraft, then it would seem highly likely that their abduction was just a story created in their imaginations.

Major Paul W. Henderson, who spoke to the Hills by telephone only a few hours after their encounter, conducted the only official investigation into the UFO sighting. It took Project Blue Book two years to produce a final report about the incident. Dated September 27, 1963, it claimed that there was insufficient evidence to determine what caused the sighting. It guessed that they probably saw Jupiter or a similar "natural" cause.

UFO researcher Robert Sheaffer agreed with Blue Book's opinion after he interviewed Betty Hill. He found that she was not able to provide a very reliable chart of the UFO in relation to the stars and planets visible at the time. She remembered seeing the bright UFO, the Moon and a planet. Sheaffer calculated that she should have seen two bright planets and the Moon, so by his reckoning, the UFO was really Jupiter. It is not unusual for drivers to see stars or planets appearing to follow their car at night, and any moving clouds can intensify the feeling that they are moving fast in the sky.

It is worth adding that in the fall of 1965, there was a spate of UFO sightings in the area of Exeter, New Hampshire. John Fuller spent a month interviewing witnesses who saw bright, flashing lights. The most notable case occurred in the early hours of September 3 when police patrolmen saw a group of lights at close range maneuver over a field. Many of the sightings were near power lines, which made some consider that they were a form of plasma discharge.

Robert Sheaffer claimed that most of the sightings were probably Jupiter, Venus and Saturn. A criticism of Fuller's book about the sightings, *Incident at Exeter*, was that it dwelled on the reactions of the witnesses rather than on details of their sightings. The same criticism can also be directed at Fuller's *The Interrupted Journey* which merely assembles information without analyzing it in much detail or putting it into a wider context.[23]

Radar

Betty Hill claimed that at 2:14 a.m. on September 20, 1961, Pease Air Force Base picked up a UFO on radar and they sent out two aircraft to investigate it. What the pilots saw, according to Betty, has remained classified ever since.[24]

The radar information is detailed in a research paper by the Air Command and Staff College dated May 17, 1974, and titled *Should the USAF Reopen Project Blue Book?* This notes that seven hours before the Hills' sighting, at 21.22 hours on September 19, Air Force radar operators at N. Concord AFS, Vermont, spotted a UFO. Their report was reviewed by the USAF's Foreign Technology Division which thought the relatively low speed and high altitude of the UFO, along with its erratic course that included hovering, ruled out a normal aircraft target. Instead, they thought it was probably a weather balloon, although this was never checked out to be established for certain.

In Blue Book file no. 100-1-61 it is stated,

> During a casual conversation on 22 September 61 between Major Gardiner B. Reynolds, 100th B S DC01, and Captain Robert O. Daughaday, Commander 1917–2 AACS DIT, Pease AFB, N. H., it was revealed that a strange incident occurred at 02.14 local [time] on 20 September. No importance was attached to the incident at the time.

The incident was the observation of an aircraft four miles out by precision approach radar. When it approached to within half a mile, it pulled up. A weak target was seen shortly afterward downwind and made a low approach, but nothing was seen by personnel in the tower at any time.

From the casual way it was reported, this does not sound like something that would cause the USAF to scramble a couple of aircraft. Indeed, on the Project Blue Book record card number 10073, the Pease radar sighting is noted in relation to the Hill's visual sighting. The conclusion was as follows:

> Both radar and visual sighting are probably due to conditions resulting from strong inversion which prevailed in area on morning of sighting. Actual source of light viewed is not known but it has all the characteristics of an advertising searchlight. Radar probably was looking at some ground target due to strong inversion [a temperature inversion can take place in a perfectly clear sky]. No evidence indicating objects were due to other than natural causes.

The authors of *Should the USAF Reopen Project Blue Book?* were disappointed that "the explanation regarding the searchlight was an example of mere speculation with no attempt at follow-up. Although a correlation between the UFO reported by the Hills and the UFO tracked on the Pease AFB radar was indicated as a possibility by Pease AFB officials, Project Blue Book officials make no further mention of it."

The report condemns Project Blue Book officials because they

> made meager attempts at "solving" the case by asking information of two other USAF offices. No attempt was made, however, to recontact the Hills or to interview them in person. No attempt was made to visit the reported UFO landing site. No attempt was made at drawing a possible correlation between the visual and radar UFO reports...

It also scathingly notes:

> The official Air Force explanation regarding the Hills' UFO sighting turned out to be almost as erratic as the radar and visual sightings themselves. The official explanations in this particular case included "weather inversion," "the Planet Jupiter," "optical condition," and finally "insufficient data." If one counts the explanation given for the N. Concord AFS UFO sighting, the explanation of "weather balloon" can also be added.[25]

Nonetheless, even if something was seen or tracked on radar, it does not mean the USAF tracked the same object or objects that the Hills said they saw.

Missing Time

When the Hills arrived home after the encounter, their watches had stopped running, and they were surprised to see that, according to their kitchen clock, it was 5 a.m, though, as we have noted before, it was not until much later that they were fully aware that they had lost two hours of time. Their watches never worked again.

Peter Rogerson noted that Barney estimated that they would certainly have arrived home by 2 or 3 a.m. if they were traveling at an average of between 50 mph and 65 mph, depending on road conditions. But he stopped to watch the UFO through binoculars, and they slowed down and stopped at other times to see the UFO, considerably cutting down his average mileage per hour. Furthermore, in his frame of mind, he could well have taken a few detours, thus the so-called two hours of missing time could easily have been accounted for without resorting to an alien abduction scenario.[26]

Other researchers like Jenny Randles have also not found any evidence to prove that witnesses have actually missed any time at all. Losing more than a few hours is very rare.

Peter Rogerson added that while the Hill investigation was underway, the November 1962 edition of *Flying Saucers* magazine contained the story of Private Gerry Irwin who went AWOL and had periods of amnesia after witnessing a UFO (or aircraft) crash.

Missing time and an abduction featuring a medical examination that was uncovered through the use of hypnosis was also featured in the fictional story "Control Somnambule" in the May 1962 edition of *Playboy*. Whether the Hills actually saw the latter is disputable, but the concept of missing time was certainly prevalent at the time.[27]

Effects on Their Car

On the advice of a physicist, who was the neighbor of Betty's sister, Betty tested the car for radiation with a compass. The compass needle seemed to move erratically over six strange, shiny spots the size of a dollar on the car's trunk. When Barney tried the same test, the needle acted normally. Whatever the behavior of the needle, this would not be an effective method for detecting radiation.

Whether these spots were radioactive or not, we must wonder how a flying saucer might have caused them. Perhaps they were created on the two occasions when they heard the strange beeping or buzzing sound coming from the trunk of their car. Perhaps the craft shot something at the trunk of the car, which made the beeping sounds and left the spots. Furthermore, these sounds came when the Hills went into and out of a drowsy trance-like condition. If they encountered a spaceship, then it would not be beyond its capabilities to be armed with this type of mind-controlling technology.

Reinforcing this idea, Jerome Clark and Loren Coleman in their book *The Unidentified* stated that many contactees reported a bee-buzzing sound that introduced and ended their encounters with Space People. Beeping sounds have been associated with other abduction cases, Bigfoot sightings, Marian visions, out-of-body experiences and other paranormal activity, implying that all these phenomena come from one source. This could be a common physiological factor involved in these experiences or it could be caused by what Bonnie Meyer suggested is a small scanning instrument "like a mind probe." This type of thinking has led some to think that the Hills heard some form of alien Morse code.[28]

Martin Cannon documented the experiences of a defense subcontractor, Rex Niles, who came under psycho-electronic surveillance. Outside Niles' home, 250 watts of microwaves were registered, and underneath the dashboard of his car, he found a radioactive disk.

According to Cannon, such disks are often used by clandestine services to act as a silent, cancer-inducing killer. He speculated that the shiny spots on the Hills' car indicated that a radioactive or electromagnetic device was fixed to it. If deployed it could have caused disorienting effects on the Hills and caused them to imagine their UFO encounter.[29]

Karl Pflock gave a more mundane explanation. He noted that when the Hills got home, they found the car trunk was not closed properly. This could have happened just before Barney's first close encounter with the UFO, when he took a handgun out of the car's trunk.

In his panic-stricken state, he could easily have left the trunk unlatched, thereby causing the strange sounds when the car roared away from Indian Head and when it hit a rough area of road a bit later on. Given the circumstances, Pflock argued that anything out-of-the-ordinary, such as the unlatched trunk, would be regarded as something to do with the UFO.[30]

Their Clothing

After the encounter, Barney found the strap of his binoculars broken. If the strap was well used, it could easily have been pulled and broken by the traumatized Barney during the sighting of the UFO. The safety of his binoculars was, after all, the least of his problems.

Following the encounter, the tops of Barney's toecaps were found to be scuffed. This seems to substantiate his statement that he was dragged by his arms toward the landed UFO when he was abducted.

The blue acetate sheath dress Betty wore during the abduction was found, after it had been stored in her closet for about three years, to be covered in a pink powder. When the powder was shaken off, it left pink stains behind. She also found the hem, lining, zipper and seams of the dress were torn. Over the years she cut sections off it to satisfy the requests of laboratories throughout the world.[31]

The chemistry department of the University of Cincinnati examined it in 1977 and concluded that the dress had not been discolored by usual reactions, such as those caused by dyes, sunlight or bleach, and it might have been due to acid treatment. Without the pink powder they were unable to positively identify what caused the stains.

Another study of the dress was initiated by Bill Konkolesky who, on July 16, 2002, sent three-by-four-centimeter sections of the fabric to the Pinelandia Biophysics Laboratory. The lab grew wheat seedlings in water with and without sections of the dress that were stained. The lab found that the wheat seedlings grown in the stained water grew much better. Their conclusion was that whatever stained the dress could "alter metabolic activity in a living organism." The report warned that the researchers did not know if the material on the dress would have any impact on other living systems, and they could not assess if the many years of storage had changed the characteristics of the stains.[32] This, like other studies of the substance, leaves us with more questions than answers. So far no one has provided any evidence that it was of exceptional, let alone extraterrestrial, origin.

Analysis by "noted biochemists" enlisted by Phyllis Budinger found two types of DNA (one area contained human, mouse or cow DNA, and the other contained Barney's DNA) and soil and water bacteria. Budinger speculated that Betty's dress was torn by the rough treatment of her alien captors, and in the process, their respiratory and natural emissions transferred to the dress and caused the stains. Significantly, no alien DNA was found.

Strange stains have been found on abductees' bodies and bedclothes. Keeping samples has proved difficult as these substances tend to evaporate or are insufficient to make any form of adequate analysis possible.[33]

Return of the Earrings

Even weirder, Betty claimed that six to eight weeks after their encounter, they returned home to find a pile of leaves on their kitchen table.

They had just been to the mountains in an attempt to find the exact location of their abduction. When cleaning up the mess she found the blue earrings she had been wearing on the night of the encounter. She quite reasonably wondered how she lost them and how they got in their home. From this we can presume there were no signs of a break-in. The problem with this story is that most accounts say they visited the mountains in the early part of 1962, and the earliest suggestion for them to make these trips was made on November 25, 1961. The earring story would indicate that they searched for the location before the end of 1961. It would not be surprising if Betty got the time of this mixed up. The most important thing is that she thought the aliens had stolen her earrings and just wanted to let her know they knew where she lived.[34]

Telepathy

There is ambiguity regarding the means of communication used during the Hill abduction. Barney seemed to think their abductors spoke through their eyes telepathically. Their thoughts came into his head without them speaking.[35]

They also had small mouths and sometimes they spoke to each other in a gurgling, humming manner.[36] Betty said that they used normal English speech. Generally, the abductee hears voices inside their head or gets an impression of what the aliens want them to do.

According to Jacobs, there are no cases of an abduction occurring that involved completely spoken communication.[37] Abductee "Arthur" asserted that you have to eliminate your fear so that you can establish telepathic communication with the aliens. Negativity of any kind blocks communication. The aliens seem to be able to look inside our minds, especially if the abductee stares into their eyes.[38]

Writing

Budd Hopkins kept a secret file of the letters, numbers and symbols that abductees remembered seeing inside UFOs. He termed them "notational symbols," and they were remarkably consistent in a wide range of abduction stories. He kept this information secret because he used it to assess the genuineness of new abduction reports.[39]

It is not very difficult to find examples of alien writing; samples are given by George Adamski and the medium Hélène Smith, who produced elaborate alien language and writing. Betty Andreasson saw a glowing book and Betty Hill gave a detailed description of an alien book containing curved and straight lines similar to Japanese writing. It is difficult to determine whether these are the product of the person's imagination or not.

According to research by Leonard Keane, the star language spoken by Betty Andreasson when she was under hypnosis was Gaelic. A translation of her speech amounted to a warning that the descendants of the Northern peoples would suffer due to the mistakes of those in high places. This suggested that the aliens are more connected to our planet than the stars.[40] Since 1999, Gary Anthony has conducted the Alien Semiotics Project. It uses linguistic analysis to review claims of spoken and written alien language. The project has not been impressed by the so-called alien origin of the material given to them so far, but it is still looking.[41]

The Star Map

Over a period of several years amateur astronomer Marjorie Fish worked to build a realistic model of the stars and lines depicted in the glowing 3-D Star Map seen on a flat TV-type screen by Betty Hill onboard the flying saucer. She methodically collected information from

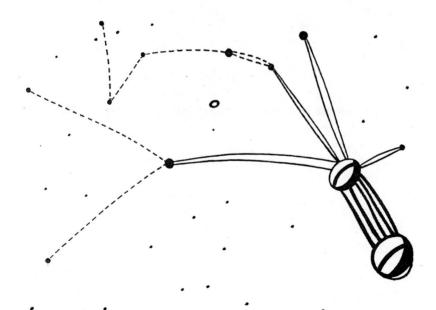

The Star Map produced by amateur astronomer Marjorie Fish based on Betty Hill's memory of a chart seen onboard a flying saucer during her abduction. This indicated the aliens came from Zeta Reticuli 2 in the Reticulus constellation (Archives for the Unexplained).

star catalogues and focused her search on stars that would be suitable and stable enough to enable life forms to evolve on planets orbiting them. She assumed that since they visited our Sun they probably originated from sun-like solar systems. There was also the assumption that they came from the stars shown at the bottom of the map and that one of the lines came from them to our Sun. After constructing models of star systems from beads hung on threads, she found a sector of space with 12 sun-like planets that matched Betty's drawing of the aliens' star map.

Her work showed that the aliens came from Zeta Reticuli 2 in the Reticulus constellation. She felt that her interpretation of the map, which was first presented in February 1973, could not be based on a hoax, as it used data from catalogues and data that were not available until the late 1960s, well after the time when Betty drew her map. Fish's "conclusion was that Betty's map could only have been drawn after contact with extraterrestrials."[42]

Critics have dismissed the Fish map since it includes non-sun-like stars that are regarded as background to the main stars that have lines indicating "trading routes" between them. Astronomer Carl Sagan showed that if you took away the trading routes, there was little similarity between the two maps. In his revised edition of *The Interrupted Journey*, John Fuller had to admit that expert opinion about the map was divided.[43]

Astrophysicist and computer scientist Jacques Vallee was crushingly skeptical of the map. He accepted that a computer simulation by Walter Mitchell, an astronomy professor at Ohio State University, confirmed the accuracy of Fish's model. For him, however, this was beside the point because the wrong question was asked.

A better approach would have been to use the computer to process and calculate the possible viewpoints from outside our Solar System that might make better matches. Out of these potentially millions of viewpoints we could more accurately judge whether Zeta Reticuli 2 was the best fit. Whateverthe outcome, Vallee noted that Betty's map did not correspond to any type of scale or to the brightness of the stars. Building to his main argument, he wondered what use a map like this would be to the pilots of an advanced spacecraft. Since our own rudimentary spacecraft use telemetry and software for navigation, he noted the map was "as ludicrous as a propeller or a rudder would have been."[44] For these reasons Vallee thought Betty was presented with this map to impress on us that the aliens were visitors from outer space, perhaps to divert our attention from other possibilities.

Another blow to the map came in 1980, when it was discovered that

Zeta Reticuli 2 was a double star rather than a single star system. As a double system, it would be less likely to support stable life forms, as we know them, and would not have met Fish's original criteria for her model. Another objection was that if the aliens originated from this system, they would have depicted it with two stars and not one.[45]

If Fish's map is wrong, it casts doubt on other abduction stories that have since claimed their aliens came from Zeta Reticuli. Those who still have faith in Betty's original map have looked for other possible matches to it. Most ufologists who have taken up this challenge have looked for other star fields and systems whereas Joachim Koch wondered if the map was really of our own planetary system. He claimed:

> Amazingly, we found out by pure astronomical analysis that the positions of the inner and middle planets and some of the major and very interesting planetoids [asteroids] in our planetary system one month around the time the abduction took place match completely the famous "Betty Star Map" pattern.

As more accurate information about the type and distance of the stars in Fish's map has been collected, it has become obvious that many of the stars no longer fit her original criteria. Brett Holman, reviewing her data, stated that at least six out of the 15 stars in the map must now be excluded, leaving it as "evidence of nothing."

If there is any validity to trying to establish an accurate map based on Betty's memories, then Holman suggests computer models rather than Fish's wire and bead models should be used to explore new possibilities. Nonetheless, ufologists continue to be fascinated by the prospect that aliens come from Zeti Reticuli.[46]

Steve Pearse in *Set Your Phaser to Stun* (2011) connects the Hill map with the details of an encounter with aliens given by Erik and Kay Wilson in Portland, Oregon, during July 1993. Erik had a conversation with a grey alien who told him they came from a star cluster to the right of and below Ursa Major on the fourth planet from their sun. This information, combined with Betty's map, led Steve to seek out new possible locations for the home of the greys and to confirm that they are indeed extraterrestrial travelers.[47]

Maps have also been seen by other UFO witnesses. Abductee Virginia Horton saw holographic, color-coded star maps during an abduction she recalled happening in 1950.[48] During the 1909 phantom airship scare in Britain, two witnesses saw an airship with a map. The men were walking on Ham Common, London, on the night of May 13 when they heard a buzzing sound and saw a 200-foot-long airship on the ground in front of them. The occupants of the craft were a Yankee, who kept shining a searchlight at them, and a German, who asked for some to-bacco for his pipe. According to their report, "The German gentleman had a cap and a beard and a map in front of him. It was fastened on a board and there were red discs on it, as though they had been stuck in the maps with pins." Once the occupants were given some tobacco, the ship left within 10 seconds. The manner in which this report was written strongly suggests it was a hoax, but it is an early equivalent of modern-day encounters.[49]

Physiological Factors

Budd Hopkins pointed out that the aliens consistently took an interest in the human head, genitals and the lower abdomen. They never took an interest in our most important organ—the heart. For him this showed that alien medical examinations and procedures were real and not the product of dreams, folklore or fantasies. The abduction experience of the Hills confirms this viewpoint.[50]

Barney Hill had neck pain, ulcers and various ailments that have been attributed to stress that had nothing to do with his encounter, according to skeptics, or they were induced by the proximity he had with the alien flying saucer, according to believers.

Betty thought that if they had seen an extraterrestrial spacecraft, then they could have been exposed to some form of radioactivity or cosmic rays. For this reason, when Barney unloaded the car, she insisted that he put their belongings on the back porch for a couple of days. They also felt very dirty and had long showers to get rid of the feeling. Indeed, the concern about what the craft might have done to their health was the main reason she reported the sighting to NICAP.[51]

Abductees are reported to find a wide range of scratches, scars and scoop marks all over their bodies when they wake up the morning after an abduction. One simple explanation is that the marks are self-inflicted. This does not mean that the abductees have made these marks deliberately—the marks could be acquired in the process of experiencing a vivid nightmare or hallucination. The abductee could inflict such injuries or report other physiological symptoms if they were suffering from Munchausen's syndrome.

Another possibility is that during sleep, all of us get marks or lines on our skin or aches and pains from remaining in the same position for a period of time. In the normal course of life, we ignore them, but abductees read them differently. A more exotic explanation is that the intense mental experience of the abduction causes a psychosomatic response, the equivalent of UFO or alien stigmata.

Missing Fetus Syndrome

The association of abduction experiences with "missing fetus syndrome" is a difficult and sensitive area of abduction research. Mary Rodwell, a trained midwife as well as an abductionist, has produced a useful list of possible medical explanations for this syndrome:

1. Blighted ovum.
   This occurs when the embryo degenerates, or is not even present in the first place, but hormones are secreted that will give a positive reading in a pregnancy test.
2. Spontaneous abortion or miscarriage.
3. Missed abortion.
   This is a non-viable fetus that can stay in the uterus for up to five months but is not rejected by the body as in two months.
4. Hydatidiform mole.
   A mass of tissue grows from a fertilized egg that has degenerated. Hormone secretions would indicate that the person is pregnant. This can be a dangerous condition that requires urgent medical attention.
5. Secondary amenorrhea.
   Periods cease or are later than usual due to stress or other physiological factors (e.g., anorexia).
6. Pseudocyesis.
   False or phantom pregnancies can be experienced by men and women. This is generally a psychological rather than a physiological condition. Phantom pregnancies could be triggered by the same psychosomatic processes used to explain UFO stigmata.[52]

Not included in her list is the process of absorption. This sometimes happens if a person is having twins but one fetus withers away and is absorbed by the other, which thrives. Rodwell, although aware of the medical explanations, believed that the missing fetus syndrome in connection with contact experiences is real.

As evidence, she noted that celibate women have had positive pregnancy results, scar tissue indicative of former unknown pregnancies has been found in some women, and the fetal heartbeat has been monitored in women before the fetus has disappeared. The rest of her evidence amounts to "strong emotions," dreams, flashbacks, visual images and the exhibition of post-traumatic stress disorder (PTSD).[53]

In such cases, we have to carefully consider the psychological status of the abductee as these physiological signs might be expressing deeper anxieties and traumas. Dennis Stacy, for example, has considered the possibility that the shame and guilt of abortion could be the reason for missing fetus syndrome and other anxieties surrounding abductions. He points out that the medical procedures of physical abortion and abduction have the same elements of rage, paralysis, and helplessness, centering on the unborn fetus. The aliens themselves also evoke the image of the fetus, as they are, according to Stacy, the "avenging angels" who blame us for our use of abortion. He proposed that abductees should be asked their thoughts about abortion in the battery of questions put to them by investigators.[54]

The most damning criticism of the missing fetus syndrome is why would aliens rape their victims and take away fetuses for their hybrid baby program? We already use in vitro fertilization techniques that avoid this trauma and pain so why can't they?

Alien Technology

Implants

The insertion of a small ball up Betty Andreasson's nose seems to have been the main catalyst for abductees to report implants in virtually every part of the body. Mary Rodwell in her book *Awakening* carefully noted that implants could have the following purposes:

1. Confirming to abductees that they have had a real experience.
2. Downloading information into the abductee's brain.
3. Monitoring and tracking the abductee's movements.
4. Monitoring the abductee's feelings and biochemical processes.
5. Controlling the actions of the abductee.
6. Boosting creativity, psychic abilities, telepathic and healing powers.
7. Facilitating the integration of alien bodies with human bodies.
8. A form of alien shamanistic initiation.[55]

And we can add another point.

9. Initiating molecular changes to allow the abductee to be transported to and into UFOs.[56]

Implants tend to be very small and elusive. Rodwell observed, "These anomalies or implants have often strangely disappeared, just as they were due to be removed, or they would dissolve or disappear just after removal from the body."[57] They also have the ability to elude magnetic resonance imaging (MRI), X-rays and CAT scans, though on occasion the odd inconclusive shadow has been spotted.

David Jacobs stated that aliens use long instruments to insert round or spiky BB-shot-sized balls into abductees' ears, nose or sinus cavity between eye and cheek. The balls cause abductees to suffer unexplained nosebleeds and ruptured eardrums.

Implants are less frequently inserted near the ovaries of women or in the penile shaft of men. One abductee reported finding an implant in his penile shaft, which turned out to consist of cotton fibers that had formed around dead human cells. Believers suggest that aliens deliberately hide their devices in this manner to avoid suspicion.[58] Despite Jacobs' confidence about these implant procedures, of the 62 abductees he interviewed, not one was able to provide proof of their existence.

Whitley Strieber described having an implant removed from his ear by a physician. On analysis, it was found to be collagen.[59] Other implant recoveries have been equally disappointing.

When the *NOVA* television program decided to examine the abduction phenomenon, it wrote to several abduction proponents saying it would pay to examine any alien artifacts that they could provide. This included MRI tests to reveal nasal or other implants. *NOVA* did not get one positive response to its request. The producer thought that ground traces used to prove that a UFO had landed on the ground were caused by common fungus, and the scaring and scoop marks on abductees' bodies were due to everyday bumps and scratches.[60] Equally, everyday contact with unnoticed objects like splinters can pierce the skin and form a membrane that might be mistaken for implants.

Invisibility

Budd Hopkins and his wife Carol Rainey in their book *Sight Unseen* report the experiences of abductee Katharina Wilson in relation to invisibility. When she arrived at Chicago O'Hare International Airport to attend a UFO conference, she was an hour late meeting the organizers, who were waiting for her. She was in a confused state before leaving the aircraft, and then in the airport restroom, she had trouble operating the washbasin taps. Her hands would not trigger the automatic sensors, and in exasperation she asked a woman, "Am I invisible or something?" The woman just ignored her. Hopkins speculated that Wilson was abducted or teleported or that her energy field had been changed.

British ufologist John Harney suggested that she suffered a mental fugue and had merely "lost" the hour by wandering around the airport.[61]

Transport Through Solid Matter

Aliens move themselves and abductees through solid matter like windows and doors. Betty Andreasson was floated through her own kitchen door when she stood behind the alien leader. Jacobs confirmed that abductees can be passed through walls or ceilings, although aliens prefer to transfer people through windows that are not blocked by boxes or similar obstacles. So far, I have not read of anyone who claims to have been passed through blinds or curtains as well as the window, though I assume this is equally possible. What bothers me is that highly intelligent aliens have not learned to open doors and windows.[62]

Martin Kottmeyer questioned the physics of two objects being able to occupy the same place at the same time and shows that passing through walls is an attribute of supernatural beings and fictional characters.

Jesus Christ was said to have had the ability to move through closed doors after his resurrection, and fiction features people moving through solid matter from Scrooge in *A Christmas Carol* (1890) to the science fiction movies of the 1950s onward.[63]

Floating and Levitation

Aliens have the ability to float people through the sky like Peter Pan or Superman. This is often carried out by some form of light beam from a flying saucer. In the case of Linda Napolitano, witnesses allegedly saw her and the three UN staff being floated into a UFO over Manhattan, though Jacobs thinks that abductees are often rendered invisible when they are floated to a UFO. This would explain the rarity of sightings of people flying about in their nightwear by independent witnesses.[64]

Elusive Evidence

Abductions never take place in public; they tend to be at night when the abductee is alone. As Jacobs put it: "The greater the victim's seclusion and the less others will miss her, the longer the experience tends to last."[65]

If other people are present during the abduction, they are "switched off" by the aliens. If it is a bedroom encounter, the person's partner will remain in a deep sleep, or if a UFO is spotted while people are riding in a car, the driver might pull over and go to sleep or become unconscious. The targeted person will then be floated through the windshield. If outdoors with a group of people, the abductee will be inclined to walk away to where a UFO is landed and experience an abduction. To hide the time she is away, the group is switched off until she returns.[66]

There are some abduction episodes that do involve more than one person, like the Betty and Barney Hill case. Unfortunately, they tend to involve close friends, family members, or partners. There tends to be a dominant abductee and a passive partner or friend. Often only one of the abductees will consent to be hypnotized. When two or more abductees are taken onboard a flying saucer, they are nearly always separated by the aliens so they cannot corroborate the main details of their abduction. There are few reports of witnesses seeing landed flying saucers taking on-board abductees, though several abductions have taken place where there has been UFO activity reported by independent witnesses.

It is intriguing that when Jacobs put a video camera in the bedroom of an abductee who had virtually daily abductions, he had very little success in capturing any images of the aliens. For days nothing happened, then the abductee had an experience late one morning at the very time the video camera had stopped recording. Her next abduction came several weeks later. It was not recorded by the camera because she was asleep in her living room.

Another abductee had a video camera installed in their bedroom, which produced the same non-results. As researchers used the video system for other abductees, they found that the equipment would suffer from malfunctions. In one case an abductee saw aliens standing out of camera view telling her to switch off the camera, which she did. Altogether, researchers used this equipment with six abductees and had similar resulting problems.[67]

Chris Kenworthy tried the same video experiment with British abductees. He found that when his subjects reported being abducted, the videotapes indicated that they were fast asleep in their beds. Two abductees were recorded getting out of bed and leaving the room, which tallied with their recollection of an abduction at the same time. In both cases it looked as if they were sleep walking.[68] This would indicate that in these cases their abductions are caused by vivid dreams rather than by physical aliens. Although the number of people tested has been small, video evidence could be a very effective means of establishing the reality of these experiences.

Attempts have been made to understand the seemingly magical technology of aliens in scientific terms. Dr. Richard D. Butler claimed that during physical abductions, abductees were tranquillized to prevent harm to themselves and to their abductors. He explained why abductees experience doorway amnesia and how aliens are able to float people through solid objects in these terms:

Subjects are transported via a small shuttle, lifting beam or direct transfer. Direct transfer utilizes a hyper-dimensional tunnel. It will appear as a large brilliant white energy gate. The subject steps through the gate and is instantly aboard the craft. Also reported is the nullification of the nuclear repulsive forces in solid objects. This allows the subject to physically pass through solid objects.[69]

This is a great explanation, if we can establish that the terminology of hyper-dimensional tunnels, nuclear repulsive forces and energy gates is more than just science fiction speak. Another way to explain the abduction experience is to say that abductees enter a different form of reality through an altered state of consciousness. The abduction experience is real, but it is controlled by "scientific" magic and in realities that we can barely understand.[70]

Hard line abductionists dismiss astral journeys and channeling, but by acknowledging the ability of aliens to levitate, use telepathy, move through walls and become invisible, they have accepted the encroachment of many paranormal factors into nuts-and-bolts ufology. John Harney observed that physical beings should not be able to ignore the laws of physics. By accepting paranormal theories or happenings, it is not "necessary for any further thought or investigation. In other words, it is merely a form of intellectual laziness."[71]

Besides working out the science or pseudoscience of alien technology, we must wonder why it is so incompetent. John Keel brought up this issue in *Operation Trojan Horse*, where he wondered why flying saucers are always crashing. Bits fall off and aliens make their repairs near highways or near farms rather than in isolated areas away from prying eyes.[72]

Regarding abductions, we are told that abductees get an inclination to walk or drive to a certain location before they are walked, half-dragged or floated to a flying saucer. On return the person is left outside their home several yards from where they were originally abducted, or they wake in their beds the next morning to find they are wearing different clothing or their clothes have been put on back to front. With technology that can float and transfer people through solid matter, why don't they simply take and return people without all this elaborate ritual? If you can move through solid matter, why do abductees report elaborate procedures to find a window to travel through, when others claim they have gone through walls and ceilings?

Furthermore, aliens are selective at covering up their activities. They can switch off people, create screen memories and elude video equipment, photography and radar, yet they cannot fully block people's memories or put their clothes back on properly.

They also leave scratches and scars all over people's bodies (even though some abductees claim the aliens have fast-acting healing powers), and their sophisticated implants drop out of people's bodies.

Looking at the UFO evidence in the early 1970s, John Keel found "that flying saucers are not stable machines requiring fuel, maintenance, and logistical support. They are not permanent constructions of matter."[73]

In stark contrast, Budd Hopkins believes that abductions are what he calls real, event-level occurrences that have provided a wealth of photographic, medical and physical evidence.[74] As we have seen, there is no photographic or video evidence for alien abductions, and other forms of evidence are based on anecdotes or generalizations rather than hard facts or data.

When working on a UFO documentary, the *NOVA* producer was frustrated by the fact that abductionists dismissed or avoided the problems of supplying conventional evidence and instead pointed at the sincerity of the witnesses, the consistency of their stories, and the scale of the abduction phenomenon.[75]

Several polls of varying reliability and quality have been conducted to try to find out the full extent of the abduction phenomenon. The results of such research would help us determine if there are only a few abductees, indicating that they are victims of some unusual delusion or that aliens are specifically targeting them. If abduction experiences are common, then they constitute, at the very least, a mental health risk that medical practitioners should be aware of so they can try to bring about a cure. In our worst imaginings, they represent a hidden invasion that needs repelling as soon as possible.

In the 1990s, David Jacobs conducted a poll of students at Temple University, which showed that 5.5 percent of those questioned might have had an abduction experience. Projecting these figures indicates that 15 million people in the United States and 60 to 200 million people throughout the world are potential abductees. Another poll by Robert Durant in 1995 revealed that five million Americans had probably been abducted in the past 50 years, which indicated that there are 2,740 abductions a day.

A more organized attempt at assessing the true extent of alien abductions began in 1991 when Robert Bigelow and an anonymous financial backer employed the Roper Organization to poll the U.S. population. Using Roper's Limobus survey, which precisely takes into account gender, political, racial, educational, age and census data, Bigelow placed questions in three separate surveys. He knew that he could not ask people directly if they had been abducted, so he worked with abduction researchers Budd Hopkins and David Jacobs to create 11 questions that would discriminate between true abductees and people with fertile imaginations.

Five key questions were put in the survey. If a person answered them positively, the person was a real abductee. When the results from the selection of 5,947 American adults were analyzed, researchers found that one in 50 people fitted the abductee profile, which would indicate that there are 3.3 million abductees living in the United States. Abductees crossed gender and ethnic boundaries but were found to be above average in terms of higher education and social awareness.

Taking a harder look at the figures, we see that only 18 people out of the 5,947 respondents fitted the abduction profile perfectly. This 0.3 percent of the sample, if projected onto the U.S. population, would indicate that 555,000 U.S. citizens have been abducted. By lowering standards to include those who only answered four out of the five abduction questions positively, researchers found that 119 met the criteria. This 2 percent of the sample, when projected onto the U.S. population, provides us with 3.7 million abductees, although the margin of error could mean that there is anywhere between 1.11 million and 6.29 million adult abductees residing in the United States.[76]

This gave the abduction researchers a big boost, but it did not last for long. Critics like Paul Devereux and Peter Brookesmith noted that the poll had a margin of error of 1.4 percent, which rendered the finding of 0.3 percent full abductees statistically meaningless. They concluded that the results "reveal absolutely nothing about the incidence of abductions by aliens in the U.S."[77]

Between March 7 and June 27, 1998, the Roper Organization conducted the survey again, using a sample of 5,955 people. This time, positive responses to the five key questions was lower than the 1991 survey results, and even positive answers to the other questions was lower or level with the 1991 figures. Only 1 percent of the sample answered four or five of the key questions positively, indicating that the number of potential abductees had halved.

No obvious reasons to account for this downward trend could be found. The 1998 survey did make one minor change, in that it replaced "Having vivid dreams about UFOs" with "Having been abducted by the occupants of a UFO." And it was found that a meaningless control word, *trondant*, which had been invented to weed out people who would answer yes to anything, was in fact a little-known real word. It was used in both surveys, so it could not be used to explain the differences in the two poll results.

Although the Roper surveys are the most scrupulous ever conducted on this subject, they still leave us with more questions than answers. One of the major flaws is that their construction assumes they can discriminate accurately between "real" and "false" abductee respondents. Nonetheless, the lower number of abductees in the second survey goes against the expectations of critics. In the period since the first survey in 1991, there was even more "contamination" of the population by images and stories about aliens in all forms of media, from books and films to the Internet.

The Roper surveys only looked at the U.S. population, but other polls have shown that there is an extensive belief in alien abductions elsewhere in the world. As a prelude to the release of the *Steven Spielberg Presents Taken* mini-series on the Asian Star Movies channel, an e-mail poll about alien beliefs was conducted between April 15 and 27, 2003. The survey was sent to 83,000 adults older than 18 living in Mainland China, Taiwan, Hong Kong and Southeast Asia. It found that 90 percent of the respondents believed that there is life beyond our planet and 51 percent believed in alien abductions. Unfortunately, the poll did not ask if anyone thought they had been the victims of an alien abduction.[78]

Whatever the validity of these polls, they have been used to prove the prevalence of the abduction phenomenon. David Jacobs, in a lecture at the 1998 MUFON UFO symposium titled "Thinking Clearly about UFO Abduction," asserted that since the 1890s, about 2 percent of the U.S. population has had 200 abductions throughout their lifetimes.

Assuming a more conservative figure of 100 abductions per lifetime, MUFON investigator Craig Lang worked out that in a metropolitan area of two million people, there would be 200 abductions every 24 hours; projecting these figures globally there would be 600,000 abductions a day. As he rightly noted, if they are "nuts-and-bolts" events, this would require thousands of aliens to operate and maintain a vast fleet of flying saucers. Lang therefore concluded that we must consider four possibilities:

1. Individual abductees have far fewer than 200 abduction experiences in a lifetime.
2. The number of abductees throughout the population is lower.
3. Alien technology is such that it can operate on this scale without (much) detection.
4. As John Keel suggested, flying saucers and abductions are non-physical "events."[79]

Sweeping statements that millions of abductees have been whisked away to have medical examinations, implants inserted, and hybrid babies do not live up to the actual details of individual abduction reports or any other evidence that has been put forward.

David E. Pritchard noted that any artifact, if it is to be convincing, must have unusual performance, composition and structure, which should be "simple enough to be deduced, and yet impossible to duplicate naturally or in the lab." As we know in the case of photographic evidence, the pedigree of the artifact is one of the most important factors. When dealing with any form of evidence and alien artifacts we have to consider important questions: Where and how it was found? Who found it? Who analyzed it? Pritchard stated, "It is the whole story, confirmed by the artifact, which will do the convincing; not the artifact by itself."[80]

When preparing information for this book, I requested evidence for alien abductions from fellow researchers or from abductees on a few Internet bulletin boards. I only got three cagey and suspicious replies. One abductee informed me that there are UFO pictures and video, but those with closed minds will argue about their authenticity. Essentially, they believed that proof resides within the abductees' mind and soul. In other words, you have to reject science and our concepts of reality to truly come to terms with the abduction phenomenon.

8

Alien Movies
and TV

UFO historian and abduction researcher David Jacobs, like many other supporters of the reality of abductions, stated categorically that Hollywood had no influence on UFO and alien reports. He acknowledged film serials like *Flash Gordon* (1936 to 1940) and *Buck Rogers* (1939), but they were about us venturing into outer space, and there was no "major" film about aliens visiting Earth until 1949. On this basis he was able to say, "UFO sightings did not spring from one of the important shapers of popular attitudes—mass media science fiction."[1]

Budd Hopkins reinforced Jacobs' statement by pointing out that the public awareness of abductions began with the publication of the Betty and Barney Hill story in 1966, and after a sprinkling of high-profile cases in the 1970s, the subject did not fully enter public consciousness until the 1980s when the abduction floodgates opened. He found it "highly significant" that many of the abduction stories he uncovered through hypnotic regression refer to experiences in the 1960s and 1970s before they could have been contaminated by the abduction books and films of the 1980s.[2]

In complete contrast, Mark Pilkington noted:

> Themes of aliens kidnapping and impregnating humans, coming from dying planets and using implants, telepathy and mind control have been consistent themes in science fiction film and literature since the pulp magazines of the 1930's, so to deny a link between popular culture and the abduction myth is entirely ridiculous.[3]

Martin Kottmeyer conducted the most convincing research into the influence of the media on UFO reports. He has taken a detailed look at Betty and Barney Hills' experiences and compared them to the media that was available to the Hills at the time.

One feature that was particularly puzzling to Kottmeyer was the Hills' description of the aliens as having wrap-around eyes. Since UFO books and magazines of that period did not contain any similar descriptions, he wondered if the Hills might have been inspired by images from science fiction films. He did find a mutant with this type of eyes in a Japanese film called *Evil Brain from Outer Space*. This had a U.S. release in 1964 but it seems unlikely that the Hills saw it.

Having drawn a blank with films, Kottmeyer was excited by the Bifrost alien in an episode of the TV series *The Outer Limits* titled "The Bellero Shield." Not only did it have wrap-around eyes, it could read and speak to human minds. The alien explained, "Learn each word just before I speak it. Your eyes teach me." This is much like Barney's confused recall of how his aliens spoke to him.

The only problem with this was that *The Outer Limits* was made in the mid–1960s, not in 1961 when the Hills had their encounter. Rechecking *The Interrupted Journey,* he found that the first mention of wrap-around eyes was made by Barney during a hypnotic regression session on February 22, 1964. This was just 12 days after the first broadcast of "The Bellero Shield." This detail could have been unconsciously inspired by the episode.

On the other hand, folklorist Thomas Bullard, argued that

> we know that the eyes troubled Barney before hypnosis and before the *Outer Limits* episode was aired. Is it so strange that he would grope for a handy visual simile, and grasp one from a recent TV show? Even if his description bent towards the image of the television alien, this fact does not negate the reality of his basic observation.[4]

If that was the only source of comparison, Bullard would have a very strong case, but there are plenty of other media productions that could have had a bearing on the Hills' story. British ufologist John Spencer noted that there were many similarities between the Hills' story and an episode of the *Fireball XL5* puppet TV series. It featured short aliens with bald heads who are able to block the memories of humans so that they can carry out their nefarious activities unmolested. The episode "Robert to the Rescue" was broadcast in 1962. He notes that even if the Hills did not see this episode, they and the program-makers were drawing on the same sources of inspiration.[5]

We can find other possible film and TV influences on the Hills' memories of the flying saucer itself. The examination rooms and operating tables are very similar to those in the flying saucer featured in *The Day the Earth Stood Still* (dir. Robert Wise). This 1951 science fiction classic features a giant robot called Gort who carries a woman into his flying saucer. Fortunately, Gort, who is controlled by a humanoid alien called Klaatu, is relatively friendly. As part of a cosmic police force, they have come here to stop humanity using atomic weapons.

On a more general level Mark Pilkington noted that *The Manchurian Candidate* (1962) contains many of the elements that could have influenced the Hill abduction story. In this film the Korean abductors use brainwashing, screen memories and mind control in the very manner that is now associated with alien abductors.[6]

The film *Invaders from Mars* (dir. William Cameron Menzies, 1953) contains the most comparisons with Betty's experience; they both feature aliens with large noses, examination tables and needles. In one scene, of the alien examination room, the curvature of the floor and a conduit give the overall impression of a hypodermic needle being inserted into an abdomen. It will be recalled that Betty Hill said she had a needle injected into her navel, although Bullard can only regard this as a "clever but unpersuasive" comparison.[7]

A star chart is even shown by a human scientist in *Invaders from Mars*. He talks about Earth's closeness to Mars even though the map itself does not show our planet. If this was the inspiration for Betty Hill's star map, then it would explain why she was also puzzled by what the map was meant to show. We have to admit that this map is not shown onboard the UFO in *Invaders from Mars* but Kottmeyer accounted for this by saying that "dreams have an odd penchant for distortion and condensation of memory materials."[8]

John Spencer made an equally strong case for the influence on the Hills of *Earth versus the Flying Saucers* (dir. Fred F. Sears, 1956). It is loosely based on Donald Keyhoe's book *Flying Saucers from Outer Space*. Spencer's comparisons can be listed as follows:

1. A UFO is encountered on a lonely road.
2. After the encounter the witnesses ask if it really was a flying saucer.
3. A buzzing sound is heard. In the film this is a high-speed voice message that has to be slowed down for humans to understand it.
4. The abductees have their minds blacked out.
5. The aliens speak English.
6. When landing, the flying saucer causes electromagnetic effects. In the Hill case their watches stopped.
7. At first the film aliens look like robots but inside their outfits they are bald and have large eyes, slightly similar to the Hills' aliens.[9]

Betty's fear of radiation from the UFO could have helped trigger her nightmare of having a medical examination by aliens. Kottmeyer compared this to the newsreels showing people in the fall-out area of the Project Bravo U.S. atomic bomb test conducted on March 1, 1954. The films show the Marshall Island victims having their hair examined and nails clipped. Their meat, vegetables and milk are considered contaminated, which might account for why the topic of such foods is discussed in Betty's nightmare. Peter Rogerson added that in September 1961, the month of the Hills' abduction, the Soviets exploded three nuclear bombs as part of a renewed testing program, causing the United States to respond by resuming their own nuclear testing.[10]

It was Kottmeyer's contention that bad movies and medical quackery were the prominent influences on Betty's imagination, rather than alien medical procedures. Cases that have followed are merely examples of cultural transmission and elaboration.[11]

It is worth adding that after his abduction experience, Charles Hickson demanded to be tested for radiation as he feared being contaminated. The police took him to Keesler Air Force Base where it was established that he had not been exposed to radiation. His fellow abductee, Calvin Parker, feared he had some bacteria on him that might affect others, so he poured bleach over himself and showered it off.[12]

Anthony R. Brown made two major points in a strident critique of Kottmeyer's exposition of the possible media influences on the Hills' experiences. First, he claimed that dream research has never revealed a case of anyone having a dream based exactly on a film. We are more likely to use the emotional tone of a film in a dream rather than its narrative and imagery. In Kottmeyer's defense, he never stated that the Hills' dreams and hypnotic recollections were ever derived from any single film or source. Indeed, as we can see from his discussion of the star map, he was postulating that their accounts include a mixture of science fiction elements that they could have picked up unconsciously. Brown's second point was more damning as he asserted that we have no proof that the Hills saw *Invaders from Mars*, *The Outer Limits* TV series or any other science fiction film or TV program.[13]

Equally, Greg Sandow had no time for theories that alien abductions were created and spread by the media. He thought anyone could cherry-pick details from old science fiction magazines and that the more serious underlying narrative of the abduction reports have never been a major feature of science fiction stories.[14] The implications of these arguments will be dealt with later in this chapter.

Whatever the influences of film and TV, the Hills repaid the favor by becoming the subject of their own well-regarded TV movie *The UFO Incident* (Richard A. Colla, 1975). It might be expected that the aliens in it would look like those in *Invaders from Mars*; instead they have small bodies and big heads. This was the first appearance of what Richard Dengrove called the "full fledged Greys" that became the normal appearance for aliens.[15] Ironically, Betty claimed the aliens shown in *The UFO Incident* "did not look like that. The real ones looked more human than their television counterparts."[16]

The TV movie encouraged more people to report abductions and nudged the whole abduction craze into mainstream popular consciousness. In Britain this film did not get much, if any, exposure at the time, which might account for the lower number and slower rise in abduction reports here.

Aliens in Fiction

To fully understand the relationship between fictional aliens and their "real" counterparts, we must return to the very first form of mythic American literature, the "captive narrative." These stories began with Mary Rowlandson's *The Sovereignty and Goodness of God* (1682). Its popularity led to hundreds of captivity narratives featuring kidnapping and life among the Indians. These captivity narratives became the stuff of folk tales, legends and pulp fiction. The genre spawned novels like James Fenimore Cooper's seminal *The Last of the Mohicans* (1829) and the theme was continued in such films as the John Wayne classic *The Searchers* (John Ford, 1956), *A Man Called Horse* (1969) and Kevin Costner's *Dances with Wolves* (1990).

The typical captive narrative usually features a woman who has to reject assimilation of the rituals of the captors and their temptations of the flesh. To marry the Indian captor or come to terms with captors is to reject Christianity. By overcoming the ordeal through belief in Christ, the victim is redeemed and is given salvation.[17]

Michael Sturma, a senior lecturer in history at Murdoch University, Perth, Western Australia, makes these comparisons between captive narratives and abduction narratives:

1. The captive/abductee is stripped naked, thereby divesting them of their culture and identity.
2. The victim is subjected to torture.
3. The abductors are regarded as evil or devilish, yet the captive/abductee can admire and identify with them.
4. The experience initiates spiritual growth in the victim.
5. The Native Americans and the aliens represent a punishment for moral and religious laxness.

For Sturma, the wildness and mythic power of the Western frontier has been displaced by our consciousness of space, the "final frontier," in the words of the original *Star Trek* television series.[18]

In the 19th century the fictional works of Edgar Allan Poe, Jules

Verne, H.G. Wells, and a whole army of long-forgotten authors helped to set the foundations for what Hugo Gernsback in 1926 termed "science fiction." Their stories often centered on marvelous machines and devices that could help us explore our world and beyond. The interest in these subjects made it easy to perpetrate several successful journalistic hoaxes in this century.

In 1835 the *New York Sun* published a series of articles by prominent astronomer Sir John Herschel about the exotic flora and fauna he could see on the Moon through a new telescope based at the Cape of Good Hope. By the time the fourth installment came out on August 28, which told of winged, hairy, men four feet in height, the circulation of the *Sun* had soared to 19,360, making it the most read newspaper in the world. Rival newspapers copied the stories, but on September 16, the *Sun* had to confess that the story was a hoax. This did not put the *Sun* off hoaxes. On April 13, 1844, it announced that after 75 hours in the air, a balloon had crossed the Atlantic Ocean. This caused a sensation for several days until the *Sun* admitted that the story was a hoax by Edgar Allan Poe. As Daniel Cohen noted, journalistic hoaxing at that time was moderately respectable and often involved scientific and technological themes, and it was certainly profitable for newspaper proprietors.[19]

Ron Miller showed that Jules Verne's 31st novel, *Robur the Conqueror* (entitled *Clipper of the Clouds* in Britain and in U.S. newspaper serializations), which was published in English in 1887, anticipates the great American airship wave of 1896–97. It tells of lights seen in the sky reported in newspapers throughout the world. It transpires that these sightings are created by a flying machine invented by Robur. He abducts three skeptics and takes them on a tour of the world, while astronomers explain the sightings of this craft as optical and celestial misperceptions. Rather than phantom airship reports or the like, Verne based his description of Robur's "Albatross" airship on the work of French aviation inventors and pioneers. The Albatross was a fast, electric-operated, boat-shape craft that carried 74 propellers mounted on 37 vertical masts; a powerful searchlight; a canon; and a winch for lifting things from the ground.

The popularity of *Robur the Conqueror* and Verne's other novels was amplified by literally hundreds of imitators who wrote these "scientific romances" for newspapers, dime novels and quality magazines like *The Strand*. After the English publication of Verne's *From the Earth to the Moon* in 1871, the number of novels with interplanetary themes rose to a peak of nearly 30 a year by the 1890s. Adventures with craft like the Albatross were churned out by fellow French author Luis Philip Senerans and Garrett Serviss, the "American Jules Verne."

When looking at the airship reports of 1896–97 Miller saw that they

The airship scare in the United States that ran from 1896 to 1897 received an incredible amount of newspaper publicity and encouraged advertisers and producers to cash in on the craze. One such production was this musical farce comedy *The Air Ship* by J.M. Gaites promoted by this poster that depicts the vessel over New York. One reviewer noted that it contains the most realistic stage scenes of a real airship ever presented (author's collection).

bore close comparison with the widely distributed designs of aircraft inventors, the fiction of Verne and his imitators, and balloons that had actually been built and flown. These visual references and stories fueled the sightings, reports and hoaxes of 1896–97 in the United States, though Miller does allow that there could be a "core phenomena" that is given airship or spaceship features according to the witnesses' terms of reference.[20]

In the 1930s pulp magazines satisfied the public demand for science fiction. The likes of *Thrilling Wonder Stories, Amazing Stories, Astounding Stories, Planet Tales, Galaxy,* and *Fantasy and Science Fiction Magazine* had garish covers of robots, spacemen and alien invaders to lure the public to their publications. As Hilary Evans puts it, these magazines covered alien visitations "from almost every conceivable angle."[21]

Showing the impact of science fiction stories, Orson Welles' *Mercury Theatre of the Air* caused a sensation when it broadcast its version of the *War of the Worlds* on Halloween eve, October 30, 1938. The radio show presented the story as an ongoing news broadcast. It told listeners that spaceships were landing in New Jersey and that Martians were coming to get them. After studying the panic psychologist Hadley Cantril thought that 1.2 million listeners had been frightened or excited by the broadcast. The reaction was so intense that a stunned and unshaven Orson Welles apologized before newsreel cameras the following day.

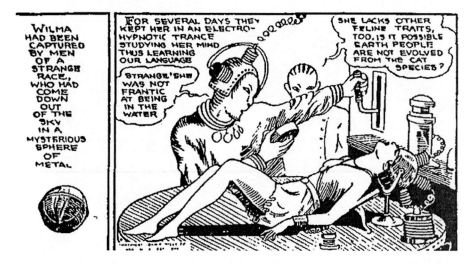

Wilma Deering was captured by alien humanoids with cat-like traits who came out of the sky in a sphere of metal. Inside it she was put into a hypnotic trance and studied by the aliens, much like a modern-day abductee, except this occurs in a *Buck Rogers* **comic strip story, "The Tiger Men from Mars," in 1930 (author's collection).**

Although the show had been presented as fiction, many listeners apparently accepted it as fact. It has been noted that the worrying political frictions in Europe, which were leading up to World War II, had made listeners more responsive to stories of attack. People were also more likely to believe what they heard on the radio, however outlandish, if presented as news. The public had been accustomed to seeing and reading about spaceships and future weapons through the likes of *Flash Gordon*, so an attack from Mars only indicated that the foreseen "future" had arrived.

Cantril's classic study of 1945 has been used to show that the public would panic if extraterrestrials ever made a mass landing or provided unequivocal proof of their existence. In the 1980s sociologists looked again at this panic and found that few listeners did more than feel worried about the broadcast.[22]

The masses did not run into the streets in a blind panic or hide in their basements. Instead, it has been suggested that this was really a product of mass delusion fueled by the media and confirmed by Cantril. Since Welles was the supreme showman, one wonders if he helped promote the idea of a mass panic and his apology the next day was just an act. The film *The Adventures of Buckaroo Banzai Across the Eighth Dimension* (dir. W.D. Richter, 1984) plays with the idea that this alien invasion really did happen in 1938 and that we were all implanted with false memories to make us believe it was all a hoax.

As we have already seen in previous chapters, science fiction magazine editor Ray Palmer (1910–1977) was instrumental in bringing the UFO myth to life. In the October 1946 edition of his *Amazing Stories*, magazine he published a story by Harold M. Sherman. Titled "The Green Man," it tells of an astronomer whose car engine is halted by a beam of energy. As he walks away from his car, he sees a cigar-shape craft that disgorges a noble, robed man who has a green complexion. He is a Christ-like figure who heals the sick. It is his mission to awaken people and to bring about worldwide peace. The story anticipates car stoppages caused by UFOs, and Loren Gross thought the story probably provided the inspiration for George Adamski's meeting with Orthon.[23]

The sensational reports of flying saucers in 1947 had such a grip on the popular imagination that authors and filmmakers could not resist dramatizing and playing with the images and theories that they brought forth.

Spencer Gordon Bennet and Thomas Carr quickly cashed in on the flying saucer craze by releasing the 15-part film serial *Bruce Gentry— Daredevil of the Skies*. This 1948 production features a Dr. Benson who is abducted by a villainous scientist who uses flying saucers to attack the Panama Canal. These flying saucers have a central dome that the rest of the craft spins around as it flies. These high-speed, remote-controlled flying saucer bombs cause the instruments of nearby aircraft to go wild. At that time there were no actual reports of flying saucers having any influence on electronic equipment, and it seems likely that this detail was taken from spy films like *Ghost Patrol* (1936) and *Sky Racket* (1937). Otherwise, it is a very forgettable film.[24]

At the same time actor Mikel Conrad decided to make a film about Russians stealing a flying saucer from a scientist in Alaska. To gain interest in his project he spread rumors that it would include scenes featuring "real" UFOs crashing to the ground. In Frank Scully's book *Behind the Flying Saucers* this story transmuted into the claim that a flying saucer had really crashed at Aztec, New Mexico. Conrad's film, imaginatively titled *The Flying Saucer* (1950), does show a craft exploding in mid-air but talk of "real" UFOs was just Hollywood hype.[25]

The extraterrestrial angle came to the fore in 1951 with the release of the film serial *Flying Disc Man from Mars* (dir. Fred C. Brannon). This re-working of a 15-part serial that appeared in 1945 has a Martian who forces a scientist to rebuild his flying saucer. The Martian, called Mota (atom spelled backward), is killed in an ironic twist by an atomic bomb launched by a young scientist.

A constant theme of 1950s science fiction films is that aliens want to invade the planet, steal our women and radically alter (if not totally destroy) the American way of life. The aliens are usually emotionless and rational. Their scientific abilities are underlined by the sleek, seamless lines of their one-piece suits, the prowess of their flying saucers and the size and power (physical and mental) of their robot helpers. It does not take a great mental leap to realize that they are (very) thinly disguised Soviet communists.[26]

The combination of scientific ability and the power to control minds was particularly potent in the climate of the Cold War. With all the marvels invented during World War II—radar, jet engines, rockets, atom bombs, and computers—it was easy to believe that the nation with the most powerful technology and science would dominate all others. These fears are reflected in the science fiction and horror films of the period that unleashed all manner of monsters on our cinema screens. At a deeper and less literal level they expressed our fundamental concerns about death, evil, science versus nature, the role of God and religion, individuality, democracy and our place in society.

The race for nuclear weapons superiority was by the 1960s disguised as the Space Race. The struggle between East and West in reality was rehearsed and executed in the cinema by the (usually) American Earthlings against the (Commie) aliens.

Most of the 1950s films can be regarded as the acting out of World War Three, albeit in a highly imaginative form. This would be no ordinary war because we now had the ability to obliterate our planet in the process. For the first time ever, we had to face the possibility of extinction. The flying saucers and their crews can be seen as messengers, literally from heaven, who warn us that we are dabbling with things we do not understand. The best example of this type of film is *The Day the Earth Stood Still* (1951). We have already noted that it provides a powerful image of the flying saucer and its associated superior technology and spirituality.

It has been suggested that the huge robot, Gort, in *The Day the Earth Stood Still* was the inspiration for the robot-aliens seen by Parker and Hickson in the Pascagoula abduction case. The pincer claws of the Mutants in *This Island Earth* (dir. Joseph Newman, 1956) are also a possible visual source for Parker and Hickson's aliens.[27] *This Island Earth* contains several other potent images that have been incorporated into ufology. The plot of this colorful movie centers on the Metalunians who have come to Earth to kidnap our top scientists. It shows a flying saucer swallow an aircraft, and it takes us to their war-stricken planet where they hope the Earth scientists can help them fight the Zahgons.

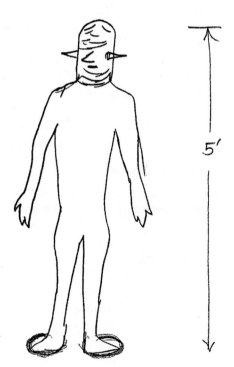

We have already looked at the possible influence of *Invaders from Mars* on the Hill case. We should also mention that it anticipates the use of implants by alien abductors. The film shows a young woman have a needle injected into her neck as she lies on the alien's operating table. By this means the aliens put implants in the back of people's necks to put them under their control. This procedure leaves a scar on the back of the neck, making it easy for us to spot who has been taken

On the evening of October 11, 1973, Charles Hickson and Calvin Parker were fishing at Pascagoula, Mississippi, when three of these mummy-like entities abducted them inside their UFO (illustration by Philip Mantle).

over and who has not. In a creepy scene near the end of the film, the boy who originally saw the aliens' flying saucer land near his home discovers that the police and those in authority have been taken over.

In the UFO literature there is the case of an abductee called Jerry who had a similar experience to that shown in *Invaders from Mars.* Under hypnotic regression, she remembered being taken inside a UFO where a sharp instrument was pushed into her neck, causing so much pain that she thought the aliens were trying to kill her. They said they had implanted a small device inside her to monitor her. This abduction occurred when she was seven years old, and 23 years later, in 1992 when she was regressed, she thought it was still inside her.[28] Joe, another of John Mack's abductees, also said he had an implant put into his neck.[29]

Help for humanity usually came in the form of religion. George Pal's *The War of the Worlds* (1953) has the remaining survivors of the invasion congregating in a church, where their prayers are miraculously answered by rainfall, which kills off the Martians. The God-given bacteria of our planet Earth kills the aliens but protects us. The power of God and His creation protects us against the evil aliens who are obviously not blessed by His protection.

The mastery of space exploration and the ongoing Space Race quickly made us wonder if we could evolve into God-like beings. In Stanley Kubrick's *2001 A Space Odyssey* (1968) humanity's technology leads to evolutionary change. On TV's *Star Trek* we would become secular rulers of the Universe (and spiritual leaders in *The Next Generation*). These ideas are parodied in *The Final Programme* (dir. Robert Fuest, 1973), in which Jerry Cornelius (Jon Finch) turns into a monster rather than a messiah.

Giving birth to devilish and monstrous creatures was to become a predominant theme of science fiction and horror films. Our own bodies incubate our worst nightmares. Such a transition can be seen by comparing *The Thing from Another World* (dir. Christian Nyby and Howard Hawks, 1951) and John Carpenter's 1982 remake. The former shows a unified male group fighting the alien enemy while in Carpenter's *Thing* everyone fends for themselves against a foe who can take over anyone.

In *Rosemary's Baby* (dir. Roman Polanski, 1968), Mia Farrow gives birth to the Anti-Christ, reflecting deep unease about pregnancy and birth. The sanctity of feminine space does not worry the traditional forces of evil; indeed, with scientific advances, there are new ways of violating it. One not-so-obvious violator is the computer if we are to believe the premise of the *Demon Seed* (dir. Donald Cammell, 1977). The machine called Phase IV keeps Julie Christie prisoner and develops the technology to rape her. The outcome is a baby, the perfect fusion of human and machine, who will lead humanity Christ-like to salvation.

Science fiction has always had an obsession with giving birth to monsters. The archetypal story is that of Dr. Frankenstein's monster, the product of our tampering with nature. Although huge and strong, the monster is also helpless and inexperienced, and his stumbling gait and constant grasping for things is reminiscent of a toddler's behavior. Partly it is the

The 1967 cover of *Beyond the Spectrum*, a pulp science fiction novel by Martin Thomas, links a disembodied brain with images of flying saucers. The cover blurb about psychic powers, invisible forces and a centuries-old cosmic battle are all themes that have infiltrated ufology (author's collection).

ignorance and arrogance of science, partly the superstitions and fears of the common people that spell his doom.

The issues of motherhood and birth are tackled in *Alien* (dir. Ridley Scott, 1979). This time the male body is impregnated by the alien, and the woman, Ellen Ripley (Sigourney Weaver), is the only one who can success-fully survive. If *Alien* shows that Ripley and her crew members are allowed to die due to the weakness of the patriarchy, then the sequel *Aliens* (dir. James Cameron, 1986) shows that Ripley has to fight both patriarchy and the alien matriarchy. In *Alien 3* (dir. David Fincher, 1992) Ripley has to sacrifice herself to kill the alien inside her for the sake of humanity.

The hero of *God Told Me To* (Larry Cohen, 1976), Peter Nicholas (Terry Lo Bianco), investigates a series of seemingly unpremeditated mur-ders. When the murderers are caught, they explain their actions by saying "God told me to." In the process of his investigation Nicholas discovers he is the outcome of an encounter his mother had with an alien when she was abducted by a UFO. Confronted by this unwelcome information, instead of killing himself like Ripley, he voluntarily enters an insane asylum.

Our institutions are so corrupt in *The Man Who Fell to Earth* (dir. Nicholas Roeg, 1976) that the alien is ruined by the U.S. government and betrayed by science. In the wake of Watergate, Vietnam and the under-mining of social and moral values, it is no wonder that films of the 1970s reflected changes in our attitudes and beliefs. There was uncertainty and fear until Steven Spielberg's *Close Encounters of the Third Kind* (1977) came to the rescue.

Close Encounters plays knowingly with government, scientific and military cover-ups maintained and perpetuated through the mass media of television and with our cinematic knowledge that aliens and UFOs are hostile. The appearance of the UFOs disrupts family life and Middle American normality, but it puts Roy Neary (Richard Dreyfuss) in touch with life and the Universe in a manner similar to a religious conversion. Darren Slade thinks that the climax of *Close Encounters*, where humanity is united with the aliens, can be regarded as an early sign of glasnost be-tween East and West, whereas Roger Sandell told me the return of the U.S. military men by the emaciated aliens can be regarded as a metaphor for the cease of hostilities between the United States and Vietnam.[30]

Spielberg took the title of his film from the 1972 book *The UFO Ex-perience: A Scientific Inquiry* by top UFO expert Dr. J. Allen Hynek.[31] He used Hynek as a technical advisor so that he could integrate real UFO cases into his story. These elements include the balls of light; the beams of light that can burn; the sightings by airline pilots that go unreported for fear of ridicule; the car chases; the abductions; the power cuts; and the psychological trauma and isolation felt by UFO witnesses.

More contentious are the spindly aliens with big heads that emerge from the UFO at the end of the film. No aliens of this type were ever reported before this film was released. They were developed by Spielberg and designer Carlo Rimbaldi. They went through a series of designs, including an alien with an "S" neck, eyes that projected laser beams and a visible brain. Fortunately, this monstrous creation was dropped in favor of the small-bodied, big-headed aliens that have now become part of UFO lore.

In 1980 *Close Encounters of the Third Kind—Special Edition* was released. This takes out some of the comic, almost hysterical, reactions to the images being projected in to the mind of Roy Neary (Richard Dreyfuss), and at the end he actually goes inside the alien spaceship.

Spielberg's companion piece to *Close Encounters, E.T. The Extra Terrestrial* (1982), also has Christian religious overtones. E.T. can be compared to Jesus because he is discovered hiding in a shed, he has the miracle of life literally at his fingertips and he suffers death and resurrection. E.T. is at one with nature and his death is "caused" by the scientists who seek to investigate and exploit, rather than understand and love.

The savior from the stars theme is also followed in *Superman—The Movie* (dir. Richard Donner, 1978). Superman is sent here to save himself and our planet from the fate that destroyed his home planet, Krypton. The sequels that followed never attained the same mythological power or box office success.

Star Wars, Alien, Superman and *Close Encounters* can be easily seen as reworkings of older science fiction films, but with production values and special effects that are as impressive as the skills and money used to create them.

In the 1980s films about aliens commented on culture and gender clashes. Such films were usually comedies about the alien not knowing how to act properly in our society and gave us a chance to see ourselves (and our ridiculous behavior) from the point of view of an alien/outsider. Examples are *My Stepmother Is an Alien* (1987), *Alien Nation* (1988) and *Earth Girls Are Easy* (1989).

Television programs provide us with an excellent benchmark for assessing popular interests and obsessions. In the 1990s U.S. producers discovered that UFO reports, particularly those involving abductions, got good audiences. The odd documentary had always done well but factional docu-dramas based on "real" cases entered prime-time TV schedules.

They can be seen as a development from the TV series of the 1960s *The Invaders*, the 1970s *UFO* and the 1980s *V*, which used UFOs as a launching point for fiction that didn't particularly care much for the factual evidence.

The Invaders (1967–68) played more on ideas of government conspiracy and paranoia surrounding such control, a theme that was used in the better, but more esoteric *The Prisoner*. The premise of *The Invaders*, according to producer Alan A. Armer, was "they're here among us now ... in your city ... maybe on your block. They're invaders ... alien beings from another planet ... but they look just like us!"[32]

Gerry Anderson's *UFO* (1970–73) despite its title had scant regard for real UFO theories or stories. Nonetheless *UFO* played with our notions of reality; one memorable episode titled "Mindbender" had one of the characters hallucinate that he was really an actor in this TV series.

Alien invasion continued being a hot topic in the 1980s. The *War of the Worlds* (1988–90) was revived as a TV series to show that the aliens, who were apparently killed off in the 1953 film, are in storage at a U.S. military base. When terrorists attack the base, they cause radiation to leak out and bring the aliens back to life. The aliens promptly inhabit the bodies of the terrorists and resume their plans to take over our world. The idea of terrorist aliens probably strikes a greater chord with us now, but the series never lived up to the ideas of the original.

In the case of *V* the producers admitted that they wanted to do a series about the rise of fascism and how freedom fighters might fight an occupying force. They ended up using this idea, in science fiction trappings, to satisfy the demands of the TV network and perceived public demand. This shows how the U.S. population quickly comes to terms with the aliens. The aliens seem friendly and humanoid, but in reality, they are evil reptilians who use the media to keep society under totalitarian rule.

The experiences of abductees as outlined by Budd Hopkins in his book *Intruders* became a three-part TV mini-series of the same name in 1992. It shows the trauma of alien abduction and the struggle abductees have to carry on normal lives. Much of the action is based on the real experiences of Kathie Davis. As might be expected, the authorities are aware of these events but they will not publicly confirm their existence. Tracy Tormé, the co-writer of the script, took an early interest in Hopkins' work after the publication of *Missing Time*.[33] They appeared together in a 1980 episode of the *Larry King Show*, and it was Tormé who introduced David Jacobs to Hopkins. Tormé was also involved in the investigation of the Davis case.

Robert Henderson noted several similarities between the original *V* mini-series of 1984 and the depiction of Davis' experiences in *Intruders*.[34] Like *Intruders* the sub-plot of *V* involved a teenage girl who was the subject of cross-breeding between humans and aliens. In both, the teenage girls give birth to a female hybrid child who has special powers. He wonders if Davis unconsciously absorbed details of *V*, which influenced her abduction story, and through the *Intruders* TV production inspired a new generation of abductees.[35]

The most successful and influential alien TV series of this period, if not of the 20th century, was undoubtedly *The X-Files* (1993–2002). The series shows that you cannot believe in any form of authority or even your own perceptions. One of the main story arcs is that there is a grand government conspiracy that involves alien colonists and the breeding of alien and human hybrids. Drawing its stories freely from tabloid headlines, science fiction films of the 1980s and obscure UFO and paranormal literature, *The X-Files* brought our most basic fears to life. For the affluent and intelligent Generation X, which had been largely neglected by the U.S. networks, *The X-Files* gave prime-time attention to such UFO and cult movie obscurities as missing time, Area 51, brain implants, mind control, and flying saucer retrievals.[36]

The success of *The X-Files* prompted others to use alien conspiracy theories for their programs. The most notable attempt was the short-lived *Dark Skies* (1996–97). It took us back to the 1960s when an organization called Majestic-12 tried to keep the alien "Hive" secret. Knowledge of Majestic 12 (MJ-12) came to light in 1987, when a top-secret government document appeared detailing its involvement with retrieving crashed UFOs and alien bodies. Ufologists are still arguing over the authenticity of MJ-12, but it has encouraged many to firmly believe that the U.S. government has obtained scientific and technological knowledge from the aliens in exchange for allowing them to abduct anyone they please.

Another great cornerstone of UFO belief, the Roswell spaceship crash of July 1947 that allegedly prompted the formation of MJ-12, has also been exploited by TV producers.[37] A TV movie, *Roswell* (a.k.a. *Incident at Roswell*, dir. Jeremy Paul Kagan, 1994) told of how Jesse Marcel spent 30 years searching for the truth about this crash. A series about teenagers who live in Roswell began in 1999. This too was called *Roswell* (a.k.a. *Roswell High* outside of the United States). It centers on three human teenagers who are friendly with three alien teenagers who survived in incubation pods after their craft crashed in 1947. Its teenage relationships mixed with concepts from ufology proved to be a popular combination.[38]

Returning to the cinema, the trend in the 1990s was to make docudramas based on "real" UFO cases. As Martin Kottmeyer noted in a letter to me dated May 25, 1993:

> *The UFO Incident, Communion, Intruders* and *Fire in the Sky* now constitute a genre. Call it True-Life Abductions. I don't know if that is enough, but I guess a category is emerging here. Comparisons seem indicated. Best by far is *The UFO Incident*. It is surprisingly honest and is compellingly presented. Worst: *Communion*. A muddle that doesn't want to be understood and makes Strieber seem off

key relative to reality and humanity. As a take on the Travis Walton case, *Fire in The Sky* is corrupt. As entertainment, the spaceship scene is wildly horrific and clever. Shrink-wrapping Travis to a table and threatening to stick a needle in his eye (cross his heart and hope to die; and suffer birth trauma) was over the top. The reaction of a girl sitting nearby in the theater was amazing to watch. She cringed, yelped, hid her eyes, and curled up into a ball. It's been years since I saw anyone react like that to a movie.

Whether corrupt or not, Tracy Tormé, who wrote and co-produced *Fire in the Sky* (dir. Robert Lieberman, 1993), intended it to be the middle-part of a UFO trilogy, which began with the *Intruders* TV mini-series and was meant to be completed by his version of Jacques Vallee's *Messengers of Deception*. So far, the latter has failed to make it to the screen.

Communion (dir. Philippe Mora, 1989) is based on Whitley Strieber's real-life abduction experiences. Whitley (Christopher Walken) has a series of vivid dreams and strange fears about insects to the extent that his wife advises him to see a psychiatrist. His psychiatrist, who seems to be modeled on Budd Hopkins and John E. Mack, encourages him to believe that his nightmares or hallucinations are real. He's abducted by monk-like aliens who seem to be of insect origin. When his wife is told by an alien, "Its time to understand," she is shown an alien hybrid that seems to be her daughter. But can we trust the word of these torturing tricksters? Are they really alien insects or just images of our own worst nightmares? *Communion*, like the abduction experience itself, is a puzzle.

The theory that aliens are insects was aired as early as 1950 by the British science writer Gerald Heard in his book *Riddle of the Flying Saucers*. In this, the first British UFO book, Heard put forward the view that the flying saucers were piloted by super bees from Mars. This theory could well have helped inspire the plot of Denis Wheatley's UFO-themed novel *Star of Ill-Omen* a couple of years later. Wheatley has giant humanoids abducting people to Mars, which is ruled by super bee-beetles who have no sting.[39]

Men in Black (dir. Barry Sonnenfeld, 1997) cleverly plays with the premise that the Men in Black (MIB) are immigration control officers who prevent visiting aliens straying from New York City. This comedy features a farmer being taken over by an alien force, giant alien cockroaches and the use of devices that can erase human memories. The MIB read sensational tabloid newspapers to keep track of the activities of the aliens. A sequel, *Men in Black II*, was released in 2002.

Independence Day (dir. Roland Emmerich, 1996) is a loose reworking of *The War of the Worlds*. Writer/producer Dean Devlin saw that, like the coming millennium, an alien invasion forces us to put our petty rivalries into perspective. Showing its awareness of the UFO literature, *Indepen-*

ALIEN ABDUCTION
NOVEMBER 5, 1975
5:49 PM
WHITE MOUNTAINS
NORTHEASTERN
ARIZONA

FIRE
IN THE
SKY
BASED ON
THE TRUE STORY

The feature film of Travis Walton's 1978 abduction experience, *Fire in the Sky* (1993), used this dramatic image of him being zapped by the beam of a UFO in its publicity material (author's collection).

dence Day uses the infamous Area 51 as its staging post to take the fight back to the aliens. Here, everyone unites to fight the invaders, including the president. In contrast, *Mars Attacks!* (dir. Tim Burton, 1996) brings the kitsch style and values of the 1950s into the 1990s. Instead of the action-man president of *Independence Day*, Burton's President Dale (Jack Nicholson) is a wimp who is all for appeasement.

As in *Earth Versus the Flying Saucers* (1956) there is considerable delight in destroying famous landmarks in both *Independence Day* and *Mars Attacks.* Such scenes lost their comic appeal after the real terrorist attacks on U.S. landmarks on September 11, 2001. As far as audiences were concerned the heroics and action of *Independence Day* won over the frantic *Mars Attacks.*

Prominent alien movies of the new century include *Signs* (dir. M. Night Shyamalan, 2002), which starts with crop circles in a farmer's field triggering a whole series of alien events. *The Mothman Prophecies* (dir. Mark Pellington, 2002) is an equally dark and sinister tale of alien encounters and psychic events that is loosely based on John Keel's factual book of the same title. *K-Pax* (dir. Iain Softley, 2001) features a mental patient who makes us wonder if he is really an alien or just a very convincing fantasist.

On television, Steven Spielberg's mini-series *Taken* (2002) covers the influence of alien encounters on three families since World War II. The Roswell crash, government conspiracies, abduction and the birth of a gifted hybrid child are woven into the plot. In 2004, Francis Ford Coppola was the executive producer of *The 4400* television series. It looks at the 4,400 people who suddenly reappear after being abducted by aliens. With the success of these programs and the forthcoming Spielberg remake of *The War of the Worlds* it looks like the alien invasion genre has not run out of steam.

Discussion

In his book *Hollywood vs. the Aliens*, Bruce Rux put forward the hypothesis that the U.S. government has actively influenced or forced Hollywood to participate in spreading disinformation about UFOs. He supported this idea by claiming that under Republican administrations Hollywood aliens tended to be depicted as dangerous, while they were friendly under Democratic administrations. This is a difficult idea to support considering that films with hostile and friendly aliens have been released in the same years.[40] Another flaw with his argument is that the most successful film with a friendly alien was Spielberg's *E.T.*, which was released during the right-wing Reagan administration. Rux nonetheless claims:

> A case could be made for *E.T.*'s being an informational movie confirming the EBE [Extraterrestrial Biological Entity] stories, but given its year of production and Reagan's unprecedented military buildup, it seems more likely it was part of the Intelligence community's increasing hold on entertainment, and its use to trump-up their disinformation ploy for exactly that reason.

A member of the intelligence community who went under the name of "Falcon" to preserve his anonymity has also claimed that since the 1950s the U.S. government has conditioned and monitored the public's reaction to the possibility of alien invasion. If, as he claims, they have been carrying out this project from *The Day the Earth Stood Still* right through to *E.T.*, we might wonder why both these films show the government and their associated authority figures as prone to violence and stupidity. Or is this a double bluff to put people off the idea that these are part of a government propaganda program?[41]

Another theory is that the aliens in Spielberg's *Close Encounters of the Third Kind* were so realistic the film worried powerful members of the Reagan government. Spielberg had got too near the truth for comfort so he was forced by government authorities to make the more pleasing and fantastic *E.T.*[42] If this is correct, then Spielberg did a poor job because when *E.T.* was screened at the White House, President Reagan was heard to say, "There are probably only six people in this room who know how true this is."[43]

Sometimes the parallels between a fictional work and a UFO story are beyond the realms of sheer coincidence. The infamous abduction of Linda Napolitano from her Manhattan, New York, apartment on November 30, 1989, has been compared to a novel titled *Nighteyes* by Garfield Reeves-Stevens. It was published in April 1989 and features government agents, abductions and other details that are very similar to the events told by Linda.[44]

It is certain that some writers have been under the sway of paranormal forces. Whitley Strieber was an established horror writer long before he wrote about his abduction experiences in *Communion*. Another important writer who had all manner of visionary experiences was Philip K. Dick (1928–82). From the very beginning his science fiction dealt with notions of reality and the power of the mind to perceive and change different realities. His own mind was invaded by an all-knowing alien intelligence in March 1974, which he termed VALIS (Vast Active Living Intelligence System). From that date it used pink light beams to fire streams of information into his mind. Dick graphically described the full power of one his encounters with VALIS:

> It seized me entirely, lifting me from the limitations of the space-time matrix; it mastered me as, at the same instant, I knew that the world around me was cardboard, a fake. Through its power I suddenly saw the universe as it was; through its perception I saw what really existed, and through its power of no-thought decision, I acted to free myself.

This force was able to supply Dick with vast resources of information dating back 2,000 years, and it was equally useful at helping Dick deal with his chaotic personal and private life. VALIS encouraged him to vacuum his apartment, sack his agent and visit his doctor for a check-up. He might have displayed classic symptoms of paranoid schizophrenia but his visions helped him create some of the best science fiction of the 20th century.[45]

His writings directly inspired Ridley Scott's ground-breaking *Blade Runner* (1982) and Paul Verhoeven's *Total Recall* (1990), and they have gone on to influence films like the *Matrix* trilogy into the 21st century.[46]

As a postscript, there have been rumors of a remake of *The UFO Incident*, and in the meantime we can enjoy the excellent 2019 short film *The Bumbry Encounter* directed and written by Jay K. Raja. It focuses on the fact that the Bumbrys, like the Hills, are a mixed-race couple and it highlights the prejudices of that period. The first season of the *Project Blue Book* TV series, episode 9, "Abduction," is also based on the Hill encounter. It changes Barney and Betty into a black couple and has Barney forcing Dr. Hynek to listen to his story at gunpoint. Like the rest of the series it is very fast and loose with the facts.[47]

We also have to add that Elizabeth Fuller, the wife of the late John Fuller, has produced a play about the case, "The Interrupted Journey: A UFO Story, a Love Story, a True Story, " with Joel Vig. The focus is on the hypnosis sessions by Dr. Simon, played by Alla Zeller, while Betty and Barney are played by Sachi Parker and Richard Pryor, Jr. A staged reading directed by Mark S. Graham took place at the Theater for the New City in New York on September 16, 2019. Hopefully it will have a proper run in the future.

9

Psychology
of Abductions

Along with the physical evidence for alien abductions, we have to consider the psychological factors and context that have a bearing on the abductee's testimony. Here we will look at the background of the Hills' life, and then we will look at the possible psychological factors that can be considered to explain their encounter and alien abductions in general.

Before I go further, I should add that psychological explanations are not an underhanded way of implying that reporters of such experiences are mentally ill or that they require any form of treatment. We should be aware that this type of explanation covers all varieties of human experience and perception. It is not a matter of labeling people sane or insane; the psychology of alien abductions is far more complex than that. I mention this because even mildly skeptical views of alien abductions are often received with very hostile opposition from ufologists and abductees. To question or probe too deeply into the story of an abductee is regarded as a cruel affront to their character and mental health. Fair enough, abductees do need protection, but I do not think you can use this as an excuse to avoid studying and honestly examining their experiences. In the long term, a less emotionally charged view of their experiences is likely to be of more help to them than soothing platitudes.

In the case of Betty and Barney Hill we have an inter-racial couple who had a good standing in their community. Barney worked for the post office in Boston, New Hampshire, which meant he had to commute a distance of 120 miles every working day. He was very active in civil rights issues connected with the police, housing and at the local shipyard. He organized the Rockingham County Community Action Program and became its director for three years. He even went to the march in Washington where Martin Luther King gave his famous "I have a dream" speech. He and Betty were also active members of their local Unitarian-Universalist Church in Portsmouth. On its behalf they acted as envoys to the United Nations. As Betty put it, "Everybody knew Barney."[1]

In Fuller's *The Interrupted Journey*, Barney comes across as someone who worried about everything. Barney had two sons from a previous marriage and was concerned about keeping in contact with them. On their car journey before the abduction, he was worried about bears coming out of the woods. He was worried about being rejected from a motel because he was black. He was wary of busy and confusing Montreal. When he and Betty went into a restaurant there, all eyes looked at them, and they saw "hoodlums" there. Although he was on his guard, the people in the restaurant were friendly. It was Barney who was most traumatized by the abduction experience. He suffered from high blood pressure, ulcers, a ring of warts around his groin and extreme headaches. The ring of warts was attributed to venereal disease after the death of Betty Hill in 2004.

Barney Hill died of a cerebral hemorrhage on February 25, 1969, at the Portsmouth, New Hampshire, hospital. Ufologists have suggested that his illness and early death at the age of just 46 was caused by his exposure to the UFO. This idea is not valid because he was already ill before the encounter. No doubt the UFO experience and its aftermath did add more to his anxiety and stress, but it can be regarded as a symptom rather than a cause of his bad health.

Betty Hill was born Eunice Elizabeth Barrett in Newton, New Hampshire, on June 28, 1919. She was the first of five children born to Raymond and Florence Rollins Barrett. In 1937 she graduated from Sanborn Seminary and went on to study at the University of New Hampshire. After two years she left to marry Robert Stewart. She had three children with Stewart. When their marriage broke up, she returned to the University of New Hampshire. Betty graduated in 1958.

She was employed as a child welfare worker in New Hampshire specializing in adoptions and training foster parents. Her career was very important to her and she rose to the post of supervisor. In the meantime, she met Barney Hill and married him in 1960. Along with Barney she was a founding member of the Rockingham County Community Action Program, and she was a community coordinator for the National Association for the Advancement of Colored People (NAACP). Betty and Barney supported Lyndon Johnson's presidential campaign, and when he won, they were invited to his inauguration.[2]

Neither of them can be accused of being publicity seekers. They feared that if their story got out, they might lose their jobs. Fortunately, the public reaction to their story did not make them the subject of ridicule, and their employers were more understanding than they expected.[3]

Betty seems to have been the one who was most interested in finding out more about their encounter, while Barney was more inclined to dismiss it as a bad dream. Barney seemed to internalize his problems, whereas Betty was far more gregarious, cheerful, quick-witted, and willing to talk about their experiences in a no-nonsense fashion. Over the years she became a minor celebrity and was affectionately called the Grandmother of Ufology.

Given the toil of work, worries about debt and family issues, it seems odd that they decided to take a short break to Niagara Falls on a whim. It involved a very long car journey, and their decision to go was so spur of the moment that they did not take much cash with them. When a hurricane was forecast for the area, they decided to go home because they were worried that the storms would block the roads and force them to stop another night. As they were short of money, they did not want the expense of staying away for an additional night.

Other Sightings

The fame of their encounter was such that many scientists visited the Hills but one of the most unusual meetings took place on July 26, 1967. A group of 26 scientists camped in the backyard of Betty's mother's home in Kingston, New Hampshire. It included Jacques Vallee, John Fuller, Dr. Simon and his son. In her interview with Peter Huston she mentioned this to show that scientists were very interested in her case.[4]

What she failed to mention is that she invited these people to Kingston because she had a strong urge that she could cause a UFO to appear. In addition, she thought that she would be able to make telepathic contact with its occupants. The UFO failed to appear, but several months later the Hills heard a radio program that described a UFO sighting at nearby Newton, New Hampshire, on the same night.

The UFO was seen at 11 p.m. by Gary Storey, a NICAP investigator, his sister Evelyn, and her husband Francis Frappier. Through a telescope they could see it was baton-shaped, had a red light on top, and a bright white at each end. Lights flashed in numerical sequences along the object. When Francis flashed his flashlight at the craft it reversed direction and flashed its lights three times in response. The craft repeated further flashes directed at it, but when a jet aircraft came into view, it simply disappeared from sight. When the jet went away the UFO briefly reappeared then flew away eastward toward the Atlantic Ocean. The witnesses were familiar with aircraft from the nearby Pease Air Force base. The UFO was nothing like them as it had no wings, moved abruptly without turning and was completely silent. The sighting was investigated by the Colorado Project but never appeared in its Blue Book report.

In his article about this sighting, Raymond Fowler wondered if this signaling UFO was responding to Betty Hill's telepathic thought waves, but for some unaccountable reason it appeared over the wrong field in front of the wrong people. He added that the aliens of the Hills abduction did say they would find them again, so perhaps this was another attempt at contact, or was it just a coincidence? If this was an alien spaceship it does show that they are as fallible as we are.[5]

After their abduction, Barney and Betty read about and also saw UFOs following police cars and fire trucks. The UFOs would mimic the flashing lights of these emergency vehicles. UFOs were also reported over the local race track and schools. After Barney's death Betty regularly saw UFOs pace her car and fly over her house. When she saw a UFO she would call out, "Hi, boys." In the neighborhood other people also saw UFOs, and there were even stories of UFOs landing nearby and discharging green-suited aliens and of aliens peeping into people's windows. It was her view that the aliens operated large mother ships that remained at the greatest distance from Earth, and they sent out the smaller craft that were spotted by UFO witnesses. George Adamski and conventional ufologists have long supported the idea of mother ships and smaller (scout) craft. Betty added a more unconventional category of UFOs that she called "sneaky ones." They landed in wooded areas and looked exactly like a house with its lights on, by this means the aliens could infiltrate populated areas without detection.

The aliens seen during Betty's abduction were not the weak, robotic and skinny creatures seen by other abductees. They ranged in height from three to five feet and were sturdy beings with different facial features and personalities. Since her encounter she had seen a group of nine dark robots with large orange heads, causing her to nickname them "pumpkin heads." Others in her silent UFO research group said they had also seen such robotic devices but they had no idea what their purpose was. In February 1976, Betty claimed that she had seen a large pumpkin head gliding beside her car as a UFO flew overhead. Since that sighting, she was full of electricity; if she touched anything she got shocked, though it eventually faded away.[6]

Berthold Schwarz met Betty at a few UFO conventions and had longer conversations with her in the early part of 1976. He found her to be a "highly intelligent, open, straight-talking, good-natured lady of unquestionable probity." His intention was to record other events in her life, before and after the abduction, that might provide a fuller picture of the UFO experience. There was no shortage of information.

After the abduction she told Schwarz that she would come home to find her coats dumped in the middle of a room. Only three months afterward she found a bowl-shaped hunk of ice underneath a newspaper. Right up to the time of the meeting with Schwarz she reported that the water supply would be found turned off or the taps would be running, electrical equipment and appliances malfunctioned, clocks stopped and restarted, the phone was tapped, prowlers seemed to be lurking inside and outside the home, bogus gas meter readers appeared at the door, and mail went missing. She saw a doppelgänger of ufologist Raymond Fowler, and she and her friends saw mystery helicopters on several occasions. He found that Betty, her family, and close friends had life-long experiences of psychic phenomena. It led Schwarz to speculate that such people have unique characteristics that enable the UFO beings or forces to initiate a "mind-matter interface experience."[7]

It was Betty's view that the aliens were trying to find out how we primitive human life forms live. In the course of this mission the occupants of a UFO telepathically contacted her during a Christmas parade to find out what was going on. When she supplied explanations for such events the aliens usually accepted them without question. At some other time her communications with the aliens were recorded on tape but they have long since disappeared.[8]

Betty gave lectures about her experiences in the United States and overseas until 1991 when she went into semi-retirement from the UFO scene. She became disillusioned with the hype surrounding alien abductions and the Roswell crash case. She believed that alien bodies had been recovered at Roswell in 1947, and she believed in some alien abduction cases, but she could not agree that thousands of people were being regularly abducted. It was her view that instead of seeking information, the media and people with "flaky ideas, fantasies and imaginations" were now dominating the subject. In an effort to fight against these trends she self-published a book titled *A Common Sense Approach to UFOs* in 1995 and she set-up a "silent network." This informal network was created to discuss and learn about UFOs away from the glare of publicity. In this period she often discussed politics and UFOs and attended related events with her niece Kathleen Marden.[9]

Besides ufology, Betty was interested in gardening, animals and researching her family tree. Any money she gained from her UFO experiences she gave to charities and organizations that reflected her interests in civil and health issues. These included UNICEF, Doctors Without Borders, the Carter Foundation, the Salvation Army, the Southern Poverty Law Center, and the Rockingham County Community Action Program.

Betty Hill died of lung cancer at her home in Portsmouth on October

17, 2004. She was mourned by the UFO community as a true pioneer. One person went so far as to say that she was the ufological equivalent of Charles Lindbergh. Others had some doubts about her credibility. Bryan Daum, who was a junior officer co-pilot stationed at Pease Air Force Base, remembered meeting her twice in the late 1970s. The first time was in the library of the base where she gave a talk about sightings in the area. About a year later he saw a box-like UFO and decided to visit Betty to see if she knew if anyone else had seen such a thing.[10] He met her in her garden, and she affirmed such sightings and added that they sometimes flap their wings. Her wild-eyed manner made him think "she was real crazy and [I] quickly got into my car and drove away."[11]

Her continued UFO sightings indicated that Betty was of special interest to the aliens and they might have been intrigued by her openness to psychic phenomena. On the other hand, to skeptics, this just indicated that she was highly imaginative and given to all sorts of way-out fantasizes. Alternatively, all these psychic incidents and sightings are just a smoke screen by the aliens to undermine the credibility of her original abduction.

Abductee Whitley Strieber was worried about his mental health and took a battery of psychological tests and had MRIs of his brain. Nothing showed any abnormalities. Intriguingly, he said that all these findings were available to qualified professionals and scientists but not to debunkers who would twist these facts for their own "emotional" purposes.[12]

Betty and Barney Hill were under several forms of stress due to their own personal problems. Like other Americans at this time they "primarily worried about personal financial and health problems: loan repayments, over-demanding children, mortgages, college finance, hospital bills, and so on. Less than 1 per cent ... [worried about] ... communism or civil liberties."[13] Unlike this 1 percent the Hills as activists in several organizations were well aware of the prevailing poor state of international affairs. Peter Rogerson elaborates the worldwide tensions of that period:

> On August 15 the Berlin Wall had been thrown up, with a further flare-up of tension during 8 to 10 September. On August 31 the Soviet Union ended its nuclear test moratorium ... on 16 September the United States resumed its tests.... On 1 September, 78 people had been killed in an airliner crash at Hinsdale, Illinois.... On 5 September there was an assassination attempt on De Gaulle. Next day, Kennedy made a speech praising the desegregation attempts at Little Rock High school. On 11 September Hurricane Clara ... struck Texas, and a United Automobile workers strike started. The Katanga crisis exploded on the 13th and that led to the death of United Nations Secretary General Dag Hammarskjold in a (probably non-accidental) plane crash on the 18th.[14]

We should also note that mentally ill people can be far from confused and chaotic in their delusional behaviors or beliefs. There is the complex story of Kirk Allen (pseudonym) who was the subject of a chapter titled "The Jet-Propelled Couch" at the end of Dr. Robert Lindner's book of psychoanalytical case histories, *The Fifty Minute Hour*.[15]

Allen was a physicist who had an important position with a U.S. government laboratory in the late 1940s. His colleagues were worried about his mental health when he was seen writing hieroglyphs and apologizing for not spending enough time on this planet. He was sent to see Dr. Lindner, a Freudian psychoanalyst based in Baltimore who found that as a teenager Allen had come to believe that he was an extraterrestrial trapped in the body of a human being. Based on his reading of the works of Charles Fort, Allen thought that he had been teleported from his home galaxy to Earth. He could return to his galaxy through astral projection, rather than physically, by means of certain psychic organs in his body. Dr. Lindner submitted him to a battery of tests, and they all gave results that rated Allen as normal.

From almost the very beginning Allen wrote about every aspect of the planets he visited, from their politics, flora and fauna, politics and civilizations to their orbital mechanics. After Dr. Lindner gained Allen's confidence, Allen showed Dr. Lindner his 12,000-page autobiography with 2,000 pages of annotations, 82 full-color scale maps of the planets he had visited, a 200-page history of the galaxy Allen ruled, several astronomical charts, a glossary, genealogical tables, architectural drawings, hundreds of drawings of alien people, animals and machines, and, for good measure, 44 files detailing different aspects of alien transport systems, anthropology and biology.

The sheer scale of his work impressed Dr. Lindner, and it was no wonder that Allen felt that his delusions were overwhelming him and distracting him from life on Earth. Dr. Lindner decided that the best way to treat Allen was to find contradictions or errors in his delusional worlds so he could be shocked back to reality. This strategy was successful; scrutinizing his delusions took his enjoyment out of them. In a strange twist, Allen continued to display a belief in his other worlds for several weeks for the benefit of Dr. Lindner, an avid science fiction fan.

It was rumored that Kirk Allen was really Dr. Paul Myron Anthony Linebarger (1913–66). Using the pseudonym Cordwainer Smith, from the 1930s he wrote science fiction stories and novels about a future history. For conspiracy theorists it is noteworthy that he was an intelligence officer in China during World War II, wrote *Psychological Warfare*, a textbook on the subject, and advised on psychological warfare techniques for the British during the Malayan conflict and for the U.S. forces during the Korean conflict.[16] Psychologist Alan C. Elms spent several years trying to establish a link between Dr. Linebarger and Kirk Allen. Although he thought they were probably one and the same person, he could find no documents or any other hard evidence to support this view.[17]

Whoever Kirk Allen was, his case shows the enormous effort and intellect that can be put into a project by a deluded person. And, as Paul Thompson pondered in his review of this case, what kind of impact would he have had on the public at that time? His knowledge and education combined with his sophisticated delusions would certainly have eclipsed the comparably shoddy and ill-thought-out tales of the contactees and caused the U.S. government great embarrassment.

Like Betty and Barney Hill, many abductees have nightmares, anxieties and other ill-defined worries that makes them seek help. It was Budd Hopkins' claim that, for these reasons, abductees were not always aware that they had been abducted until they had some form of therapy.[18]

John Mack reinforced this concept by stating that the post-traumatic stress displayed by abductees was caused by their abduction and not by the stress itself.[19] This is one of those chicken-and-egg conundrums that skeptics and believers can wrestle over for years to come. To nudge it in favor of the skeptics, we have to consider what type of counseling or treatment the abductee received. So-called abductees might not be aware of being abducted by aliens because they were not abducted by them. Enthusiastic abduction researchers could be responsible for introducing these ideas to people especially under the influence of hypnotic regression and other forms of suggestion.

Dr. Alvin Lawson and William McCall's theory that alien abductions were caused by birth trauma caused considerable controversy in the late 1970s. They hypnotically regressed a group of people who had no intimate knowledge of the UFO subject and found that their accounts matched those of "real" abductees. To explain these similarities they postulated that we all have the common experience of birth. As a validation of this view they found that people who had normal births tended to recall UFO encounters that involved tubes and tunnels, which are symbolic of or memories of the birth canal. Those who were born by Caesarean section do not seem to report UFO encounters with these elements.[20] But not everyone was convinced. As British ufologist Ian Creswell put it:

> Dr. Lawson's theory poses more questions than it answers, leaving too many strands untied and open. He admits that "a causal nexus between specific events of one's biological birth and particular images has yet to be established," and that "we cannot yet explain what stimulates the sequence of visual imagery and events which makes up an abduction."[21]

Hypnotic Regression

The main case against abduction stories is that they are mainly obtained through the use of hypnotic regression. Under hypnotic regression, the subject is easily open to suggestion and can be swayed by what they think the questioner wants to hear. The extent to which abductionists give leading questions to abductees under hypnotic regression has been hotly debated, but the very context of being regressed to discover more about a UFO sighting can in itself set the scene for a person's imagination to run riot. Indeed, an early case of hypnotic regression elicited a spontaneous abduction account without any form of prompting. A 10-year-old school girl called Janet had gone through a series of hypnosis sessions to deal with a slight nervous disorder. Out of the blue she spoke of being inside a flying saucer. This craft took her to another planet where she saw people in a city. The Adelaide–based hypnotist took the case to the newly formed Australian Flying Saucer Research Society (AFSRS) in February 1955. At first, they thought it was a hoax either by the hypnotist or the girl, but convinced that the claim was genuine, they put her under hypnosis to obtain more information about the flying saucer. She said that inside the craft there were three men wearing colored overall outfits. They were on couches to help them "go into gravity," and she saw a planet appear on a screen. The craft went inside a mountain where she was taken in an elevator to a city. It was full of black-haired people and glass buildings that contained long corridors. She was shown machinery that made flying saucers. The questioners asked her if the aliens have heard of George Adamski, and they replied that he is an important man. The travel to a planet and a city with glass buildings was very similar to the story told by Betty Andreasson, without the mystical elements.[22] We can only assume at this distance in time that something in the media or conversation with other people might have triggered this fantasy. Or was she recalling a real event?

Some people seem to easily recall an encounter unprompted, but others are more resistant. Some investigators will persist in hours of questioning so that they can piece together a coherent story of an alien abduction. I saw a videotape of one such interview, which consisted of a subject under considerable pressure giving very short and fragmented answers. How the investigators managed to put the answers together to form a "story" was a work of art.

Reading John Mack's *Abduction* or Jacobs' *Secret Life*, the power of the emotions displayed by abductees under hypnosis is certainly very clear and potent. Although these emotions are no doubt real, it does not mean the events described are real.

With regard to the Hill case, Dr. Simon was skeptical of the Hills' claims and used every method possible to get them to find mundane explanations for their experiences. Many of the sessions were highly traumatic, especially for Barney, and Dr. Simon simply failed to make any real progress with them. He accepted that they might have seen a UFO but the rest was either a *folie a deux* (a shared psychosis) or based on Betty's dreams. Dr. Simon favored the idea that the abduction memories were based on Betty's dreams.

In contrast, Dr. Leo Sprinkle thought the Hills had an actual encounter based on its similarity with elements of other UFO events. He could not accept the "dream hypothesis" as there was the difficulty of explaining how Barney's perception of the beings inside the UFO transferred to Betty, who dreamed of the abduction and in return transferred this to Barney.[23] Like Sprinkle, other investigators claimed some form of ESP or telepathy would have been required for them to share this experience if it had not been a real event.

Many UFO experts make much of the fact that the Hills were hypnotized separately and that they could not have influenced each other's testimony. The flaw with this argument is that Betty's nightmares were very similar to the story that they eventually told under hypnosis. Even if they had not discussed her dreams, they had several years of thinking and talking together about UFOs and aliens. Given the fact that they talked with UFO investigators and gave public lectures on their encounter long before the hypnosis sessions, I don't think any fanciful notions of ESP or telepathy were required for them to arrive at a similar story.

In her many interviews Betty Hill always insisted that she and Barney told their stories under medical hypnosis conducted by a respected professional. She poured scorn on the many abductees who had been put under light hypnosis by unqualified amateurs. Indeed, it is very worrying that some ufologists have taken it upon themselves to hypnotize people rather than rely on qualified professionals.

In defense of hypnosis, abduction researchers note that abductees often consciously recall much of their experience. Underlining this point John Mack et al. noted that nearly 30 percent of alien abduction accounts were recounted without hypnosis.[24]

In his review of hypnosis in UFO research Dr. Leo Sprinkle listed six main reasons for its use:

1. To relax and reduce the anxiety suffered by UFO witnesses.
2. Gaining more information about their encounter and the person's ideomotor responses.
3. Cross-checking information given prior to hypnosis.
4. Gaining information about "missing time" events.

5. Training to experience out-of-body events and to project them to UFO locations.
6. Training to initiate clairvoyant and telepathic communication with aliens.[25]

Sprinkle claimed the various uses would depend on the requirements of the investigator and the UFO observer. Points 5 and 6 sound more like those employed by contactees and channelers, though even the hard-core abductionists of today seem to veer into this territory even if they are not overtly training the witnesses to do so.

Although it is commonly stated by ufologists that hypnosis is *not* a key to uncovering the truth about missing time events or other aspects of alien encounters, it is still frequently employed by experts and amateurs, especially in the United States. If used correctly, it can help ease the anxieties and concerns of UFO witnesses or abductees, but all too often it seems to be callously used to winkle out information for the benefit of UFO investigators at the mental harm and cost of the subject.

Auto Hypnosis

Australian psychologist Mark Moravec put forward the idea that UFO witnesses enter an involuntary or self-induced autohypnotic state. It might be far-fetched to think that two people could simultaneously enter such a state, yet David Jacobs reported a case that is very pertinent to the Hills' experience. From his own files he retrieved a case from 1972 that involved an elderly couple who saw a UFO near Madison, Wisconsin. When they stopped to look at this object in front of their car, they had the urge to go to sleep. When they woke up, the UFO had gone and they carried on with their journey. On reflection, Jacobs thinks that on further investigation it could have revealed an abduction experience.

He could be right since it parallels the Hill encounter, as they experienced drowsiness at the beginning and end of their abduction experience. We might postulate that, like the elderly couple, the Hills fell into an autohypnotic or sleeping state and that was the reason for their amnesia and missing time.[26]

Moravec made the point that staring at a UFO could have put the Hills into an autohypnotic state but added that the use of hypnotic regression and Betty's dreams were probably more important in shaping their abduction experience.[27]

It is argued that Barney Hill suffered a short psychotic episode that made him remember the incident as real. Because he worked in an office environment and worked under stress, this mini nervous breakdown was caused by Subliminal Peripheral Vision Psychosis (SPVP). The author of this theory did not think this happened when Barney viewed the UFO through binoculars. Although this was an obvious moment when he seemed to be at his most agitated, the author thought that if it occurred, Barney would not have been able to drive home. The missing time is dismissed for the same reasons Peter Rogerson gave (see Chapter 7) and the UFO was possibly a star or the Moon that looked as if it was following him, which is an illusion commonly reported by "UFO" witnesses. He thought that the combination of recalling the *Outer Limits* TV episode "The Bellero Shield" (see Chapter 8) and hypnosis created "a paranoid psychotic delusion."[28]

There are several assumptions and suppositions about SPVP and the Hill case itself for this theory to work, plus it does not account for Betty's experiences. Did she also suffer SPVP or some other syndrome?

Sleep Paralysis

Dr. Susan Blackmore regarded sleep paralysis experiences as the main explanation for alien abductions. She described typical sleep paralysis as waking up to find yourself as the name suggests, paralyzed. You might hear strange buzzing sounds, see strange lights and feel terrified about an undefined presence. An entity might appear, or sometimes it might be invisible, to sit on your chest or to strangle and prod you. It is all the more frightening because it is very difficult to fight the paralysis.

If the person is not aware that they are undergoing a sleep paralysis experience, the perception of lights, buzzing sounds and the appearance of an entity can be interpreted in the form of an alien abduction encounter. In this state, knowledge of aliens from TV, films and other media can help shape their recollection of the experience. When the person is hypnotized their experience is more likely to fit the expected abduction scenario.[29]

These experiences have been interpreted differently throughout history and in different cultural contexts. The perception of demons and the incubus and succubus that have sexual intercourse with their victims are regarded as classic examples of sleep paralysis.[30]

Sleep paralysis can feature hypnagogic or hypnopompic experiences. They are extremely clear visual and auditory images that are generated within the mind of the percipient. They can include the perception of temperature, touch and smells. Hypnagogic imagery occurs in the stage between waking and sleep, while hypnopompic imagery occurs before waking fully. They can be so vivid to the percipient that they are virtually indistinguishable from reality, except that they feature bizarre or unusual images.

The argument against this explanation is that abductions do not just take place indoors, they occur while people are awake, driving on highways or taking part in other outside pursuits. Sleep paralysis does not have the sequence of events reported by abductees nor do they have the same sense of realism or emotional charge.

Undermining this argument is the study by Spanos et al. that found the majority of abduction experiences occurred at night, and of these 60 percent were sleep related.[31] Almost a quarter of them could be regarded as symptomatic of sleep paralysis. In a group of six abductees Cox found that they experienced more sleep paralysis than the control groups.[32]

These studies involve only a few subjects, but it is clear that most abduction experiences that occur in the bedrooms or homes of abductees are triggered by sleep paralysis.

The work of Dr. Jorge Conesa confirmed that sleep paralysis (SP) could involve vividly experiencing floating, going through tunnels, seeing lights and hearing noises. Furthermore, these types of experiences could be triggered by anxiety, tiredness and sleep deprivation, making it common in shift workers, truck drivers, hospital workers and other people who work long and odd hours. In this context, it is possible that the Hills and Antonio Villas Boas were subject to this phenomenon. Conesa suggested that geomagnetic activity might trigger SP experiences and that birth trauma memories might shape the imagery of those who interpret their SP experience in terms of an alien abduction. He also indicated that these experiences run in families and that people can learn to use SP to have out-of-body experiences, lucid dreams and shamanic journeys.[33]

Temporal Lobe Epilepsy

The work of Penfield and Perot found that if the temporal lobes are stimulated by electricity, they can cause auditory hallucinations. Studies have found that people who suffer involuntary temporal lobe epilepsy report shadowy figures, auditory hallucinations, strange feelings in the genital and anal regions, strange smells, the sensation of flight, anxiety and even missing time. Since these experiences sound like symptoms of alien abduction, Michael Persinger put forward the idea that abductees might have a higher degree of abnormal temporal lobe activity. To test this theory he applied weak magnetic fields to the heads of human subjects. These induce feelings of disorientation, the sensation of the limbs being pulled, anger and fear according to Susan Blackmore, who submitted herself to this procedure. Using this technique Persinger and his colleagues were able to induce the false experience of an apparition. This was still a long way from inducing anything like an abduction experience or explaining how it occurs in the natural or supernatural world.[34]

Tectonic Strain Theory

To answer the question of how our temporal lobes might be stimulated in the real world, Persinger postulated that geophysical phenomena—not flying saucers or space ships—could induce witnesses to view UFOs and experience other paranormal events including alien abductions.

He claimed that in areas of tectonic strain the crushing of rocks by these forces could release energy that would be visible as a light in the sky. Close proximity to such energy might induce epileptic fits in susceptible people, causing them to experience hallucinations and other sensations that could be interpreted as an alien abduction.

To prove his tectonic strain theory (TST) he statistically correlated UFO reports with earthquake areas. Even though the quality of his UFO database has been disputed, Persinger was convinced that such a correlation existed. He might have been correct in asserting that people with labile temporal lobes were more likely to report out-of-body experiences and visions, psychic and mystical experiences, but studies have shown that UFO reporters and abductees do not seem to have any greater temporal lobe lability than control groups.[35]

Earthlights

Besides TST, lights in the sky have been associated with earthquakes, mountain peaks and ball lightning. Significantly, Mount Shasta is the location for light phenomena as well as contactee events; similarly, George Adamski's first UFO sightings were of spheres of light coming out of the peak of Mount Palomar. These natural phenomena could conceivably trigger assumptions about them based on the witnesses' cultural preconceptions and elaborations.[36]

Electronic Pollution

Albert Budden has put forward the concept that we can become allergic to electronic and electrical pollution. These sources of pollution can cause up to 20 percent of the population to suffer hallucinations. There is a growing body evidence that living near power lines can cause certain health risks, but Budden goes further by stating that EM pollution also has an effect on our bodies via the food we eat. Sensitive people build up an allergy to this pollution through the combination of nutritional, chemical, and electromagnetic factors interacting on their body. Furthermore, hallucinations caused by this pollution symbolically represent these threats to our health. The main downfall of this complex theory is that Budden offers no empirical evidence to support it.[37]

Mass Hysteria

The late Carl Sagan suggested that alien abductions are a form of mass psychosis, hysteria, or hallucination. To test such explanations, Robert E. Hall compared MPI (mass psychogenic illness) criteria with EAT (experienced anomalous trauma) cases. Out of 12 criteria he only found resemblances between two of them. This made him conclude that there is something to EAT and that the psycho-sociological theory is up the creek. Once you start looking at the various criteria you can see that Hall's ability to make comparisons is rather faulty. He suggests that those experiencing MPI "select others as their models for belief and behavior" but EAT victims don't. It doesn't take a great UFO expert to easily know this is false—what about the support groups propagated by Hopkins or the role of Strieber et al.? The other sets of criteria can be as easily applied to EAT cases, which would seem to indicate that MPI is at work and that Hall effectively supplies ammunition for the psycho-sociologists.[38]

David Jacobs also claimed that alien abductions do not fit the mass hysteria model because the abductees have no common relationship to each other or close contact that would reinforce hysterical contagion. It was his view that abductees are isolated people who do not realize that other people have had similar experiences.[39] Again, we have to be aware of the role of the many formal and informal support groups that have appeared and that the "contagion" can also be spread by the many books, magazines, websites and other media about all aspects of this subject that goes beyond local geographical areas.

Social Context

Peter Rogerson made a good case that the Hills' personal circumstances and social factors had a great bearing on their experience:

The Hill's aliens are very poor aliens indeed, they are just far too human. They look more or less like us, except for a few minor anatomical differences, far less than the differences between humans and their very close cousins the chimpanzees. They act like people, they have books, and maps, and mutinous crews, they wear uniforms. Their technology was getting old fashioned in 1960, its levers and wall map positively antiquated by now. Their conversations are self contradictory.

The Hill story reads like a product of the human imagination, replete with human imagery and human concerns, and that is what it almost certainly is. Its story line must be derived from the lives, hopes and fears of the Hills. There are clues here, some more obvious than others. Right on the surface is the fact that Betty and Barney Hill were not Mr. and Mrs. Average, they were very unusual people indeed. Even today interracial marriage is far less common in the United States than the UK, in 1960 when the Hills got married they were very rare indeed. The black population of New Hampshire was small, the Hill's may well have been the only black/white couple in the whole state. That took a lot of guts, and a lot of risk taking.

Betty was a professional woman with a higher status job than her husband, again rare. She had been divorced, and her first husband had also been married before, was she the cause of his first divorce? We don't know, nobody has asked. We do know that Barney's divorce was bitter and that the first Mrs. Hill loathed Betty and would not let her children meet her. To have lost her husband to a white woman would, one imagines, have been a very humiliating and enraging experience for a black woman of her time. One can perhaps imagine the insults that were thrown and the suggestions made, for example that Betty and her white liberal friends were using Barney as a token 'negro' to show how progressive and enlightened they were, but might one might think that their real thoughts were somewhat uglier?

To rub it in, Betty in her dreams becomes the heroine who stands up to the grey meanies, tells them off (after all she is a Barrett of New Hampshire). Don't these dreams emphasize who wears the trousers and has the balls in this family?

What is Barney afraid of, but which Betty Barrett of New Hampshire can stand up to? Look at the pictures of the aliens with their caps and jackets and trousers, remember those charts and that mutinous crew. Charts aren't much use in space ships hopping between stars through wormholes, using space warp or the Z process which no human mind could ever understand. These are images of ships and the sea. These are sailors. What kind of sailors steal people, slavers of course. We have all overlooked this because we are not black. This is the central fear which grips Barney, the terrible others who are both us and not us are going to take him back into slavery. Betty comes from the dominant white culture, she cannot feel the fear of being turned back into a slave. She can stand up to the crew. In her vision the sailors are more like a chaotic pirate crew.

The alien motif points to the distinctive character of Anglo-American slavery. Traditional societies, which did not pay lip service to human equality, could treat slaves as subordinate groups of human beings with their own status, allied to that of serfs for example. However liberal, individualistic Anglo-American society, with its Christian belief and its lip service to "all men being created equal" could only give conscience to slavery by reducing the slaves to a subhuman status.

The medical examination and the symbolism for the fertility test for Barney are images of the farmyard, the prodding and probing on the auction block. For Betty they are perhaps medical procedures to test for the presence of radioactivity following the resumed nuclear tests. Betty has incorporated Barney's fear of capture into her dreams but she cannot really understand what it is about. Her aliens let them go, and Barney takes this on board, because it means that he has escaped, these aren't slavers after all.

Yet is he going to be really free? What for Barney was an event of unadulterated horror, becomes for Betty a grand adventure, one which will take her far from the shores of planet reality. Betty went into some very strange places indeed, seeing flying saucers all over the place and recounting many an unlikely adventure, becoming a sort of cult leader. To put no finer point on it, she was becoming a contactee.

As the stories change the aliens become friends, and begin to develop supernatural powers, such as leaving leaves in a neighbors apartment, appear over another's house in answer to Betty's prayers. The iron wall that some ufologists believe exists between the contactees and the abductees looks more like a paper curtain.[40]

Discussion

From this review of some of the major psychological explanations we can see that UFO sightings can be explained by the misperception of ambiguous stimuli, such as stars or aircraft. They can also be triggered by internal psychological processes. Whatever the stimuli this is inter-

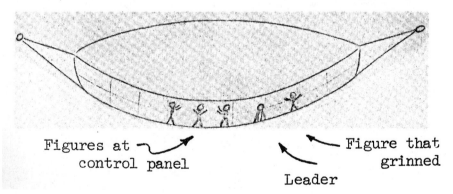

Sketch by Barney Hill of the UFO and aliens he saw on the fateful night of September 19, 1961. The one he pointed out as the leader, stared intently at him and looked like a German Nazi. The others worked on a large control panel inside the craft (author's collection).

preted in terms of the prevailing UFO mythology by the witness and/or the investigator.

This helps explain sightings of just a light or even a structured craft in the sky. For abductions we also have to consider the more important role of fabrication, psychopathology, hypnotic regression, fantasy proneness, false memory syndrome and mass hysteria.

The main problem with the psychological (and sociological) explanations for alien abductions is that we have to consider a complex interaction between our mental processes that are subject to illness, misperception, genetic predisposition, intoxication and trauma with our culture, society, myths, beliefs, peer pressures, and preconceptions.

Even the methods by which we use psychology to examine these processes in pursuit of alien abduction investigation can be conditioned by our culture. In the United States there has been far more credence given to results from polygraph tests and hypnotic regression techniques whereas in Britain these methods have been rarely used for extracting alien "evidence."

Whether they are accessible to scientific analysis or not, psychologists have increasingly taken up the challenge of examining alien abductions. At the University of London, Katharine J. Holden and Christopher C. French have considered this subject even though they regard alien abductions as "almost certainly untrue." At the end of their paper "Alien Abduction Experiences: Some Clues from Neuropsychology and Neuropsychiatry" they concede that

> even excluding the minority of cases based on serious psychopathology or deliberate hoaxes, there are still many cases on which the neurosciences can currently cast little light. To give but one example, many alleged abductions occur when people are driving in their cars. There are many anecdotal accounts of so-called "highway hypnosis" in which, especially during long monotonous drives, individuals may enter a dissociated state. In mild forms, this may simply produce the experience of missing time familiar to most experienced drivers. In some cases, however, it appears to form the basis of full abduction experiences. Clearly, this is an area that deserves further consideration by neuroscientists.[41]

10

Reviewing
the Hill Case

The Hills' abduction continues to fascinate believers and skeptics alike. In recent years the best defense of the reality of their encounter is given by Kathleen Marden and the late Stanton T. Friedman in their book *Captured! The Betty and Barney Hill UFO Experience*. Kathleen is Betty and Barney's niece, and their experience triggered her lifelong interest in UFO research leading her to lecture on the subject and become director of MUFON's Director of Experiencer Research.

Kathleen also has a website that contains several pages about the Hill case, one of which tells us "Where the Debunkers Went Wrong."[1] Here she claims debunkers have spread false and misleading information for the reasons listed below accompanied by my response to them:

1. Betty did not have a prior knowledge of UFOs or science fiction.

Kathleen does admit that her family was interested in the space race and that her mother, Janet, saw a UFO one night in 1957. Her mother was the first person Betty telephoned to talk to about her encounter.

"The Immanuel Velikovsky Archive" website contains a copy of a letter from Betty dated March 9, 1968, to Dr. Velikovsky:

> Since 1950 I thought that some day I would write to you, for at that time I discovered your "Worlds in Collision." At that first reading, my emotional experience was one of shock, but I accepted your theories quickly, for they answered many of my own questions: If man has been in existence for so many ages, where has he been and what has he been doing? These theories helped me to solve this riddle.[2]

The book claims that in the 15th century BC, Venus was blasted from Jupiter, and as it passed Earth, it caused numerous catastrophes that are recorded by worldwide mythologies and religions. His thesis intrigued the public, which made the book a bestseller, but scientists have found it unconvincing. James Fitton, who was working on his Roman history dissertation at McMaster University in the early 1970s, wrote:

> In at least three important ways Velikovsky's use of mythology is unsound. The first of these is his proclivity to treat all myths as having independent value; the second is the tendency to treat only such material as is consistent with his thesis; and the third is his very unsystematic method.[3]

This shows Betty had more than a passing interest in space topics and what have become known as Ancient Alien theories. Indeed, she even told Swedish UFO researcher Clas Svahn that in 1959, two years before her abduction, she saw a UFO crash with her relatives. She kept the debris in her wardrobe for some time before throwing it out. She speculated that she was abducted because "they" knew she had debris of one of their crashed vehicles.[4]

Betty Hill (pictured here April 13, 1987) with a color painting of her alien visitors created by David G. Baker in 1967. This now resides in the Hill Archives at the University of New Hampshire (photograph by Clas Svahn, Archives for the Unexplained).

2. Betty was not fantasy prone.

Even her most ardent supporters admit that she saw literally thousands of lights or UFOs in the sky that could be easily explained. Some claim that she became obsessed with UFOs and aliens after the death of Barney as a way of keeping his spirit alive, but it seems she regularly saw UFOs long before that date.

3. Barney was not tired and stressed on their trip back to Portsmouth.

This goes against every account of their journey home on the night of their abduction and the evidence that he suffered ill health before and after the encounter. The whole reason for their hypnosis sessions was to help alleviate Barney's stress.

4. Barney did not see Nazis inside the UFO.

I agree he merely saw a figure inside the UFO that reminded him of a Nazi soldier. This indicates how fearful Barney was of the UFO crew and its intentions.

5. The two hours of missing time was not caused by them getting lost.

This is hard to verify. They certainly must have slowed down to watch the UFO and they stopped at least once to get a better view of it. Barney did make a diversion during the journey, so this combined with the confusion or excitement caused by seeing the UFO could well have made them lose track of time.

6. "The Bellero Shield" episode did not influence their story.

Kathleen calls this ridiculous speculation and argues that the Bifrost alien in this episode of *The Outer Limits* does not look or behave much like the alien Barney described under hypnosis. She notes, "It sounds like the Bellero shield explanation is another 'anything but ET' hypothesis."

7. Betty's dreams are a red herring.

They did not have an overdue impact on Barney's recollection of events under hypnosis, according to Kathleen, and do not have a bearing on his account.

8. Symbols provide further scientific evidence.

Betty drew the symbols she saw inside the alien leader's book for Kathleen's files. These were compared with symbols collected by Budd Hopkins and they looked "remarkably" similar, leading Kathleen to conclude that this "is yet another piece of scientific evidence" that they "were abducted by non-human entities." This does not constitute scientific evidence at all, merely that a collection of symbols match some Betty "remembered." This is the same problem we have with the star map; it is based on Betty's memory and nothing more tangible than that.

In September 2000, Karl Pflock and Peter Brookesmith organized a symposium at the Indian Head Inn, New Hampshire, near the site of the abduction, sponsored by Joe Firmage (at that time a Silicon Valley multi-millionaire). Invited UFO experts included Marcello Truzzi, Robert Sheaffer, Dennis Stacey, Eddie Bullard, Hilary Evans and Greg Sandow. Betty and Kathleen made a guest appearance.

This became the basis for the book *Encounters at Indian Head: The Betty and Barney Hill UFO Abduction Revisited*, which has contributions from those at the symposium and by Martin Kottmeyer and Walter N. Webb.[5]

Moderator Marcello Truzzi reviewed the arguments pro and con and the kinds of inferences that can be made as to what makes a claim remarkable. The other contributors reflect the division of opinion about the case, from the outright skepticism of Sheaffer, the psychosociological discussion by Brookesmith, Evans and Kottmeyer, to the belief of Bullard, Pflock and Webb in an extraterrestrial encounter.

In his detailed review of the symposium, Robert Scheaffer pulled no punches by stating: "Not a single participant in the symposium was willing to describe the Betty Hill we heard first-hand as a credible witness; none-theless, a number of them still were inclined to accept her story of alien abduction..." At the end of the day, not surprisingly, no consensus was agreed over whether the Hills had a real encounter with aliens or imagined it.[6]

11

Questions
and Conundrums

When Betty and Barney Hill saw a UFO following their car in the early hours of September 20, 1961, they never guessed that it would change their lives and fundamentally alter the popular perception of UFOs and alien encounters.

Under hypnosis they convincing recalled being medically examined onboard a flying saucer and their whole story seemed to confirm that extraterrestrials were conducting a systematic and scientific reconnaissance of our planet.

The Betty and Barney Hill case as a foundation for abduction research has several flaws and contradictions. Although it involves two abductees, the key elements of the experience happened when they were separate from each other. There are many contradictions in the story, and the facts are that they probably did not experience any missing time, the aliens they saw were more like humans than the greys of today, and most of the story was based on Betty's dreams. This indicates that subsequent cases that have included these and ever-more elaborate features are equally insubstantial in relation to physical reality.

We can go on to object to the general reality of alien abductions by considering these points:

1. Why do aliens continue to carry out so many medical examinations? They could get the information from reference books, medical schools, and corpses or by reading the minds of doctors.
2. Their surgical skills are next to useless. They insert implants in the nasal cavity, which causes headaches, bleeding and the ejection of the implant. They leave scars and bruises all over the abductees' bodies. A butcher would do a better job than an alien examiner or surgeon.

The alien inseminators also make many elementary mistakes. They were puzzled when they found something missing when they examined Betty Andreasson, who had to explain that she had had a hysterectomy.[1] Carl Higdon was also useless for their breeding program because they found he had had a vasectomy. Johannes Fiebag disputed the idea of a breeding program for two reasons:

    a. If the aliens have been visiting us for millennia, they would have completed the program by now.

    b. Even if they were conducting a program, they would only need a few human cells from hair or skin samples. The would not have to conduct what amounts to raping humans.[2]

3. If aliens use screen memories and other forms of memory blocking, why are these techniques so selective or downright ineffectual?

4. The widespread use of hypnotic regression to "recall" an abduction experience is the weakest link in the chain of evidence. The brain does not record memories and playback memories like a "biological tape recorder" as Raymond Fowler put it in *The Andreasson Affair*.[3]

    Under hypnosis the subject easily says what is expected of them. When a ufologist organizes, or even conducts, the hypnotic sessions, he or she biases the outcome because either consciously or sub-consciously the people involved in these sessions expect an abduction experience to be revealed.

5. Ufologists argue that literally thousands of people have been abducted and they all cannot be wrong. True, hundreds of cases in the literature are fairly consistent, but since this information and knowledge is so widespread, it is contaminated by these influences. Any evidence gained merely mimics what has gone before, perhaps with an odd new slant or twist for the sake of novelty.

    We can also dispute the assertion that literally millions of U.S. citizens have been abducted without their knowledge.

6. If there are so many abductions involving people floating through the sky to hovering spaceships, why are they never seen by independent witnesses?

7. Why is the physical evidence for them so elusive?

    Implants disappear before they are X-rayed or scanned. Video cameras do not operate when people are being abducted. Why are abductees never allowed to bring home any evidence? Why are they never given any useful scientific knowledge?

8. Why do the aliens always confirm and reflect the prejudices and preoccupations of the abductees and/or the abduction investigators?
9. Why are abductions so similar to those imagined in films and other media?
10. Abductees have been seen sleeping or in an unconscious state during a supposed abduction.

These are just some of the objections that lead us to consider three main possibilities.

The Alien Abductors Are Real

The criticisms of the reality of abductions assume that the aliens think like we do. To us the antics of the aliens might seem horrifying, silly, comic and downright ludicrous. But we must remember that they are alien in every sense of that word. The evidence shows that there is more than one type of alien species visiting us, so some might be better at abducting us than others. As humans, we can only dimly glimpse their motives. The aliens are manipulating our ideas and beliefs all the time and perhaps they want us to think that their methods are crude. Their superior technology would seem like magic to us and explains why they can do things that we would regard as physically impossible.

They might be allowing us a trickle of information here and there, knowing that it is not enough for total belief in their existence by the whole of humanity, but enough for fair-minded people to grasp and understand.

The Aliens Are Phantoms

This concept argues that the so-called aliens are an intimate part of our environment. They are not really beings from outer space; instead, they are elemental or ultraterrestrial beings that can emerge from their realms and interact with our reality. This theory considers them insubstantial phantoms who can conjure up solid spacecraft that can be photographed and leave landing traces. The religions, myths and legends of history, fairy lore, shamanism and stories of witchcraft are used to support the contention that these forces have always been with us and that the flying saucers crewed with aliens are their latest manifestation. If the aliens appeared in a too outlandish or extraordinary manner, we might ignore them or become literally insane by the dramatic loss of our grasp of reality. This theory suggests that they are trying to educate and inform us in a way that only believers will come to understand. It also suggests that they have manipulated our view of the world since time began and that they continue to do so.

Aliens Are a Psychosocial Phenomenon

The two theoretical frameworks listed above, and their various combinations that include the idea that the U.S. government is conspiring to aid and hide the activities of the abductors, is countered by psychosociological theories.

This broadly argues that abductions are caused by individual psychological factors:

a. A trigger event that could be a misinterpretation of a celestial or aerial object, geomagnetic phenomena, illusion or hallucination.
b. The "observation" or experience can be due to neurosis or other pathological states of mind, abuse, trauma, stress, sleep paralysis, drugs, sensory deprivation, lack of sleep, dreams, trance states and other psychological factors.
c. The abduction story can be a hoax, an invention, a friend-of-a-friend rumor, or the outcome of hypnotic regression techniques.

On a social and cultural level these individual factors are shaped and conditioned by friends and family, UFO investigators, the religious, political and social milieu, and the mass media.

The accounts of mythology, religion, fairy lore, witchcraft, shamanism and legends are similar to those of ufology because they were subject to similar psychosociological factors and mechanisms.

Discussion

The belief in and reporting of alien abductions can be seen as having evolved from the science fiction and séances of the 19th century through the contactees of the 1950s to the abduction of the Hills in 1961. The abduction research of Budd Hopkins, David Jacobs and John Mack combined with abduction as entertainment cultivated by Steven Spielberg, Tracy Tormé (*Fire in the Sky*) and *The X-Files* has cultivated a world where we can no longer escape the stereotyped image of the grey aliens and their attendant abduction activities.

Hilary Evans made the point that the abduction scenario provides a ready-made framework that allows extraordinary experiences, personal concerns and dispositions to be played out in accordance with this "authorized myth." As he put it, "Each of us, given the appropriate circumstances, could find ourselves living a fantasy with the total conviction that we are really experiencing events we are actually imagining, or recalling imagined experiences with such vividness that we are convinced they took place in reality."[4]

The gruesome stories of aliens abducting, raping and torturing have condemned thousands of people to believe that they are victims of alien breeding projects.

This is all based on a very few cases that have relied on hypnotic regression to obtain the evidence for these suppositions. As with the Hill case and other abduction reports, it is never a clear matter of determining whether supposed abductees are telling the truth or not.

When there is no physical evidence to support these stories, the abductionists claim that the aliens use invisibility, hologram projections, telepathy and screen memories or other convenient techniques to hide them from our scrutiny.

Whatever the reality of the abduction phenomenon, flying saucers and aliens act as a metaphor for personal and/or social, psychological and/or physical alienation and despair. As Mark Pilkington put it, "the Greys are an unconscious portrait of Western Man itself; many see our times as colorless and emotionless, ruled by grey leaders and grey technology and driven by the cold desire for wealth and property. The beings resemble human fetuses, so perhaps they are representations of our future children, born out of the current state of humanity."[5]

At other times the flying saucers have, through the eyes of the contactees, acted as a symbol for optimism, beauty and a means of going beyond our Earth to find new wonders to marvel at. Those days are long gone as the greys stare down at us in the night and haunt our minds.

Glossary

Abductee: Person who is involuntarily abducted by aliens.

Abductionist: Person who investigates or believes in alien abductions.

APRO: Aerial Phenomena Research Organization.

AR: Army regulation.

ASC: Altered state of consciousness.

Astral Travel: A non-physical form of travel unlimited by time and space.

BSRA: Borderland Sciences Research Association.

CAS: Classic Abduction Syndrome (or Scenario).

CAUS: Citizens Against UFO Secrecy.

Channeler: Person who uses paranormal means to contact aliens.

CIA: Central Intelligence Agency.

Close Encounter of the Fourth Kind (CE4K): An addition to Dr. Allen Hynek's classification system to denote an abduction case.

Colorado Project: Investigation headed by Edward Condon to determine the scientific value of UFO reports. His Condon Report justified the cancellation of Project Blue Book.

Contactee: Person who voluntarily meets aliens.

CSICOP: Committee for the Scientific Investigation of Phenomenon.

CUFOS: Center for UFO Studies.

Cultural Tracking: UFOs mimic our social and cultural expectations.

Direct Contactee: Contactee who has face-to-face encounters with aliens.

Doorway Amnesia: Abductees often do not remember how they arrived inside a flying saucer.

EAT: Experienced Anomalous Trauma.

EBE: Extraterrestrial Biological Entity.

ESP: Extra Sensory Perception.

ET: Extra-terrestrial.

ETH: Extraterrestrial hypothesis.

Etherean: A being that lives in the invisible world of Etheria.

FBI: Federal Bureau of Investigation.

Flap: An intense period of UFO activity.

Flying Saucer: An aerial craft presumably operated by aliens.

FOIA: Freedom of Information Act.

Fortean: A person interested in the philosophy, and curiosities collected by, Charles Fort.

FSR: *Flying Saucer Review.*

Grey: Large-headed, small-bodied alien.

GSW: Ground saucer watch.

Implant: Object inserted into the body of an abductee.

Incubatorium: Room onboard a flying saucer that contains fetuses that are being incubated.

Indirect Contactee: Person who does not meet aliens face-to-face but via astral travel, etc.

IUR: *International UFO Reporter*, journal published by CUFOS.

Ley Lines: Lines linking ancient sites and buildings. Claimed to be conduits of magical or electromagnetic energy along their pathways or at strategic points.

Leys: See Ley Lines.

LITS: Lights in the sky.

Magonia: Alleged historical home of alien beings, and name of British UFO magazine, now a website.

Majestic 12: See MJ-12.

MIB: Men in Black.

MJ-12: Alleged secret U.S. government agency that deals with UFOs and aliens.

Mothership: Large alien spaceship that does not land on Earth. It dispatches scoutcraft to Earth.

MUFON: Mutual UFO Network.

NDE: Near death experience.

NICAP: National Investigations Committee on Aerial Phenomena.

Nuts and bolts: Physically and literally real spacecraft or aliens.

Oz Factor: Time and reality seems frozen when a UFO is encountered.

Pelicanist: Usually a derogatory term for a UFO skeptic.

Project Blue Book: United States Air Force project to investigate UFO reports. It ran from 1953 to 1969.

Scoutcraft: Small flying saucer that is dispatched from a mothership.

Screen Memory: Aliens distort our perceptions to present themselves as animals or people.

Silent Contactee: Person who does not make public their voluntary contact with aliens.

SP: Sleep paralysis.

Spooklights: Apparently intelligent or intelligently controlled balls of light.

Switched Off: While an abductee encounters aliens, the people around them seem to go into some form of trance state.

Telepathy: Mental communication between people and/or aliens.

Trigger Event: Something that causes a person to believe they have been abducted by aliens.

UAP: Unidentified aerial phenomena.

UFO: Unidentified flying object.

UFOIN: UFO Investigators Network.

Ufologist: Person who studies the subject of UFOs.

Ufology: The study of UFOs.

Ufonaut: Alien associated with a UFO encounter.

Ultraterrestrials: Intelligent alien beings who secretly seek to control human society.

USAF: United States Air Force.

Wave: An intense period of UFO activity over a period of days, weeks or months.

Window Area: A location where UFOs and other phenomena are seen on a regular basis.

Wise Baby: A hybrid human/alien baby.

Further Reading
and Notes

Chapter 1

Books and Periodicals

Friedman, Stanton T., and Marden, Kathleen. *Captured! The Betty and Barney Hill UFO Experience*, New Page Books, 2007.

Fuller, John G. *The Interrupted Journey: Two Lost Hours Aboard a Flying Saucer*, Souvenir Press, London, 1980.

Spencer, John. *Perspectives*, Futura, London, 1989.

Watson, Nigel. "Betty and Barney Hill—Abduction Pioneers," *Magonia Supplement*, No. 56, May 25, 2005, 1–6.

Webb, Walter N. *A Dramatic UFO Encounter in the White Mountains, New Hampshire. The Hill Case—Sept. 19–20 1961*, www.nicap.org/reports/610919hill_report2.pdf.

Websites

Koenig, Sarah. "Aliens Made Them Famous," https://www.ufocasebook.com/aliensfamous.html.

Price, Joan. "The Betty and Barney Hill Story 1961," Members.ozemail.com.au/~vufors/pdfs/BettyBarneyHill1961.PDF.

Watson, Nigel. "The Hill Abduction: Milestone or Millstone?" http://greyfalcon.us/The%20Hill%20Abduction.htm.

Notes

1. John G. Fuller, *The Interrupted Journey: Two Lost Hours Aboard a Flying Saucer* (London: Souvenir Press, 1980).

2. Major William E. Brummett and Captain Ernest R. Zuick, Jr., *Should the USAF Reopen Project Blue Book? Air Command and Staff College Research Study. Air University Report No. 0450-74* (Auburn: The Graduate Faculty of Auburn University, May 1974), www.cufon.org/cufon/afrstdy1.htm.

3. Major Donald Keyhoe, *The Flying Saucer Conspiracy* (New York: Henry Holt, 1955).

4. Fuller, *The Interrupted Journey*, 36.

5. Hilary Evans, *From Other Worlds* (London: Carlton, 1998), 134.

6. Fuller, *The Interrupted Journey*, 47.

7. *Ibid.*, 60.

8. Peter Huston, "Interview with Betty Hill," October 1, 1998, https://web.archive.org/web/20030225011548/http://www.capital.net/com/phuston/bettyhill.HTML.

9. Ben H. Swett, "Betty & Barney Hill. Testimony," www.bswett.com/1963–09BettyAndBarney.html.

10. Fuller, *The Interrupted Journey*, 90.

11. Jacques Vallee, *Dimensions: A Casebook of Alien Contact* (London: Souvenir Press, 1988), 121.

12. Huston.

13. *Ibid.*

14. *Ibid.*

15. Swett.

Chapter 2

Books and Periodicals

Pilkington, Mark. "What's on Your Mind?" *Magonia*, No. 58, January 1997, 3–5.

Sachs, Margaret. *The UFO Encyclopedia*, Corgi, 1981, 191–192.

Thomas, Kenn. *Maury Island UFO: The Crisman Conspiracy*, Last Gasp, 1999.

Wilkins, H. T. *Flying Saucers from The Moon*, Peter Owen Ltd., 1954, 53–65.

Wilson, Robert Anton. *Everything Is Under Control*, Pan, 1998, 310–311, 386.

Websites

Brasilia, Anthony. "Maury Island No Longer a Mystery: A UFO Hoax Exposed," https://www.ufoexplorations.com/maury-island-no-longer-a-mystery.

Constantine, Alex. "Project Paperclip and the Kennedy Assassination," https://www.stopeg.com/tinet.nl/public/browse-online/raven1-eleanor-white/mcf/hambone/paperclip.html.

Cooper, Timothy S. "The CIA, UFOs, MJ-12, JFK & James Jesus Angleton," www.nexusmagazine.com/angleton.html.

"The Dulce Files," www.thewatcherfiles.com/dulce/chapter1.htm.

Maccabee, Bruce. "June 24, 1947: How It All Began. The Story of the Arnold Sighting," https://www.456fis.org/HOW_IT_ALL_BEGAN.htm.

"Premonitions of the Future, Part I. Support for 'New Revelations' in Early UFO Material: The Arnold Case," www.v-j-enterprises.com/arnold.html.

Project 1947. "The Kenneth Arnold Page," www.project1947.com/fig/1947ka.htm.

Notes

1. Peter Rogerson, phone conversation with the author, 4 July 2004.

2. Berthold Schwarz, "MEN IN BLACK: A Classic Case," https://mankindresearchunlimited.weebly.com/berthold-eric-schwarz-md.html.

3. "The Sad Truth Behind an MIB Story," pelicanist.blogspot.com/2009/02/sad-truth-behind-mib-story.html.

4. John Keel, *Operation Trojan Horse* (London: Abacus,1976), 237.

5. Jenny Randles, *MIB: Investigating the Truth Behind the Men in Black Phenomenon* (London: Piatkus, 1997), 33–34.

6. *Ibid.*, 39–40.

7. Dr. Robert M. Wood and Ryan S.

Wood, "Majestic Documents: Evidence We Are Not Alone. Fred Crisman," www.majesticdocuments.com/personnel/crisman.php.

8. Randles, *MIB*, 36.

9. *Ibid.*, 32.

10. Kenneth Arnold, "The Maury Island Episode," in *Proceedings of the First International UFO Congress*, ed. Curtis G. Fuller, Mary Margaret Fuller, Jerome Clark, and Betty Lou White (New York: Warner Books, 1980), 41.

11. Paul B. Thompson, "UFO Continuing Tales No. 5—The Maury Island Case," www.parascope.com/nb/cautionarytales/mauryIsland.htm (this link is no longer active).

12. *Ibid.*

13. John A. Keel, "The Maury Island Caper," in *UFOs 1947–1987: The 40-Year Search for an Explanation*, ed. Hilary Evans and John Spencer (London: Fortean Tomes, 1987), 40–43.

14. Randles, *MIB*, 38.

15. Thompson.

16. Ron Halbritter, "Before the UFO Crash at Roswell, There Was ... Maury Island. The Hoax on You," *Steamshovel Press*, No. 12, 1995, 23, http://files.afu.se/Downloads/Magazines/United%20States/Steamshovel%20Press%20(Kenn%20Thomas)/Steamshovel%20Press%20-%20Issue%2012.pdf.

17. Harold T. Wilkins, *Flying Saucers from the Moon* (London: Peter Owen Ltd., 1954), 54.

18. Captain Edward Ruppelt, *The Report on UFOs* (New York: Ace, 1956), quoted in Randles, *MIB*, 37.

19. Keel, "The Maury Island Caper," 40–43.

20. Wood and Wood.

21. Robert Morningstar, "The Death of Dorothy Kilgallen," https://highstrangeness.blogspot.com/2010/03/death-of-dorothy-kilgallen-by-robert-d.html.

22. Dougllas Woodward, "Connecting the Killing of Kennedy with German UFOs," https://faith-happens.com/connecting-the-killing-of-kennedy-with-german-ufos-part-one/.

23. Thomas Kenn, *Maury Island UFO: The Crisman Conspiracy* (Lilburn, GA: Illuminet, 1999).

24. Fuller, *The Interrupted Journey*, 87.

25. The Group, edited by Branton, "The

Secrets of the Mojave," www.v-j-enterprises.com/mojave1.html.

26. Don Ecker, "The Uncover-Up. Part 1," *Fortean Times*, No. 121, April 1999, 40–31.

27. Dennis Stacy, "Moore and the Military," *Magonia*, No. 34, October 1989, 8–11.

28. David Barclay, *Fatima: A Close Encounter of the Worst Kind?* (Irchester: Mark Saunders Publications, 1987).

29. Tim Swartz, "The Mysterious Life and Death of Philip Schneider," https://www.ufodigest.com/article/the-bizarre-fate-of-phil-schneider/.

30. Thomas Kenn, *The Octopus: Secret Government and the Death of Danny Casolaro* (Lilburn, GA: Illuminet, 1998).

31. Fuller, *The Interrupted Journey*, 41–42.

32. Coral Lorenzen, "UFO Occupants in the United States," in *The Humanoids*, ed. Charles Bowen (London: Futura, 1977), 163–164.

33. Keel, "The Maury Island Caper," 237.

34. The Group, edited by Branton.

35. Anthony Roberts and Geoff Gilbertson, *The Dark Gods* (London: Rider/Hutchinson, 1980), 166.

36. Dr. Helmut Lammer, "Alien Abductions Via MKUltra to an Implanted Cyber-Situation," http://fc0.co/all.net/journal/deception/MKULTRA/www.vegan.swinternet.co.uk/articles/conspiracies/milabs.html

37. Lammer.

38. Nicholas Redfern, *The F.B.I. Files* (London: Simon & Schuster, 1998), 111–115.

39. Adam Gorightly, "PKD, The Unicorn and Soviet Psychotronics," http://tinet.nl/public/browse-online/raven1-eleanor-white/mcf/mindnet/mn191.htm.

40. Jacques Vallee, *Messengers of Deception: UFO Contacts and Cults* (Berkeley: And/Or Press, 1979).

Chapter 3

Books and Periodicals

Bartholomew, Robert E. *Little Green Men, Meowing Nuns and Head-Hunting Panics*, McFarland, Jefferson, NC, 2001.
Bartholomew, Robert E., and Howard,

Professor George S. *UFOs and Alien Contact: Two Centuries of Mystery*, Prometheus Books, Amherst, NY, 1998.
Bullard, Thomas E. *The Airship File*, privately published, Bloomington, Indiana, 1982.
Bullard, Thomas E. *The Airship File, Supplement I; Supplement II*, 1990; *Supplement III*, 1997.
Bullard, Thomas, "Prehistoric UFOs: A Review," *MUFON UFO Journal*, No. 243, July 1988, 14–16.
Busby, Michael. *Solving the 1897 Airship Mystery*, Pelican Publishing, Gretna, LA, 2004.
Fort, Charles. *The Complete Books of Charles Fort*, Dover, New York, 1974.
Medway, Gareth J. "Beyond the Reality Barrier. Part One: Many Mansions," *Magonia* 94, January 2007, http://magoniamagazine.blogspot.com/2014/02/barrier1.html
Watson, Nigel. *UFOs of the First World War*, The History Press, Stroud, 2015.
Winkler, Louis. *Analysis of UFO-Like Data Before 1947*, Fund for UFO Research, Mount Rainier, WA, 1984.

Websites

Barry Greenwood UFO Archive: UFO Historical Review, http://www.greenwoodufoarchive.com/.
Collins, Curt. "UFO History: The Saucers from Atlantis," *Blue Blurry Lines* blog, 13 July 2018, https://www.blueblurrylines.com/2018/07/ufo-history-saucers-from-atlantis.html?.
Mr. X, Consulting Resologist. The Fortean Web Site of Mr. X, contains hypertext editions of the works of Charles Fort, www.resologist.net/.
Sourcebook Project, www.science-frontiers.com/sourcebk.htm.

Notes

1. Michel Bougard, "UFOs Throughout History," in *UFOs 1947–1987: The 40-Year Search for an Explanation*, ed. Hilary Evans and John Spencer (London: Fortean Tomes, 1987), 20–25.

2. Eric Inglesby, *UFO's and the Christian* (London: Regency Press, 1978), 125–133.

3. Erich Von Daniken, *Chariots of the*

Gods? (New York: G. P. Putnam's Sons, 1970).

4. Jacques Vallee, *Magonia: From Folklore to Flying Saucers* (London: Tandem, 1975).

5. Daniel Cohen, *The Great Airship Mystery* (New York: Dodd, Mead, 1981), 79.

6. Robert G. Neeley, *UFOs of 1896/1897: The Airship Wave* (Mount Rainier, WA: Fund For UFO Research, 1988), 66–67.

7. Whitley Strieber, *Communion: A True Story* (London: Arrow Books, 1988), 240.

8. Neeley, 189.

9. Cohen, 79.

10. Keel, *UFOs: Operation Trojan Horse*, 74–75 and 171–174.

11. "Air Ship Takes a Cow. The Thrilling Experience of a Woodson Stockman," *The Farmer's Advocate* (Yates Center, KS), April 23, 1897.

12. Cohen, 98.

13. Thomas Bullard, *The Airship File* (Bloomington: privately published, 1982), 104.

14. Jerome Clark, "The Great Airship Hoax," *Fate*, February 1977.

15. Jerome Clark and Loren Coleman, *The Unidentified: Notes Toward Solving the UFO Mystery* (New York: Warner, 1975), 157–158; Keel, *UFOs: Operation Trojan Horse*, 80.

16. "Golden Haired Girl Is in It. The Airship Discovered in Southwest Missouri. What Hopkins Said He Saw," *Post Dispatch* (St. Louis), April 19, 1897.

17. Neeley, 59–61 and 66.

18. Nigel Watson, "Down to Earth," *Magonia*, No. 43, July 1992, 3–11.

19. Charles K. Hofling, "Percival Lowell and the Canals of Mars," *British Journal of Medical Psychology*, Vol. 37, part 1, 1964, 33–42.

20. Loren E. Gross, *Charles Fort, the Fortean Society & Unidentified Flying Objects* (Fremont, CA: privately published, 1976), 55.

21. Peter Haining, *The Legend and Bizarre Crimes of Spring Heeled Jack* (London: Frederick Muller Ltd., 1977).

22. J. Vyner, "The Mystery of Springheel Jack," *Flying Saucer Review*, Vol. 7, No. 3, May-June 1961, 3–6.

23. Donald M. Johnson, "The 'Phantom Anesthetist' of Mattoon: A Field Study of Mass Hysteria," *Journal of Abnormal and Social Psychology*, No. 40, 1945, 175–186.

24. Willy Smith, "Mattoon Revisited," *Magonia*, No. 48, January 1994, 3–6.

25. Scott Maruna, *The Mad Gasser of Mattoon: Dispelling the Hysteria* (Jacksonville, IL: Swamp Gas Book Co., 2003).

26. Nigel Watson, "Before the Flying Saucers Came," in *UFOs 1947–1987: The 40-Year Search for an Explanation*, ed. Hilary Evans and John Spencer (London: Fortean Tomes, 1987), 26–31.

27. Anders Lilegren and Clas Svahn, "The Ghost Rockets," in *UFOs 1947–1987: The 40-Year Search for an Explanation*, ed. Hilary Evans and John Spencer (London: Fortean Tomes, 1987), 32–38; Gross, 40 and 53.

28. *Ibid.*, 53.

29. *Ibid.*, 54–55.

30. John Keel, "The Man Who Invented Flying Saucers," *Fortean Times*, No. 41, Winter 1983, 52–57; Jerome Clark, "60 Years of Fate Magazine," *Fortean Times*, No. 237, special edition, 2008, 44–49.

31. Mark Chorvinsky, "Vincent Gaddis: 1913–1997," *Strange Magazine*, No. 19, Spring 1998, 29 and 58.

32. Gross.

Chapter 4

Books and Periodicals

Evans, Hilary, ed. *Frontiers of Reality*, Guild Publishing, London, 1989.

Lewis, James R., ed. *The Encyclopedic Sourcebook of UFO Religions*, Prometheus Books, London, 2004.

Redfern, Nick. *Contactees: A History of Alien-Human Interaction*, New Page Books, 2010.

Websites

Davenhall, Clive. "Mars and the Mediums," https://sophiacentrepress.com/2018/06/26/mars-and-the-mediums/.

Hallet, Marc. "Why I Can Say That Adamski Was a Liar," http://old.ufo.se/english/articles/adamski.html.

Notes

1. Jacques Vallee, *Anatomy of a Phenomenon: UFOs in Space* (London: Tandem, 1974), 90.

2. *Ibid.*, 124.

3. Waveny Girvan, "Trained Minds," *Flying Saucer Review*, Vol. 10, No. 3, May-June 1964, 1.

4. Vallee, *Anatomy of a Phenomenon: UFOs In Space*, 129.

5. Jacques Vallee, *Messengers of Deception: UFO Contacts and Cults* (Berkeley: And/Or Press, 1979).

6. *Ibid.*, 55–56.

7. T. Flournoy, *From India to the Planet Mars* (New York: Harper & Brothers, 1900).

8. T. Flournoy, *Nouvelles observations sur un cas de somnambulisme avec glossolalie* (Geneva: C. Eggimann, 1902).

9. Nandor Fodor, "A Martian Revelation," https://www.survivalafterdeath.info/library/fodor/chapter4.htm.

10. Anthony Roberts and Geoff Gilbertson, *The Dark Gods* (London: Rider/Hutchinson, 1980), 85 and 173–175.

11. Timothy Good and Lou Zinsstag, *George Adamski—The Untold Story* (Beckenham: Ceti Publications, 1983), 191; Chris Aubeck, "Desperately Seeking Rudolph," *Magonia*, No. 79, October 2002, 10.

12. Steven Mizrach, "The UFO Phenomenon in History," http://www.thinkaboutit-ufos.com/the-ufo-phenomenon-in-history/.

13. George Hunt Williamson, *Other Tongues, Other Flesh* (London: Neville Spearman, 1965).

14. Good and Zinsstag, 191.

15. *Ibid.*, 5.

16. Hilary Evans, *Gods, Spirits, Cosmic Guardians: A Comparative Study of the Encounter Experience* (Wellingborough: Aquarian Press, 1987), 132.

17. Harold T. Wilkins, *Flying Saucers Uncensored* (New York: Citadel Press, 1955), 43–44.

18. "The Inner Circle Teachers of Light," https://www.metaphysicalarticles.org/2012/09/portraits-and-profiles-of-inner-circle.html.

19. Trevor James, *They Live in the Sky* (Los Angeles: New Age Publishing Co., 1958).

20. Aubeck, 10.

21. Wilkins, 288–289.

22. B. J. Booth, "Subject: The State Department and the Venusians," www.ufocasebook.com/adamski.html.

23. Jerome Clark and Loren Coleman, *The Unidentified: Notes Toward Solving the UFO Mystery* (New York: Warner, 1975), 198.

24. Good and Zinsstag, 106.

25. Nicholas Redfern, *The F.B.I. Files* (London: Simon & Schuster, 1998), 289–317.

26. Good and Zinsstag, 48–153.

27. Redfern, 307–308.

28. Eileen Buckle, *The Scoriton Mystery* (London: Neville Spearman, 1967; Norman Oliver, *Sequel to Scoriton* (London: privately published, 1968)..

29. Leon Festinger, Henry Riecken and Stanley Schachter, *When Prophecy Fails* (New York: Harper and Row, 1966).

30. Jacques Vallee, *UFOs: The Psychic Solution* (London: Panther, 1977), 74–78 and 87.

31. Nigel Watson, *Portraits of Alien Encounters* (London: Valis Books, 1990), 163.

32. Good and Zinsstag, 70.

33. John Keel, *Operation Trojan Horse* (London: Abacus,1976), 302.

Chapter 5

Books and Periodicals

Beckley, Timothy Green, and Casteel, Sean. *Screwed by the Aliens: True Sexual Encounters with ETs*, Conspiracy Journal Productions, New Brunswick, 2018.

Bowen, Charles, ed. *The Humanoids*, Futura, London, 1977.

Chalker, Bill. *Hair of the Alien: DNA and Other Forensic Evidence of Alien Abductions*, Paraview, 2005.

Jacobs, David M. *Alien Encounters: First-Hand Accounts of UFO Abductions*, Virgin, London, 1994 (orig. pub. 1992 as *Secret Life*).

Mack, John E. *Abduction: Human Encounters with Aliens*, Pocket Books, London, 1995.

Notes

1. Howard Menger, *From Outer Space to You* (Clarksburg, WV: Saucerian Books, 1959).

2. Hilary Evans, *Gods, Spirits, Cosmic Guardians: A Comparative Study of the Encounter Experience* (Wellingborough: Aquarian Press, 1987), 142–143.

3. Truman Bethrum, *Aboard a Flying Saucer* (Los Angeles: De Vorss, 1954).

4. Laura Mundo, "Sex and the UFO," https://newtotse.com/oldtotse/en/fringe/abductees_contactees/sexufo1.html.

5. Elizabeth Klarer, *Beyond the Light Barrier* (Cape Town: Timmins, 1980).

6. John Keel, *Operation Trojan Horse* (London: Abacus,1976), 295.

7. "The Betty & Barney Hill Case," http://nicap.org/610919indianhead_dir.htm.

8. Coral Lorenzen, "UFO Occupants in the United States," in *The Humanoids*, ed. Charles Bowen (London: Futura, 1977), 161–162.

9. Harold T. Wilkins, *Flying Saucers from the Moon* (London: Peter Owen Ltd., 1954).

10. Harold T. Wilkins, *Flying Saucers Uncensored* (New York: Citadel Press, 1955), 47.

11. Brad Steiger and Joan Whritenour, *New UFO Breakthrough: The Allende Letters* (New York: Award Books, 1968).

12. Nick Redfern "UFOs: Microwaved to Death," *Mysterious Universe* website, 25 March 2015, https://mysteriousuniverse.org/2015/03/ufos-microwaved-to-death/.

13. John Keel, *Visitors from Space* (St. Albans: Panther, 1976), 211.

Chapter 6

Books and Periodicals

Larsen, S. J. *Close Encounters: A Factual Report on UFO's*, Raintree, 1978.

Lorenzen, J., and C. E. Lorenzen. *Abducted!*, Berkley, 1977.

Steiger, Brad. *The Star People*, Berkley, 1981.

Walton, Travis. *The Walton Affair*, Berkley, 1978.

Notes

1. Charles Bowen, "Interesting Comparisons," in *The Humanoids*, ed. Charles Bowen (London: Futura, 1977), 244.

2. *Ibid.*, 245.

3. Loren Gross, *The Fifth Horseman of the Apocalypse. UFO's A History. 1957* (Fremont, CA: privately published, 2003), http://www.cufos.org/UFO_History_Gross/1957_10–11–2nd_HistorySN.pdf.

4. Peter Rogerson, "Fairyland's Hunters. Notes Towards a Revisionist History of Abductions. Part 1," *Magonia*, No. 46, June 1993, 7.

5. Gordon Creighton, "The Amazing Case of Antonio Villas Boas," in *The Humanoids*, ed. Charles Bowen (London: Futura, 1977).

6. Jacques Vallee, *UFOs: The Psychic Solution* (St. Albans: Panther, 1975), 65–67.

7. *Ibid.*, 65.

8. Peter Rogerson, "Sex, Science and Salvation. Notes Towards a Revisionist History of Abductions. Part 3," *Magonia*, No. 49, June 1994, 17.

9. Charles Hickson and William Mendez, *UFO Contact at Pascagoula* (Tuscon: Wendelle C. Stevens, 1983).

10. James Oberg, *UFOs and Outer Space Mysteries* (Norfolk: Downing, 1982).

11. Philip J. Klass, *UFOs Explained* (New York: Random House, 1974).

12. John Rimmer, *The Evidence for Alien Abductions* (Wellingborough: Aquarian Press, 1984), 60–61.

13. Jerome Clark and Loren Coleman, *The Unidentified: Notes Toward Solving the UFO Mystery* (New York: Warner, 1975), 185–188.

14. Carol and Jim Lorenzen, *UFOs Over the Americas* (New York: Signet, 1968).

15. Hickson and Mendez.

16. Martin Kottmeyer, "The Curse of the Space Mummies," *Promises and Disappointments*, Issue One, circa 1996, 4–8.

17. Steve Sessions, "Claw Men from Outer Space," *Fortean Times*, No. 119, February 1999, 38–43.

18. Calvin Parker, *Pascagoula—The Closest Encounter. My Story* (Pontefract, Flying Disk Press, 2018).

19. Stefanos Panagiotakis, *The Road to Pascagoula (A Research Trip—1981)* (Pontefract, Flying Disk Press, 2018).

20. Leo Sprinkle, "Preliminary Report on the Investigation of an Alleged UFO Occupant Encounter," *Flying Saucer Review*, Vol. 21, No. 3 /4, November 1975, 3–7.

21. Pam Owens, "Weird Space Beings Examined Me and My Unborn Baby on a UFO," *National Enquirer*, January 8, 1980.

22. Raymond E. Fowler, *The Andreasson Affair* (New York: Bantam, 1980), 51.

23. Budd Hopkins, *Missing Time* (New York: Richard Marek, 1981).

24. Debbie Jordan and Kathy Mitchell, *Abducted: The Story of The Intruders Continues* (New York: Carrol & Graf, 1994).

25. Whitley Strieber, *Communion: A True Story* (London: Arrow Books, 1988).

26. *Ibid.*

27. Jenny Randles, *The Pennine UFO Mystery* (London: Granada, 1983), 106.

28. Thomas Bullard, *UFO Abductions: The Measure of a Mystery* (Mount Rainier, WA: Fund for UFO Research, 1987).

29. David M. Jacobs, *Alien Encounters: First-Hand Accounts of UFO Abductions* (London: Virgin, 1994), 217–219.

30. *Ibid.*, 50.

31. Rimmer, 103.

32. Fowler, *The Andreasson Affair*, 89.

33. Nigel Watson, "Enigma Variations: Mind Games," *Fortean Times*, No. 30, Autumn 1979, 43–44.

34. Nigel Watson, "Enigma Variations: A Star Is Born," *Fortean Times*, No. 30, Autumn 1979, 43.

35. Budd Hopkins, *Witnessed* (New York: Pocket Books, 1996).

36. John Rimmer, "Hold the Back Page," *Magonia*, No. 44, October 1992, 24.

37. John Rimmer, "Manhattan Transfer," *Magonia*, No. 45, March 1993, 15–17.

38. Jacobs, *Alien Encounters*, 27–28 and 329–330.

39. *Ibid.*, 43.

40. *Ibid.*, 319–320.

41. Jenny Randles, "My View of Abductions," www.anomalist.com/commentaries/abductions.html.

42. John E. Mack, *Abduction: Human Encounters with Aliens* (London: Pocket Books, 1995), 27 and 31.

43. Budd Hopkins, *Intruders: The Incredible Visitations at Copley Woods* (London: Sphere Books Ltd., 1988), xi.

Chapter 7

Books and Periodicals

Evans, Hilary, and Spencer, John, eds. *UFOs: 1947–1987*, Fortean Tomes, London, 1987.

Notes

1. John Fuller, *Incident at Exeter* (New York: Putnam, 1966), 334.

2. *Ibid.*, 308.

3. Peter Hough, "The Development of UFO Occupants," in *Phenomenon: From Flying Saucers to UFOs—Forty Years of Facts and Research*, ed. Hilary Evans and John Spencer (London: Macdonald & Co., 1988), 109–120.

4. "Alien Races and Descriptions," www.burlingtonnews.net/secretsufo.html.

5. Kevin Randle, *Faces of the Visitors* (New York: Fireside, 1997).

6. Patrick Huyghe, *The Field Guide to Extraterrestrials* (New York: Avon Books, 1996).

7. Hilary Evans, *Visions, Apparitions, Alien Visitors* (Wellingborough: Aquarian Press, 1984), 154.

8. *Ibid.*, 154.

9. Truman Bethurum, *Aboard a Flying Saucer* (Los Angeles: De Vorss, 1954).

10. Don Elkins with Carla Rueckert, *Secrets of the UFO* (Louisville: L/L Research, 1977), 14.

11. Martin Kottmeyer, "What Colour Are the Greys?" *Magonia Supplement*, No. 43, 19 November 2002, 1–4.

12. Nigel Watson, *Portraits of Alien Encounters* (London: Valis Books, 1990), 73–74.

13. Frank Scully, *Behind the Flying Saucers* (New York: Henry Holt, 1950), 209.

14. Whitley Strieber, *Transformation: The Breakthrough* (London: Arrow Books, 1989), 157.

15. Robert Dickhoff, *Homecoming of the Martians: An Encyclopedia on Flying Saucers* (Mokelumne Hill, CA: U.S. Health Research, 1964), 10–11.

16. Jason Gammon, "Alien Technology," http://www.ufoupdateslist.com/2013/jun/m04–002.shtml.

17. Strieber, *Transformation: The Breakthrough*, 73–74.

18. Elkins with Rueckert, 11.

19. John E. Mack, *Abduction: Human Encounters with Aliens* (London: Pocket Books, 1995), Chapter 8.

20. "The Reptilian Agenda," http://www.reptilianagenda.com/menu.shtml.

21. Strieber, *Transformation: The Breakthrough*, 227–228.

22. David M. Jacobs, *Alien Encounters: First-Hand Accounts of UFO Abductions* (London: Virgin, 1994), 221–228.

23. John Fuller, *Incident at Exeter* (New York: Putnam, 1966); Kim Hansen, "UFO Casebook," in *UFOs 1947–1987: The 40-Year Search for an Explanation*, ed. Hilary Evans and John Spencer (London: Fortean Tomes, 1987), 69–72.

24. Peter Huston, "Interview with Betty Hill," October 1, 1998, https://web.archive.org/web/20030225011548/http://www.capital.net/com/phuston/bettyhill.HTML.

25. Major William E. Brummett and Captain Ernest R. Zuick, Jr., *Should the USAF Reopen Project Blue Book? Air Command and Staff College Research Study. Air University Report No. 0450–74* (Auburn: The Graduate Faculty of Auburn University, May 1974), www.cufon.org/cufon/afrstdy1.htm.

26. Peter Rogerson, "Fairyland's Hunters. Notes Towards a Revisionist History of Abductions. Part 2," *Magonia*, No. 47, October 1993, 6.

27. *Ibid.*

28. Jerome Clark and Loren Coleman, *The Unidentified: Notes Toward Solving the UFO Mystery* (New York: Warner, 1975), 76.

29. Martin Cannon, "The Controllers: A New Hypothesis of Alien Abduction," https://www.constitution.org/abus/mkt/cannon_controllers.pdf.

30. Karl Pflock, "'Beep-Beep!' Went the Saucer?" *Saucer Smear*, Volume 47, No. 10.

31. Avis Ruffu, "UFO Evidence—Betty Hill, the Grandmother of Ufology," https://rense.com/general42/bettyhillgrandmother.htm.

32. "Alien Abduction Experience and Research: Examination of Stain Area on Betty Hill's, 1961 Abduction Dress," http://www.abduct.com/research/r15.php.

33. Jacobs, *Alien Encounters*, 240–242.

34. Huston.

35. Fuller, *The Interrupted Journey*, 201–202.

36. *Ibid.*, 308.

37. Jacobs, *Alien Encounters*, 87–88.

38. Mack, *Abduction*, 371–372 and 162–163.

39. Budd Hopkins, "Abductions as Physical Events," *UFO Brigantia*, No. 50, November 1991, 22.

40. Strieber, *Transformation: The Breakthrough*, 251–252.

41. Mark Newbrook, "The Aliens Speak—and Write," *Magonia*, No. 85, July 2004, 3–8.

42. Marjorie E. Fish, "Journey into The Hill Star Map. MUFON UFO Symposium 1974," https://www.nicap.org/reports/hill-map.htm.

43. Fuller, *The Interrupted Journey*, 326.

44. Jacques Vallee, *Dimensions: A Casebook of Alien Contact* (London: Souvenir Press, 1988), 266.

45. John Rimmer, *The Evidence for Alien Abductions* (Wellingborough: Aquarian Press, 1984), 88–92.

46. Joachim Koch and Hans-Juergen Kyborg, "New Discoveries in Betty Hill's Star Map," http://www.kochkyborg.de/BBHill/hill02.htm.

47. Steve Pearse, *Set Your Phaser to Stun* (Bloomington: Xlibris Corporation, 2011).

48. Budd Hopkins, *Missing Time* (New York: Richard Marek, 1981), 209.

49. "'Invasion,' Yarn of an Aeroplane in the Night. On Ham Common," *The Star* (London), May 15, 1909.

50. Hopkins, "Abductions as Physical Events," 22.

51. Huston.

52. Mary Rodwell, *Awakening: How Extraterrestrial Contact Can Transform Your Life* (Leeds: Beyond Publications, 2002), 159–165.

53. *Ibid.*, 163–164.

54. Dennis Stacy, "Alien Abortions: Avenging Angels," *Magonia*, No. 44, October 1992, 12–17.

55. Rodwell, 180–183.

56. Jacobs, *Alien Encounters*, 95.

57. Rodwell, 180.

58. Jenny Randles, "Implants: A Brief Story," *Northern UFO News*, No. 172, Christmas 1995, 16.

59. Whitley Strieber, *Confirmation* (New York: Simon & Schuster, 1998).

60. A Letter from the Producer, "Kidnapped by UFOs? Where's the Physical

Evidence?" www.pbs.org/wgbh/nova/ aliens/wheresphysev.html.

61. Budd Hopkins and Carol Rainey, *Sight Unseen: Science, UFO Invisibility and Transgenic Beings* (New York: Atria Books, 2003); John Harney, "Literary Criticism," *Magonia Supplement*, No. 49, February 16, 2004, 3.

62. Jacobs, *Alien Encounters*, 51.

63. Martin Kottmeyer, "If that someone's from outer space, they'll just go through the wall anyways," *Magonia Supplement*, No. 53, November 2004, 1–5.

64. Jacobs, *Alien Encounters*, 51.

65. *Ibid.*, 50.

66. *Ibid.*, 55, 63 and 71.

67. *Ibid.*, 259–260.

68. Christopher Kenworthy, "Abduction Evidence," *Alien Encounters*, No. 25, 1998, 68.

69. Richard D. Butler, "Abduction Experience Classifications," https://www.beyondweird.com/ufos/Richard_Butler_Abduction_Experience_Classifications.html.

70. Jim Mortellaro, "To Those Who Don't Believe Alien Abductions Are Occurring," ufocasebook.com/abductionsoccurring.html.

71. John Harney, "Off the Wall, Through the Wall and Up the Wall: The Abduction Researchers," *Magonia ETH Bulletin*, No. 3, May 1998.

72. John Keel, *Operation Trojan Horse* (London: Abacus,1976), 178.

73. *Ibid.*, 182.

74. Hopkins and Rainey.

75. A Letter from the Producer.

76. B. Hopkins, D.M. Jacobs and R. Westrum, *Unusual Personal Experiences: An Analysis of Data from Three National Surveys Conducted by the Roper Organization* (Las Vegas: Bigelow Holding Corporation, 1992).

77. Peter Brookesmith and Paul Devereux, *UFOs and Ufology: The First 50 Years* (London: Blandford, 1997), 170.

78. "Asians Believe in Existence of ET: Star Movies Poll," www.indiantelevision.com/headlines/y2k3/may/may197.htm.

79. Craig R. Lang, "The Logistics of UFO Abduction," *Journal of Abduction-Encounter Research*, First Quarter 2007, https://www.nicap.org/images/humrep/JAR_2007_1st_Qtr1.pdf.

80. Rima Laibow, Robert Sollod and John Wilson, eds., *Anomalous Experiences & Trauma. Current Theoretical, Research and Clinical Perspectives. Proceedings of TREAT II* (Dobbs Ferry, NY: The Center for Treatment and Research of Experienced Anomalous Trauma, 1992), 190.

Chapter 8

Books and Periodicals

Aldiss, Brian, with Wingrove, David. *Trillion Year Spree: The History of Science Fiction*, Paladin, London, 1988.

Biskind, Peter. *Seeing Is Believing*. Random House, New York, 1983.

Graham, Robbie. *Silver Screen Saucers: Sorting Fact from Fantasy in Hollywood's UFO Movies*, White Crow, Hove, 2015.

Hardy, Phil, ed. *The Aurum Encyclopedia of Science Fiction Movies*, Aurum, London, 1995.

Kyle, David. *A Pictorial History of Science Fiction*. Hamlyn, London, 1977.

Skal, David. J. *The Monster Show*, Plexus, London, 1994.

Slade, Darren, and Watson, Nigel. *Supernatural Spielberg*, Valis Books, London, 1992.

Websites

The Astounding B Monster, www.bmonster.com/indexa.html.

The *Internet Movie Database (IMDb)*, https://www.imdb.com/.

Mitchell, Timothy. "It Came from Inner Space: Faith, Science, Conquest and the War of the Worlds," Georgetown University, PhD thesis, 23 April 2001, https://www.scribd.com/document/173779241/Timothy-Mitchell-It-Came-From-Inner-Space-Faith-Science-Conquest-and-The-War-of-the-Worlds.

The Science Fiction Chronicles, www.web-scifi.com/.

Sci-Fi Movie Page, http://www.scifimoviepage.com/.

Starburst, https://www.starburstmagazine.com/.

Talking Pictures, www.talkingpix.co.uk.

Notes

1. David M. Jacobs, *Alien Encounters: First-Hand Accounts of UFO Abductions* (London: Virgin, 1994), 30.

2. Budd Hopkins, "Abductions as Physical Events," *UFO Brigantia*, No. 50, November 1991, 19–20.

3. Mark Pilkington, "Screen Memories: An Exploration of the Relationship Between Science Fiction Film and the UFO Mythology," www.hedweb.com/markp/ufofilm.htm.

4. Thomas Bullard, "America Strikes Back," *Magonia*, No. 37, October 1990.

5. John Spencer, *Perspectives: A Radical Examination of the Alien Abduction Phenomenon* (London: Futura, 1990), 184.

6. Pilkington.

7. Bullard, 8.

8. Martin Kottmeyer, "Entirely Unpredisposed: The Cultural Background of UFO Abduction Reports," *Magonia*, No. 35, January 1990, 3–10.

9. John Spencer, *Gifts of the Gods? Are UFOs Alien Visitors or Psychic Phenomena?* (London: Virgin, 1995).

10. Peter Rogerson, "Letters," *Magonia Monthly Supplement*, No. 13, March 1999, 3–4.

11. Martin S. Kottmeyer, "Betty Hill's Medical Nightmare," *Magonia Monthly Supplement*, No. 12, February 1999, 1–3.

12. Calvin Parker, *Pascagoula—The Closest Encounter. My Story* (Pontefract, Flying Disk Press, 2018), 31–32 and 63.

13. Anthony R. Brown, "The Decline and Fall of the Psychosocial Empire," *Magonia*, No. 72, October 2000, 5.

14. Greg Sandow, "The Abduction Conundrum," http://www.gregsandow.com/ufo/Contents/Abduction_Conundrum/abduction_conundrum.htm.

15. Richard Dengrove, "Evil Aliens and H.G. Wells," *Challenger: A Science Fiction Fanzine*, Autumn/Winter 2003–2004; Curtis Peebles, *Watch the Skies: A Chronicle of the Flying Saucer Myth* (Washington: Smithsonian Press, 1994).

16. Joe Nickell, "Extraterrestrial Iconography," *Skeptical Inquirer*, September/October 1997, 18–19.

17. Donna M. Campbell, "Early American Captivity Narratives," https://public.wsu.edu/~campbelld/amlit/captive.htm.

18. Michael Sturma, "Alien Abductions—Historical Aspects," *History Today*, January 2000.

19. Daniel Cohen, *The Great Airship Mystery* (New York: Dodd, Mead, 1981), 122–142.

20. Ron Miller, "Jules Verne and the Great Airship Scare," *International UFO Reporter*, Vol. 12, No. 3, May/June 1987, 4–10; Jess Nevins, "Fantastic, Mysterious, and Adventurous Victoriana," http://www.oocities.org/jessnevins/vicintro.html.

21. Hilary Evans, *From Other Worlds* (London: Carlton, 1998), 29–30.

22. Robert A. Bartholomew, "The Martian Panic Sixty Years Later," *Skeptical Inquirer*, December 1998, https://skepticalinquirer.org/1998/11/the_martian_panic_sixty_years_later/.

23. Loren E. Gross, Charles Fort, *The Fortean Society & Unidentified Flying Objects* (Fremont, CA: privately published, 1976), 71–72.

24. Martin S. Kottmeyer, "Bruce Gentry, Serial Filler," *Magonia Monthly Supplement*, No. 18, August 1999, 1–2.

25. Frank Scully, *Behind the Flying Saucers* (New York: Henry Holt, 1950); Andy Roberts, "Saucerful of Secrets," in *UFOs: 1947–1987: The 40-Year Search for an Explanation*, ed. Hilary Evans with John Spencer (London: Fortean Tomes, 1987), 157.

26. David Skal, *The Monster Show: A Cultural History* (London: Plexus Books, 1994).

27. Dave Baker, "Re: Abduction—Media Influence," http://ufoupdateslist.com/1999/feb/m08–027.shtml.

28. John E. Mack, *Abduction: Human Encounters with Aliens* (London: Pocket Books, 1995), 123–124.

29. *Ibid.*, 182.

30. Darren Slade and Nigel Watson, *Supernatural Spielberg* (London: Valis Books, 1992).

31. Dr J. Allen Hynek, *The UFO Experience: A Scientific Inquiry* (Chicago: Henry Regnery, 1972).

32. Gary Gerani and Paul H. Schulman, *Fantastic TV* (Godalming, Surrey: LSP Books Ltd., 1977), 115.

33. Budd Hopkins, *Missing Time* (New York: Richard Marek, 1981).

34. Budd Hopkins, *Intruders: The Incredible Visitations at Copley Woods* (London: Sphere Books Ltd., 1988).

35. Letter to the author dated March 1994.

36. Paul Cornell, Martin Day and Keith Topping, *X-Treme Possibilities: A Comprehensively Expanded Rummage Through*

Five Years of The X-Files (London: Virgin, 1998).

37. Charles Berlitz and William L. Moore, *The Roswell Incident* (London: Granada, 1982).

38. Keith Topping, *High Times: An Unofficial and Unauthorised Guide to Roswell* (London: Virgin, 2001).

39. Gerald Heard, *The Riddle of the Flying Saucers* (London: Carroll and Nicholson, 1950); Dennis Wheatley, *Star of Ill-Omen* (London: Hutchinson, 1952).

40. Bruce Rux, *Hollywood Vs. the Aliens: The Motion Picture Industry's Participation in UFO Disinformation* (Berkeley: Frog Ltd., 1997).

41. Timothy Good, *Alien Liaison: The Ultimate Secret* (London: Arrow Books, 1992), 121.

42. Dragan Antulov, "Close Encounters of The Third Kind. A Film Review," http://www.all-reviews.com/videos-4/close-encounters.htm.

43. Good, 65.

44. Pilkington.

45. Colin Wilson and Damon Wilson, *Unsolved Mysteries* (Chicago: Contemporary Books, 1992).

46. *Ibid.*

47. Nigel Watson, "The Hill Abduction on Screen," *Fortean Times*, No. 384, October 2019, 44–47.

Chapter 9

Books and Periodicals

Appelle, Stuart. "The Abduction Experience: A Critical Evaluation of Theory and Evidence," *Journal of UFO Studies*, n.s. 6, 1995/1996, 29–78.

Haines, Richard (ed.). *UFO Phenomena and the Behavioral Scientist*, Scarecrow, Lanham, MD, 1979.

Hufford, David J. *The Terror That Comes in the Night: An Experience-Centered Study of Supernatural Assault Traditions*, University of Pennsylvania Press, Philadelphia, 1982.

Moravec, Mark. "UFOs as Psychological and Parapsychological Phenomena," in *UFOs 1947–1987*, compiled and edited by Hilary Evans and John Spencer, Fortean Tomes, London, 1987, 301–302.

Parina, Kaja. "Alien Abductions: The Real Deal?" *Psychology Today*, March/April 2003. www.psychologytoday.com/htdocs/prod/PTOArticle/PTO-20030527–000002.asp.

Saliba, John A. "The Psychology of UFO Phenomena," in *UFO Religions*, edited by Christopher Partridge, Routledge, London, 2003, 329–345.

Segal, Robert A. "Jung On UFOs," in *UFO Religions*, edited by Christopher Partridge, Routledge, London, 2003, 314–328.

Notes

1. Peter Huston, "Interview with Betty Hill," October 1, 1998, https://web.archive.org/web/20030225011548/http://www.capital.net/com/phuston/bettyhill.HTML.

2. "Obituaries for Tue. October 19, 2004," *Portsmouth Herald*, October 19, 2004, https://www.seacoastonline.com/article/20041019/obituaries/310199990; Margalit Fox, "Betty Hill, 85, Figure in Alien Abduction Case, Dies," *The New York Times*, October 23, 2004.

3. Ben H. Swett, "Betty & Barney Hill. Testimony," www.bswett.com/1963–09BettyAndBarney.html.

4. Huston.

5. Raymond E. Fowler, "Telepathy and a UFO: Coincidence or Contact?" *Official UFO*, Vol. 1 No. 5, January 1976, 14–15 and 43–44.

6. Berthold Eric Schwarz, "Talks with Betty Hill: 2—The Things That Happen to Her," *Flying Saucer Review*, Vol. 23, No. 3, October 1977, 12.

7. Berthold Eric Schwarz, "Talks with Betty Hill: 3—Experiments and Conclusions," *Flying Saucer Review*, Vol. 23, No. 4, January 1978, 30.

8. Avis Ruffu, "Betty Hill," podcast, http://www.jerrypippin.com/UFO_Files_betty_hill.htm.

9. Margalit Fox, "Betty Hill, 85, Figure in alien Abduction Case, Dies," *New York Times*, October 23, 2004; Bruno Matarazzo, Jr., "Portsmouth's Betty Hill Dies; 'Alien Abduction' Made Her Famous," *Foster's Daily Democrat*, October 19, 2004.

10. "Sighting Report," www.nuforc.org/webreports/020/S20008.html.

11. Bryan Daum, "Betty Hill Credible?" http://ufoupdateslist.com/2004/oct/m22–006.shtml.

12. Whitley Strieber, *Transformation: The Breakthrough* (London: Arrow Books, 1989), 245–248.

13. Dale Carter, *The Final Frontier* (London: Verso, 1988), 101.

14. Peter Rogerson, "Fairyland's Hunters. Notes Towards a Revisionist History of Abductions. Part 2," *Magonia*, No. 47, October 1993, 5.

15. Robert Mitchell Lindner, *The Fifty-Minute Hour: A Collection of True Psychoanalytic Tales* (New York: Jason Aronson, 1983); Robert Lindner, "The Jet-Propelled Couch," *Magazine of Fantasy and Science Fiction*, January 1956.

16. Doctor Strangemind, "Paul Linebarger—Cordwainer Smith," https://doctorstrangemind.com/2017/11/10/paul-linebarger-cordwainer-smith/.

17. Alan C. Elms, "Cordwainer Smith Scholarly Corner," http://www.cordwainer-smith.com/scholarly.htm.

18. Budd Hopkins, *Missing Time* (New York: Richard Marek, 1981).

19. John E. Mack, *Abduction: Human Encounters with Aliens* (London: Pocket Books, 1995), 19.

20. Dr. Alvin H. Lawson, "The Abduction Experience: A Testable Hypothesis," *Magonia*, No. 10, 1982, 3–18.

21. Ian S. Creswell, "Objections to the Birth Trauma Hypothesis," *Magonia*, No. 11, 1982.

22. Harold S. W. Chibbett, "UFOs and Parapsychology," *UFO Percipients. Flying Saucer Review*, Special Issue No. 3, September 1969, 36–38.

23. Leo Sprinkle, "Some Uses of Hypnosis in UFO Research," *Flying Saucer Review*, Special Issue No. 3, September 1969, 18.

24. Caroline McLeod, Barbara Corbisier and John E. Mack, "A More Parsimonious Explanation for UFO Abduction," *Psychological Inquiry*, Vol. 7, No. 2, 1996.

25. Sprinkle, 17–19.

26. David M. Jacobs, *Secret Life: Firsthand Accounts of UFO Abductions* (London: Virgin, 1994), 307.

27. Mark Moravec, "The Psychology of Close Encounters," in *Frontiers of Reality*, ed. Hilary Evans, 147 (London: Guild Publishing, 1989).

28. "'Interrupted Journey' Barney and Betty Hill Abduction," www.visionand-psychosis.net/Barney_Betty_Hill_Interrupted_Journey.htm.

29. Dr. Susan Blackmore, "Abduction by Aliens or Sleep Paralysis?" *Skeptical Inquirer*, May/June 1998.

30. D. J. Hufford, *The Terror That Comes in the Night: An Experience-Centered Study of Supernatural Assault Traditions* (Philadelphia: University of Pennsylvania Press, 1982).

31. N. P. Spanos, P. A. Cross, K. Dickson and S. C. DuBreuil, "Close Encounters: An Examination of UFO Experiences," *Journal of Abnormal Psychology*, No. 102, 1993, 624–632.

32. M. Cox, *The Prevalence of Sleep Paralysis and Temporal Lobe Lability in Persons Who Report Alien Abduction* (Bristol: Unpublished thesis, University of the West of England, Department of Psychology, 1995).

33. Dr. Jorge Conesa, "Lucid Dreaming and Sleep Paralysis," http://www.geocities.ws/jorgeconesa/Paralysis/sleepnew.html.

34. W. Penfield, and P. Perot, "The Brain's Record of Auditory and Visual Experience: A Final Summary and Discussion," *Brain*, 86, 1963, 595–696; M.A. Persinger, "Propensity to Report Paranormal Experiences Is Correlated with Temporal Lobe Signs," *Perceptual and Motor Skills*, No. 59, 1984, 583–586; Susan Blackmore, "Alien Abduction: The Inside Story," *New Scientist*, 19 November 1994, 29–31; M. A. Persinger, S. G. Tiller, and S. A. Koren, "Experimental Simulation of a Haunt Experience and Elicitation of Paroxysmal Electroencephalographic Activity by Transcerebral Complex Magnetic Fields: Induction of a Synthetic 'Ghost'?" *Perceptual and Motor Skills*, No. 90, 2000, 659–674.

35. M. A. Persinger and K. Makarec, "Temporal Lobe Epileptic Signs and Correlative Behaviors Displayed by Normal Populations," *Journal of General Psychology*, No. 114, 1987, 179–195.

36. Paul Devereux, "Earthlights," in *Phenomenon: From Flying Saucers to UFOs—Forty Years of Facts and Research*, ed. Hilary Evans and John Spencer (London: Macdonald & Co., 1988), 322.

37. Albert Budden, *Allergies and Aliens. The Visitation Experience: An Environmental Health Issue* (Trowbridge: Discovery Times Press, 1994).

38. Rima Laibow, Robert Sollod and John Wilson, eds., *Anomalous Experiences & Trauma. Current Theoretical, Research and Clinical Perspectives. Proceedings of TREAT II* (Dobbs Ferry, NY: The Center for Treatment and Research of Experienced Anomalous Trauma, 1992).

39. Jacobs, *Secret Life*, 288.

40. Peter Rogerson, "Encounters at Indian Head," http://mrobsr.blogspot.com/2012/08/encounters-at-indian-head.html.

41. Christopher C. French and Katharine J. Holden, "Alien Abduction Experiences: Some Clues from Neuropsychology and Neuropsychiatry," *Cognitive Neuropsychiatry*, Vol. 7, No. 3, 2002, 163–178.

Chapter 10

Books and Periodicals

Friedman, Stanton T., and Marden, Kathleen. *Captured! The Betty and Barney Hill UFO Experience*, New Page Books, 2007.

Pflock, Karl, and Brookesmith, Peter, eds. *Encounters at Indian Head: The Betty and Barney Hill UFO Abduction Revisited*. Anomalist Books, 2007.

Notes

1. Kathleen Marden, "Where the Debunkers Went Wrong," http://kathleen-marden.com/where-the-debunkers-went-wrong.php.

2. *The Immanuel Velikovsky Archive,* https://www.varchive.org/cor/various/680309hillv.htm.

3. "The Lost Critique," http://defend-gaia.org/bobk/vfitton.html.

4. Robert Sheaffer, "Betty Hill's UFO Crash Debris," *Bad UFOs blogspot*, https://badufos.blogspot.com/2018/07/betty-hills-ufo-crash-debris.html.

5. Karl Pflock and Peter Brookesmith, eds., *Encounters at Indian Head: The Betty and Barney Hill UFO Abduction Revisited*, Anomalist Books, 2007.

6. Robert Sheaffer, "Betty Hill's Last Hurrah—A Secret UFO Symposium in New Hampshire," *Bad UFOs blogspot*, https://badufos.blogspot.com/2015/05/betty-hills-last-hurrah-secret-ufo.html.

Chapter 11

Notes

1. Raymond E. Fowler. *The Andreasson Affair* (New York: Bantam, 1980), 43.

2. K. Wilson, "UFO Abductions in Germany, Austria and Switzerland. A Lecture by Johannes Fiebag, Ph.D," http://alien-jigsaw.com/et-contact/Fiebag-Abductions-Germany-Austria-Switzerland-I.html.

3. Fowler, 32.

4. Hilary Evans, "Beyond the UFO Horizon," *Magonia Supplement. Special Issue*, No. 58, August 10, 2005, 10.

5. Mark Pilkington, "Screen Memories: An Exploration of the Relationship Between Science Fiction Film and the UFO Mythology," www.hedweb.com/markp/ufofilm.htm.

Bibliography

In April 2009 the University of New Hampshire celebrated the opening of the Betty and Barney Hill Collection. This consists of thousands of items stored in 87 files that feature correspondence, notebooks, manuscripts, news clippings, photographs and artifacts related to their case. Details are given at www.library.unh.edu/find/archives/collections/betty-and-barney-hill-papers-1961–2006#series-3.

This is a small selection of books about abductions and contactees. They provide a broad range of views about this phenomenon, from extreme belief to unflinching skepticism.

Adamski, George, and Leslie, Desmond. *Flying Saucers Have Landed*, Werner Laurie, 1953.

Appleyard, Bryan. *Aliens: Why They Are Here*, Scribner's, 2005.

Bowen, Charles, ed. *The Humanoids*, Futura, 1977.

Brookesmith, Peter, and Devereux, Paul. *UFOs and Ufology*, Blandford, 1997.

Brookesmith, Peter, and Pflock, Karl, eds. *Encounters at Indian Head: The Betty and Barney Hill UFO Abduction Revisited*, Anomalist Books, 2007.

Bryan, C.D. *Close Encounters of the Fourth Kind*, Weidenfeld & Nicolson, 1995.

Bullard, Thomas E. *UFO Abductions: The Measure of a Mystery*, Fund for UFO Research, 1987.

Clancy, Susan. *Abducted: How People Come to Believe They Were Kidnapped by Aliens*, Harvard University Press, 2005.

Clark, Jerome. *The UFO Encyclopedia* (three volumes), Ominigraphics, 1990–1996.

Clark, Jerome, and Coleman, Loren. *The Unidentified*, Warner, 1975.

Evans, Hilary. *Gods, Spirits, Cosmic Guardians*, Aquarian Press, 1987.

Evans, Hilary. *Visions, Apparitions, Alien Visitors*, Aquarian Press, 1986.

Fowler, Raymond E. *The Andreasson Affair*, Prentice-Hall, 1979.

Friedman, Stanton T., and Marden, Kathleen. *Captured! The Betty and Barney Hill UFO Experience*, New Page Books, 2007.

Fuller, John G. *The Interrupted Journey: Two Lost Hours Aboard a Flying Saucer*, Souvenir Press, 1980 (new edition; orig. pub. 1966).

Hill, Betty. *A Commonsense Approach to UFOs*, self-published, 1995.

Hogan, David J. *UFO FAQ: All That's Left to Know About Roswell, Aliens, Whirling Discs, and Flying Saucers*, Backbeat Books, 2016.

Hopkins, Budd. *Intruders*, Random House, 1987.

Hopkins, Budd. *Missing Time*, Richard Marek, 1981.

Jacobs, David M. *Secret Life*, Simon & Schuster, 1992.

Jung, Carl G. *Flying Saucers: A Modern Myth of Things Seen in the Sky*, Harcourt Brace, 1959.

Keel, John. *UFOs: Operation Trojan Horse*, Abacus, 1973.

Klass, Philip J. *UFO Abductions—A Dangerous Game*, Prometheus, 1988.

Lorenzen, J., and Lorenzen, C.E., *Abducted!*, Berkley, 1977.
Mack, John E. *Abduction: Human Encounters with Aliens*, Simon & Schuster, 1994.
Pflock, Karl, and Brookesmith, Peter, eds. *Encounters at Indian Head: The Betty and Barney Hill UFO Abduction Revisited*, Anomalist Books, 2007.
Pope, Nick. *The Uninvited: An Expose of the Alien Abduction Phenomenon*, Dell, 1997.
Randles, Jenny. *Abduction*, Robert Hale, 1988.
Rimmer, John. *The Evidence for Alien Abductions*, Aquarian Press, 1984.
Rogo, D. Scott, ed. *Alien Abductions*, New American Library, 1980.
Rutkowski, Chris A. *Abductions and Aliens: What's Really Going On*, Dundurn, 1999.
Sachs, Margaret. *The UFO Encyclopedia*, Perigee/Putnam, 1980.
Schnabel, Jim. *Dark White*, Hamish Hamilton, 1994.
Spencer, John. *Perspectives*, Futura, 1990.
Steiger, Brad. *The UFO Abductors*, Berkley, 1988.
Strieber, Whitley. *Communion*, Morrow, 1987.
Strieber, Whitley. *Transformation: The Breakthrough*, Morrow, 1988.
Tonnies, Mac. *The Cryptoterrestrials*, Anomalist Books, 2010.
Vallee, Jacques. *The Messengers of Deception*, And/Or Press, 1979.
Vallee, Jacques. *Passport to Magonia*, Tandem, 1975.
Watson, Nigel. *Portraits of Alien Encounters*, Valis Books, 1990.

Websites

There are literally hundreds of websites about UFOs and abductions that vary greatly in quality and validity. Use your favorite search engine for information or use the links below as a good starting point for further research.

As with all web links they are subject to temporary or even permanent disappearance from virtual reality.

About.com ufos.about.com/od/aliensabductions/.
Alien Abduction Case Files www.ufocasebook.com/alienabductions.html.
The Alien Jigsaw—True Experiences of Alien Abduction www.alienjigsaw.com/.
The Center for UFO Studies (CUFOS) cufos.org/.
Flying Saucer Review www.fsr.org.uk.
Fortean Times www.forteantimes.com.
International Center for UFO Research (David Jacobs' website) www.ufoabduction.com.
Intruders Foundation (Budd Hopkins' website) www.intrudersfoundation.org/.
John E. Mack Institute www.johnemackinstitute.org/.
Magonia website http://magonia.haaan.com/.
Magonia Supplement http://www.users.waitrose.com/~magonia/index.htm.
Mutual UFO Network (MUFON) www.mufon.com.
National Investigations Committee on Aerial Phenomena (NICAP) www.nicap.org/.
Paranormal Magazine http://www.paranormalmagazine.co.uk/.
Spirit Writings.com provides full texts of famous and obscure contactee literature and psychic-related writings www.spiritwritings.com.
UFO Evidence www.ufoevidence.org.
UFO Magazine www.ufomag.com/.
UFOInfo www.ufoinfo.com/contents.shtml.
UFOseek.com www.ufoseek.com.

Index